Microsoft® Windows® 2000 Professional Lab Manual

Ted L. Simpson

COURSE
TECHNOLOGY

Thomson Learning™

25 THOMSON PLACE, BOSTON, MA 02210

Australia • Canada • Mexico • Singapore • Spain • United Kingdom • United States

Microsoft® Windows® 2000 Professional Lab Manual is published by Course Technology.

Managing Editor	Stephen Solomon
Senior Product Manager	David George
Production Editor	Jennifer Goguen
Developmental Editor	Deb Kaufmann
Quality Assurance Manager	John Bosco
Marketing Manager	Susan Ogar
Text Designer	GEX Publishing Services
Composition House	GEX Publishing Services
Cover Designer	Joseph Lee, Black Fish Design

Disclaimer

Course Technology reserves the right to revise this publication and make changes from time to time in its content without notice.

The Web addresses in this book are subject to change from time to time as necessary without notice.

For more information, contact Course Technology, 25 Thomson Place, Boston, MA 02210;

or find us on the World Wide Web at www.course.com.

For permission to use material from this text or product, contact us by

- Web: www.thomsonrights.com
- Phone: 1-800-730-2214
- Fax: 1-800-730-2215

ISBN 0-619-01512-8

Printed in Canada

1 2 3 4 5 WC 04 03 02 01

TABLE OF CONTENTS

INTRODUCTION

The objective of this lab manual is to assist you in preparing for the Microsoft certification exam # 70-210: *Installing, Configuring, and Administering Microsoft Windows 2000 Professional* by applying the Windows 2000 Professional exam objectives to simulated business environments. It is designed to be used in conjunction with and extend the *MCSE Guide to Microsoft Windows 2000 Professional* (0-619-01513-6), but can also be used to supplement any MCSE courseware. While this manual is written with the intent of being used in a classroom lab environment, it may also be used for self-study on a home network.

In this lab manual you will be playing the role of a computer technician working for Computer Technology Services (CTS), a consulting firm with a range of clients including educational institutions, small businesses, manufacturing companies, and legal offices. You have been hired to provide Windows 2000 support for CTS clients. In each of the labs you will gain hands-on experience with the skills and knowledge required to meet the Windows 2000 Professional test objectives by applying them to business situations.

FEATURES

In order to ensure a successful experience for instructors and students alike, this book includes the following features:

- **Lab Objectives** – Every lab has a brief description and list of learning objectives.
- **Microsoft Windows 2000 Professional MCSE Certification objectives** – For each lab, the relevant objectives from MCSE Exam # 70-210 are listed.
- **Activity Sections** – The labs are broken down into manageable sections.
- **Step-by-step instructions**
- **Review questions** help reinforce concepts presented in the lab.
- **Forms and Student Answer Sheets** accompany labs, and can be submitted either electronically or on hard copy.

HARDWARE REQUIREMENTS

- A Pentium 200 MHz CPU or higher
- 64 MB of RAM
- A 2 GB hard disk
- An optional second disk drive with at least 500 MB of storage
- A fax-compatible modem
- A CD-ROM drive

NETWORK REQUIREMENTS

- A network card installed and attached to a cable system
- At least one other Windows 2000 or Windows 95/98 system attached to the network segment

SOFTWARE/SETUP REQUIREMENTS

- Windows 95/98 installed in a 500-900 MB partition (In order to perform the automatic installation in chapter 2, the Windows 95/98 drive should have no less than 700 MB of free space.)
- Access to a Windows 2000 Professional CD
- Access to a Windows 2000 Professional Resource kit CD
- Windows 2000 Professional installed in a second logical drive with at least 1 GB of storage space
- At least 100 MB of free space on the extended disk partition containing Windows 2000

CHAPTER ONE

A FIRST LOOK AT WINDOWS 2000 PROFESSIONAL

Labs included in this chapter

➤ Lab 1.1 Making a Windows 2000 Proposal

➤ Lab 1.2 Documenting a Windows 2000 System

➤ Lab 1.3 Working with Virtual Memory

➤ Lab 1.4 Monitoring Application and System Performance

➤ Lab 1.5 Using Event Viewer

➤ Lab 1.6 Documenting Your Windows 2000 Network Configuration

➤ Lab 1.7 Sharing Network Information

Microsoft MCSE Exam #70-210 Objectives	
Objective	Lab
Perform an attended installation of Windows 2000 Professional	1.1
Configure and troubleshoot desktop settings	1.2
Optimize and troubleshoot performance of the Windows 2000 Professional desktop	
Optimize and troubleshoot memory performance	1.2, 1.3, 1.4
Optimize and troubleshoot processor utilization	1.4
Optimize and troubleshoot application performance	1.4, 1.5
Optimize and troubleshoot network performance	1.6
Configure and troubleshoot the TCP/IP protocol	1.6
Connect to shared resources on a Microsoft network	1.7

Student Answer Sheets to accompany the labs in this chapter can be downloaded from the Online Companion for this manual at *www.course.com*.

LAB 1.1 MAKING A WINDOWS 2000 PROPOSAL

Objective

The Animal Care Center is a veterinary clinic owned by Dennis Geisler and specializes in health-care services and products for both small and large animals. In addition to Dennis, there is another veterinarian, an assistant, and three clerks. Currently they have a small store and clinic that contains four Windows-based computers and a Novell NetWare 3.11 server networked to a 10-Megabit Ethernet hub. The Novell NetWare 3.1 server is used to perform file and print services for the other computers. Two Windows 95 computers located at the main counter process customer calls and checkouts. Two computers running Windows for Workgroups 3.11 are located in the veterinarians' offices. In addition to word-processing and spreadsheet software, all computers currently run a Windows 16-bit veterinary program that is used for customer billing, inventory, and pet-treatment tracking. Dennis recently asked Computer Technology Services to provide him with information about the benefits and costs of Windows 2000 Professional. He wants to replace the Windows for Workgroups computer in his office with a fast Windows 2000 Professional computer that could act as a file and print server for the other computers. His plan is to replace the NetWare server after moving the files and programs to the new Windows 2000 system. He also is considering the purchase and installation of a new network-attached printer to replace the printer attached to the NetWare file server. After completing this lab, you will be able to:

➤ Identify Windows 2000 features and benefits.

➤ Identify hardware requirements to install Window 2000 Professional.

➤ Use the HCL to determine hardware compatibility.

➤ Identify Windows 2000 network protocol options.

➤ Identify clients supported by Windows 2000 Professional.

Estimated completion time: **30–60 minutes**

ACTIVITY

1. CTS wants you to write a proposal for Dennis that identifies the following features. Record your answers on the Lab 1.1 Student Answer Sheet.

   a. The features of Windows 2000 that would support a high-speed computer running Windows 2000 in his office. What type of system would you recommend for Dennis's office server?

   b. Windows 2000 features that would provide reliability by preventing a program from crashing the server.

   c. Windows 2000 security features that would help prevent an unauthorized user from gaining access to files and programs stored on the Windows 2000 computer.

2. In order to act as the file and print server, the computer in Dennis' office must be fast and reliable. On the Student Answer Sheet, identify the hardware requirements for such a computer.

3. Dennis needs to be able to share files and a printer with both Windows 95 and Windows 3.x computers. On the Student Answer Sheet, identify which client computer operating systems can be used to access data and printers on the Windows 2000 computer.

4. Dennis is concerned about his ability to run the veterinary software on the Windows 2000 computer in his office. On the Student Answer Sheet, discuss Windows 2000 support for 16-bit and 32-bit applications.

5. In addition to communicating with the Windows 3.x and Windows 95 computers, Dennis has files on his Novell NetWare server that will need to be copied to the Windows 2000 computer. He also wants to obtain a network-attached printer to replace the one currently on the main counter. On the Student Answer Sheet, identify the communication protocols that Windows 2000 supports, along with which protocols you recommend to provide the connectivity necessary to communicate with the Novell server, the network-attached printer, and the Windows computers.

6. Dennis currently has some equipment that he would like to use with his Windows 2000 computer. Use the Windows 2000 Hardware Compatibility List (HCL) to see if the following components are compatible with Windows 2000. On your Student Answer Sheet, identify the path leading to the HCL.TXT file on the Windows 2000 Professional CD-ROM. Record the results of your search for each of the following components:

- Adaptec 1520A SCSI controller
- Lexmark Optra R Plus series printer
- NetGear FA310TX Fast Ethernet adapter

LAB 1.2 DOCUMENTING A WINDOWS 2000 SYSTEM

Objective

A month before you started working at Computer Technology Services, one of the employees at your company replaced all five of the Windows 95-based computers at the Melendres and Associates law firm with Windows 2000 Professional systems. Currently these computers are attached to a peer-to-peer network and are used to enter and access client case information. Although all of these computers are supposed to be the same, the legal assistants think one of the systems performs slower than the others. You have been asked to document the settings on these computers to help determine what might be different. In Labs 1.2 through 1.5 you use Windows 2000 features and utilities to determine system configuration settings that could affect the performance of a computer system. After completing this lab, you will be able to:

➤ Access the Computer Management console.

➤ Use the Computer Management console to record system hardware configuration information, including processor type and speed, amount of RAM, and video settings on your computer.

➤ Use Device Manager to check for any device configuration errors.

➤ Use the Disk Management tool to document drive capacity and format.

Estimated completion time: **10 minutes**

ACTIVITY

1. Start your Windows 2000 computer and log on as Administrator.

2. Right-click **My Computer** to display a shortcut menu.

3. Click the **Manage** option from the shortcut menu to open the Computer Management console (MMC) shown in Figure 1-1. The MMC has two major panes. The left pane is the tree pane and is used to navigate the console hierarchy. The right pane is the results pane and shows the details of the utility or container selected in the tree pane.

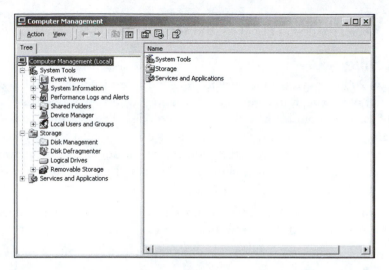

Figure 1-1   Computer Management console window

4. Double-click the **System Information** option, or single-click in the expansion box to expand its contents.

5. Click **System Summary** in the left tree pane and, on the Lab 1.2 Student Answer Sheet, record the system processor information shown in the results pane.

6. Expand the **Components** container in the tree pane.

7. Click **Display** and on your Student Answer Sheet, record the video system information shown in the results pane.

8. Expand the **Storage** container in the tree pane.

9. Click **Drives** and on your Student Answer Sheet, record the required disk drive information shown in the results pane.

10. Expand the **Multimedia** container in the tree pane.

11. Click **CD-ROM** and on your Student Answer Sheet, record the required CD information from the results pane.

12. Click **Device Manager** in the tree pane.

13. On your Student Answer Sheet, identify any device that has an exclamation mark (!). Double-click any of the devices marked with an exclamation mark and record the message on the Student Answer Sheet.

LAB 1.3 WORKING WITH VIRTUAL MEMORY

Objective

Windows 2000 uses virtual memory to store and access software and data that would not otherwise fit in RAM. Virtual memory works by paging less frequently used information from RAM to a paging file on disk. The location and size of the paging file can affect the system performance. Therefore, when a system does not seem to be performing well, the performance can sometimes be improved by increasing the size of the paging file, or by relocating the paging file to a separate disk drive. After completing this lab, you will be able to:

➤ Use the System program from Control Panel to check system processing priority and record the size and location of page files.

➤ Use Performance Monitor to view the number of page file accesses occurring every second.

➤ Use Task Monitor to monitor processor performance.

Estimated completion time: **10 minutes**

ACTIVITY

1. Click **Start**, **Settings**, **Control Panel**, and then double-click **System** to display the System Properties window.

2. Click the **Advanced** tab, and then click the **Performance Options** button. Record the total page size on the Lab 1.3 Student Answer Sheet.

3. Click the **Change** button, and record the page file information for each drive.

4. Click **Cancel** three times to return to the Windows desktop.

5. To record pages per second, you run the Performance Monitor utility and select the pages/sec counter as described below:

   a. Click **Start**, **Settings**, **Control Panel**, and double-click **Administrative Tools** to display a list of administrative tools.

   b. Double-click **Performance** to display a Performance monitor window, as shown in Figure 1-2.

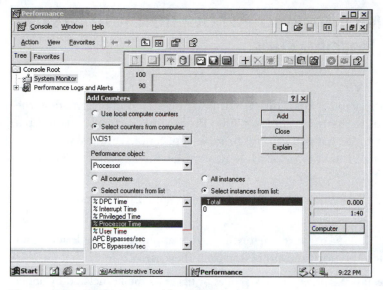

Figure 1-2   Performance Monitor window

   c. Right-click in the space under the Color column to display an action menu.

   d. Click **Add Counters**.

   e. In the Performance Object box, use the scroll bar to select the **Memory** object.

   f. In the Counter box, verify that **Pages per second** is highlighted.

   g. Click the **Add** button.

   h. Click **Close**.

   i. Observe the graph, and note the red line illustrating the number of pages/second.

   j. On the Student Answer Sheet, record the current maximum pages per second.

   k. Start **WordPad** (**Start**, **Programs**, **Accessories**, **WordPad**).

   l. On the Student Answer Sheet, record the pages per second for loading WordPad. Leave WordPad open.

   m. Start **Notepad** (**Start**, **Programs**, **Accessories**, **Notepad**), and on the Student Answer Sheet, record the pages per second. Note that as more programs are loaded into memory the pages per second increases.

   n. Close WordPad and Notepad.

   o. To end the Performance monitor, click **Exit** from the Console menu.

LAB 1.4 MONITORING APPLICATION AND SYSTEM PERFORMANCE

Objective

Application and system software running on a computer can affect the performance of the system. Windows 2000 Professional includes task and performance monitor tools that you can use to view applications and tasks currently in memory and the processor usage percentage. After completing this lab, you will be able to:

➤ Use the System option from Control Panel to determine application priority settings.

➤ Use Task Manager to determine what applications are loaded and how much memory and processor time they use.

➤ Use Task Manager to track processor usage by the kernel and by applications.

➤ Use Task Manager to unload applications.

Estimated completion time: **15–20 minutes**

ACTIVITY 1

Windows 2000 can be configured to provide priority to either applications or background server tasks. Configuring the system for background tasks provides better performance for processing requests from client computers. However, this configuration slows down applications running on the system, and also could be the reason the computer seems to be running slower. Follow the steps below to document the performance settings on your computer.

1. Click **Start**, **Settings**, **Control panel**, and double-click **System** to open the System Properties window.

2. Click the **Advanced** tab, and then click the **Performance Options** button to display the Performance settings.

3. Record the Application Response setting on the Lab 1.4 Student Answer Sheet.

4. Click **Cancel** twice to close all windows and return to the desktop.

ACTIVITY 2

Because Windows 2000 Professional can support up to two processors using Symmetric Multiprocessing (SMP), knowing the performance of your processor is useful to help you determine whether adding a second processor is necessary. Follow the steps below to use the Task Manager to figure processor utilization time for running applications.

1. To determine what applications are automatically loading, click the **Start** menu, click **Shutdown**, and then select the **Restart** option.

2. After the system restarts, log on using your assigned username and password.

3. Right-click over the taskbar to display the taskbar window.

4. Click **Task Manager** to display the Task Manager window shown in Figure 1-3.

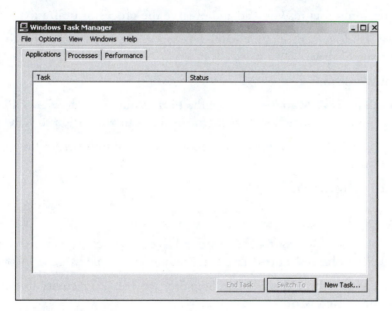

Figure 1-3   Task Manager window

5. Click the **Applications** tab, and on the Lab 1.4 Student Answer Sheet, record any automatically loaded applications.

6. Click the **Processes** tab, and on your Student Answer Sheet, record three processes that use the most CPU time.

7. Click the **Performance** tab to view the processor and memory usage graphs. To include the amount of processor time used by the Windows 2000 system kernel software, click the **View** menu and then, if necessary, place a check mark in front of **Show Kernel Times** by clicking it. The amount of kernel time is shown in red on the graph. On your Student Answer Sheet, record the minimum and maximum CPU times along with memory usage.

8. Star **Notepad** and record the processor and memory utilization.

9. Start **WordPad** and record the processor and memory utilization.

10. Click the **Applications** tab.

11. Click **Notepad** and then click the **End Task** button to exit the application.

12. Click **WordPad** and then click the **Switch To** button.

13. Enter some data in WordPad and observe the processor utilization.

14. Save the document in a file named **Temp** in the My Documents folder on your C: drive.

15. Exit WordPad.

16. Switch to **Task Manager** and use the **Performance** tab to view CPU usage history. Notice how kernel time increases in proportion to CPU usage.

17. On your Student Answer Sheet, record the maximum kernel time and CPU usage.

18. Exit Task Manager.

ACTIVITY 3

The Performance Monitor tool you used in Lab 1.3 to track pages per second also can be used to obtain a more detailed view of processor time usage, as follows.

1. Use the procedure described in Step 5 of the Lab 1.3 Activity to start **Performance Monitor**.

2. Select the **% Processor Time** counter from the **Processor** object.

3. Start **WordPad** and record the maximum processor time utilization on the Lab 1.4 Student Answer Sheet.

4. Start Task Manager, and on your Student Answer Sheet, record the maximum processor time utilization.

5. Exit WordPad and Task Manager.

6. Exit Performance Monitor, and close all windows.

LAB 1.5 USING EVENT VIEWER

Objective

Windows 2000 includes an Event Viewer utility that allows you to view any warnings and error messages issued by the operating system or application software. Warning and error messages may indicate failing or faulty components or application configuration problems that could affect system performance. After completing this lab, you will be able to:

➤ Start Event Viewer from either the Computer Management console or from the Control Panel.

➤ Use Event Viewer to view and record any system messages.

➤ Use Event Viewer to view and record any application messages.

Estimated completion time: **5–10 minutes**

ACTIVITY

1. Start Event Viewer from the Control Panel.

   a. Click **Start**, **Settings**, **Control Panel**, and click **Administrative Tools** to open the Administrative Tools window.

   b. Double-click **Event Viewer**.

   c. On your Student Answer Sheet, record the three types of logs shown in the right console tree.

   d. Exit Event Viewer.

2. Start Event Viewer from the Computer Management Console.

   a. Right-click **My Computer** and click **Manage** to view the Computer Management console.

   b. Expand **System Tools** to see the Event Viewer object.

   c. Double-click **Event Viewer**.

3. Click **System** from the left console tree. The three types of messages that may be recorded in event logs are:

   - *Informational* messages indicated by an "i" enclosed in a circle
   - *Warning* messages indicated by an exclamation mark enclosed in a triangle
   - *Error* messages indicated by an x enclosed in a red circle

4. From the System Log display, record any error messages on the Student Answer Sheet.

5. Double-click the most recent informational message from the Browser and record it on your Student Answer Sheet. (If you do not have any browser messages, record the first Informational message on the Student Answer Sheet.)

6. Click **Application** from the left console tree and on your Student Answer Sheet, record the most recent application message.

7. If auditing is enabled, the Security Log is used to record any events that you might be auditing, such as users logging on, or access attempts on secured files. Click the **Security** Log and determine if there are any audit messages. If there are any messages, record the most recent message on the Student Answer Sheet.

8. Exit the Computer Management console, and close all windows.

LAB 1.6   DOCUMENTING YOUR WINDOWS 2000 NETWORK CONFIGURATION

Objective

A major feature of Windows 2000 is its ability to access the Internet and participate in a local area network as a member of either a domain or a workgroup. In order to access a local area network, a Windows 2000 computer needs a network interface card and appropriate driver, a network protocol, and identification information including a unique computer name and membership in a domain or workgroup. A Windows 2000 domain requires the network to have one or more server computers running Windows 2000 Server and acting as domain controllers. After completing this lab, you will be able to:

➤ Determine if your computer is a member of a domain or workgroup.

➤ Document your computer's name along with its domain or workgroup name.

➤ Determine your network card type and model.

➤ Identify what protocol(s) are loaded.

➤ Access information on another computer on the network.

Estimated completion time: **10 minutes**

ACTIVITY

1. Identify your computer's name along with your domain or workgroup membership.

   a. Right-click **My Computer** and click the **Properties** option to display the System Properties window.

   b. Click the **Network Identification** tab.

   c. Record your computer name and domain or workgroup membership on your Lab 1.6 Student Answer Sheet.

   d. Close the System Properties window.

2. Determine your network card type and model.

   a. Right-click **My Network Places** and click **Properties** to display the Network and Dial-up Connections window.

   b. Double-click **Local Area Connection** to display the Local Area Connection Status window.

   c. On your Student Answer Sheet, record the number of packets sent and received by your computer.

   d. Click the **Properties** button and on your Student Answer Sheet, record the network card type and protocol information.

   e. Click **Internet Protocol (TCP/IP)**, and then click the **Properties** button.

   f. Record your IP address information on your Student Answer Sheet.

   g. Click **Cancel** twice to return to the Local Area Connection Status window.

   h. Click **Close**.

   i. Close the Network and Dial-up Connections window.

3. Access computers in a workgroup.

   a. Double-click **My Network Places**.

   b. Double-click **Entire Network** and then click the **view entire network** link.

   c. On your Student Answer Sheet, record the workgroups.

   d. Double-click your workgroup.

   e. Double-click the computer named **Instructor** (or your own if no others are present).

   f. On your Student Answer Sheet, record any shared folders.

   g. Close all windows.

LAB 1.7 SHARING NETWORK INFORMATION

Objective

A potential use of implementing workgroups in your network is allowing users within a department to access each other's documents. For example, one of the legal assistants at the Melendres and Associates law firm needs to access a legal document stored on Mr. Melendres's computer. You can simulate this activity by working with another student or computer on your network. Designate one student's computer to be Mr. Melendres's computer, and designate the other computer to be the legal assistant's computer. If working alone, you can use your computer for both roles. After completing this lab activity, you will be able to:

➤ Create and share a folder from a Windows 2000 computer.

➤ Check security to determine what users have permissions to access a folder.

➤ Access a shared document on the network.

Estimated completion time: **10 minutes**

ACTIVITY

1. Share a folder on Mr. Melendres's computer.

   a. Double-click **My Computer**.

   b. Double-click your **C:** drive to open it.

   c. Create a folder named **Shared**, as follows:

   - From the File menu click **New**.

   - Click **Folder**.

   - Press the **Backspace** key and enter the name **Shared**.

   - Press **Enter** to save the folder name.

   d. Right-click the new folder and click **Sharing**.

   e. Click the **Share this folder** option.

   f. Click the **Permissions** button.

   g. On your Student Answer Sheet, record default access permissions to this folder.

   h. Click **Cancel** to return to the Shared Properties dialog box, and then click **OK** to share the folder.

2. Save a legal document in the Shared folder on Mr. Melendres's computer.

   a. Double-click **My Network Places**.

b. Open **WordPad** and call up the document you created in Lab 3. Be sure your name is included in the document contents.

c. Save the document in your Shared folder.

d. Exit WordPad, and close all windows.

3. Access the document from the legal assistant's computer (or another computer on the network).

a. Double-click **My Network Places**.

b. Double-click **Entire Network** and then click the **view entire network** link.

c. Double-click your workgroup.

d. Double-click the computer acting as Mr. Melendres's system (or your own if no others are present).

e. On your Student Answer Sheet, record the shared folders.

f. Double-click the WordPad document saved in the Shared directory and read the contents.

g. Exit WordPad, and close all windows.

h. Use **Start**, **Shutdown** to log off, or shut down the computer.

INSTALLING WINDOWS 2000 PROFESSIONAL

Labs included in this chapter

➤ Lab 2.1 Removing Windows 2000 Professional

➤ Lab 2.2 Performing an Attended Installation from CD-ROM

➤ Lab 2.3 Installing the Windows 2000 Professional Resource Kit

➤ Lab 2.4 Creating an Unattended Installation File

➤ Lab 2.5 Modifying an Unattended Installation File

➤ Lab 2.6 Performing an Unattended Installation

Microsoft MCSE Exam #70-210 Objectives	
Objective	Lab
Perform an attended installation of Windows 2000 Professional	2.2
Create unattended answer files by using Setup Manager to automate installation of Windows 2000 Professional	2.3, 2.4
Configure Window 2000 Professional for multiple locations	2.4
Perform an unattended installation of Windows 2000 Professional	2.4, 2.5, 2.6

 Student Answer Sheets to accompany the labs in this chapter can be downloaded from the Online Companion for this manual at *www.course.com*.

Lab 2.1 Removing Windows 2000 Professional

Objective

Prior to practicing the Windows 2000 Professional installation on your computer, you need to remove the existing Windows 2000 Professional. After completing this lab, you will be able to:

➤ Create a set of four Windows 2000 Professional setup floppy disks.

➤ Remove Windows 2000 Professional from a dual-booting computer.

➤ Verify that Windows 2000 has been removed.

Requirements

This Requirements section covers all the labs in this chapter. In order to perform the labs in this chapter, you should verify the following:

➤ Your computer meets the requirements specified in the Introduction to this book.

➤ Windows 95/98 is installed on drive C:.

➤ Your existing Windows 2000 is installed on logical drive D:.

➤ You have access to a Windows 2000 Professional CD-ROM.

➤ You have access to a Windows 2000 Resource Kit CD-ROM.

➤ You have four blank floppy disks for Lab 2.1.

➤ In order to perform the unattended installation lab (Lab 2.4), you should have less than 760MB of free space on your Windows 95/98 partition.

Estimated completion time: **30–45 minutes**

 ## Activity

1. Create a set of four Windows 2000 boot disks as follows:

   a. Obtain four blank, formatted high-density floppy disks.

   b. Place your Windows 2000 Professional CD in the CD-ROM drive, and click **No** to avoid upgrading your system. If necessary, close the Windows 2000 Install window.

   c. Open the Run command (**Start**, **Run**).

   d. Type **<CD-ROM drive>:\bootdisk\makeboot** (where *<CD-ROM drive>* is the letter of your CD-ROM drive), and click **OK**.

   e. Place the first disk in drive A:, and type **A** to indicate the drive letter.

    f. Press any key to start the creation process.

    g. Once a disk is completed, label it and place the next disk in the drive.

    h. Repeat this process for all remaining disks.

2. Create a Windows 95/98 startup disk as follows.

    a. Start your computer with Windows 95/98.

    b. To open the Control Panel, click **Start**, point to **Settings**, click **Control Panel**.

    c. Double-click **Add/Remove Programs**.

    d. Click the **Startup Disk** tab.

    e. Insert a blank disk in the drive, and click the **Create Disk** button.

    f. Click **OK** when you receive the Insert Disk message.

    g. Specify the path to your Windows 95/98 CD-ROM or .cab files, and click **OK**.

    h. Click **OK** when you receive the Insert Disk message.

    i. After the disk has been created, click **OK** to close the Add/Remove Programs window.

3. Remove Windows 2000 hidden and system files as follows:

    a. Use Windows Explorer or My Computer to open a window to your C: drive.

    b. Display hidden file types and file extensions as follows:

- From the **Tools** menu click **Folder Options**.
- Use the **View** tab to select the **Show all files** option.
- To view file extensions, remove the check from the **Hide file extensions for known file types** option.
- Click **OK** to return to the C: drive window.

    c. Remove the Read-only and Hidden attributes from the following files:

- Boot.ini
- Ntdetect.com
- Ntldr
- Bootsect.dos

    d. Delete the following Windows 2000 startup files:

- Boot.ini
- Ntdetect.com
- Ntldr
- Bootsect.dos

4. Close all windows, and restart your computer from the Windows 95/98 startup disk. If necessary, select the option to start without CD-ROM support.

5. After the computer has started from the Windows 95/98 startup disk, you will be presented with an "A:>" command prompt. To replace the Windows 2000 loader files with the Windows 95/98 system files, type **SYS C:** and press **Enter**.

6. Remove the Windows 95/98 startup disk and use the **Ctrl+Alt+Del** key combination to restart your computer.

7. Remove the Windows 2000 partition.

   a. Obtain the four Windows 2000 installation disks.

   b. Insert the first Windows 2000 installation disk in your computer, and start your computer. Insert the other disks as requested.

   c. If necessary, press **Enter** to bypass the Evaluation software message and to continue the installation process.

   d. Press **Enter** to perform a Windows 2000 setup.

   e. If necessary, insert the Windows 2000 Professional CD, and press **Enter**.

   f. Press **F8** to agree to the license agreement.

   g. If you are asked if you want to repair the partition, press **Esc**.

   h. Highlight your existing Windows 2000 partition, and press **D** to delete it.

   i. Press **L** to confirm the deletion.

8. Remove any disk from your computer and press **F3** twice to exit the installation process and restart your computer. Verify that the computer now starts Windows 95/98 without displaying the Windows 2000 startup options.

LAB 2.2 PERFORMING AN ATTENDED INSTALLATION FROM CD-ROM

Objective

The Animal Care Center recently purchased a computer from your company, Computer Technology Services (CTS). Dennis wants to have the computer installed in his office with Windows 2000 Professional. One of your employees previously installed a beta copy of Windows 2000 on this computer, and now it is your job to remove this copy and do a new installation of Windows 2000 for Dennis. As described in Lab 1.1, this computer will be used as the office server to replace the aging Novell server. After completing this lab, you will be able to:

➤ Perform a new installation of Windows 2000 from a CD-ROM.

➤ Install both Novell and Microsoft client services on Windows 2000.

➤ Configure Windows 2000 Professional to use both TCP/IP and Novell IPX protocols.

Estimated completion time: **50–60 minutes**

ACTIVITY

Before beginning this activity, you need to work with your instructor to fill out the Lab 2.2 Installation Planning Worksheet that follows this lab. It is recommended that your computer have Windows 95/98 installed on drive C: and Windows 2000 installed in a separate logical drive.

1. Obtain the four Windows 2000 Professional startup disks you created in Lab 2.1.

2. If necessary, remove the Windows 2000 Professional CD-ROM and insert the Windows 2000 floppy boot disk number 1.

3. Perform the text-based phase of Windows 2000 installation.

   a. Boot your computer from Windows 2000 boot disk number 1.

   b. Insert disks 2 through 4 as requested.

   c. When you see the Welcome to Setup screen, insert the Windows 2000 Professional CD-ROM and press **Enter** to start the text-mode portion of the Windows 2000 setup, and display the Windows 2000 Licensing Agreement.

   d. Press **F8** to accept the license agreement. A setup screen showing the existing partitions is shown. Record the existing partition information on the Lab 2.1 Student Answer Sheet.

   e. Highlight the **Unpartitioned space** option in the partition selection screen, and type **C**.

   f. Enter the size of the Windows 2000 partition, or press **Enter** to accept the size shown. Record the partition size. The partition list screen is shown again with the New (Unformatted) partition.

   g. Highlight the **New (Unformatted)** partition and press **Enter**. You see a setup screen that gives you the choice of formatting the new partition as NTFS or FAT.

   h. Select the format specified on your Installation Planning Worksheet, and press **Enter**. Wait while setup formats your partition. After the formatting process is completed, the setup process creates a list of files to be copied and begins copying files to the newly formatted partition. This whole process may take several minutes, so if you're a multitasking kind of person, it's a good time to take a short break or do some reading. However, if there is a floppy disk in your computer, you should remove it before you leave. The computer automatically reboots after completing the text-mode portion of the installation.

4. Perform the graphical user interface (GUI) portion of Windows 2000 installation as follows:

a. After rebooting, the GUI portion of the installation begins, and the installation program automatically installs devices detected on your computer.

b. After the detected devices have been installed, the GUI setup process displays the Regional Settings window. Click the uppermost **Customize** button to see the options you have in controlling how the system formats numbers, currency, and dates.

c. Click the tabs necessary to record the options requested on the Lab 2.1 Student Answer Sheet.

d. Select the following options:
- Display negative numbers in parentheses.
- Do not display leading zeros before decimal points.
- Display the date using the MM/dd/yyyy format.

e. Click **OK** to return to the Regional Settings window.

f. Click the **Customize** button next to the keyboard settings to display the Input Locales tab.

g. Click the **Properties** button and record the keyboard layouts.

h. Click **Cancel** twice to return to the Regional Settings window.

i. Click **Next** to continue the installation with the Personalize your Software window.

j. Enter the user name along with the organization specified on the Installation Planning Worksheet.

k. Click **Next** to continue to the Product Key window.

l. Enter your product key, and click **Next** to display the Computer Name and Administrator password window.

m. Enter the computer name you specified on the Installation Planning Worksheet, and type **password** for the administrator password. Type **password** again to confirm the password. (Remember that passwords are case-sensitive.)

n. Click **Next** to continue.

o. If the installation program detects a modem in your computer, the Modem Dialing Information window appears. If this happens, enter your area code, and verify that Tone dialing is selected and click **Next**.

p. The Date and Time Settings window should now be displayed.

q. If necessary, update the date and time and select your correct time zone.

r. Verify that Automatically adjust clock for daylight saving time is checked, and click **Next** to configure the network settings.

2

s. Because you need to configure access to a Novell NetWare server, on the Network Settings window click the **Custom settings** option, and then click **Next** to continue. On your Student Answer Sheet, record the network information.

t. Set a TCP/IP address. (You can skip this step if DHCP—automatic IP addressing—is specified on the Installation Planning Worksheet instead of an IP address.)

- Click **Internet Protocol (TCP/IP)** and click the **Properties** button to display the Internet Protocol general properties tab.
- Click the **Use the following IP address** option.
- Enter the four octets of the IP address specified on the Installation Planning Worksheet, separated by periods.
- Enter the four octets of the subnet mask specified on the Installation Planning Worksheet.
- Click **OK** to return to the Networking Components window.

u. For the computer to be able to copy files from the Animal Health Center's Novell NetWare server, you need to follow the steps below to install the Novell IPX Protocol and NetWare Client.

- Click **Install**.
- Select **Protocol** and click **Add**.
- Select the **NWLink IPX/SPX/NetBIOS Compatible Transport Protocol** and click **OK**.
- Click **Install**.
- Select **Client** and click **Add**.
- Select **Client Service for NetWare** and click **OK**.

v. Click **Next** to display the Workgroup or Computer Domain window.

w. Verify that the computer is being installed in a workgroup and *not* a domain. Enter the workgroup name specified on your Installation Planning Worksheet and click **Next** to install and configure the networking components.

x. Wait while the setup program copies the necessary files from your CD and performs final setup tasks. This will take several minutes, so it may be another good time to take a break or read.

y. If necessary, verify that your time and date settings are correct. Click **Finish** after all processes are completed. Your system then reboots.

5. Finalize the Windows 2000 installation as follows.

   a. After rebooting, a Network Identification Wizard welcome screen is shown. Click **Next** to display the Users of This Computer window. On your Student Answer Sheet, record the user logon options.

   b. Click the option that allows multiple users to log on to this computer, and click **Next** to continue.

   c. Click **Finish** to complete the Network Identification Wizard. You should be presented with a Windows 2000 Logon window.

   d. Enter the password you established for the Administrator, and press **Enter** to log on.

   e. Leave the preferred NetWare Server box empty, and click **OK** to continue to log on.

6. Have your instructor verify your installation and sign off on the Lab 2.1 Student Answer Sheet.

   a. Check that the NetWare Client is installed, as follows:

      - Double-click **My Network Places**.
      - Double-click **Entire Network** and click the **entire contents** option. Verify that both Microsoft and Novell options are visible.
      - If you have a Novell server on your network, double-click the **NetWare** option, and verify that the server is shown.
      - Close the Entire Network window.

   b. Verify the TCP/IP address as follows:

      - Right-click **My Network Places** and click **Properties**.
      - Double-click the **Local Area Connection** icon and click **Properties**.
      - Click **Internet Protocol (TCP/IP)** and click the **Properties** button.
      - Verify that the correct TCP/IP address and mask are entered.
      - Click **Cancel** twice to return to the Local Area Connection Status window.
      - Click **Close**, and then close the Network and Dial-up Connections window.

   c. Check the computer name and workgroup:

      - Right-click **My Computer** and click **Properties**.
      - Click the **Network Identification** tab. Verify the computer and workgroup names.
      - Click **Cancel** to close all windows.

   d. Remove the Windows 2000 Professional CD-ROM.

Lab 2.2 Performing an Attended Installation from CD-ROM

Installation Planning Worksheet

Name: _____ Computer ID: _____

Work with your instructor to identify the following installation information.

Computer name to be used for your installation: _____

User name: _____ (example: your name)

Organization: _____ (example: Animal Health Center)

Drive (partition) to contain Windows 2000 Professional: _____

Format:

_____ NTFS (Select this format if your computer already has a FAT partition on drive C:.)

_____ FAT (Select this format if Windows 2000 is the only operating system; you will convert to NTFS later.)

Product key: _____
(Enter the product key provided with your Windows 2000 CD-ROM.)

TCP/IP information:
    IP address: _____ . _____ . _____ . _____

    Subnet mask: _____ . _____ . _____ . _____

Workgroup name: _____ (example: AHC)

LAB 2.3 INSTALLING THE WINDOWS 2000 PROFESSIONAL RESOURCE KIT

Objective

The Windows 2000 Professional Resource Kit contains many utilities to assist you in installing, configuring, and troubleshooting Windows 2000 systems. Because of its many uses in supporting the Windows 2000 environment, your organization recently acquired the Windows 2000 Professional Resource Kit, along with a subscription to Microsoft TechNet. With the TechNet subscription you receive monthly Windows 2000 and Windows NT service packs, technical support tools, beta copies of software, and the Microsoft technical information database that includes reported problems and fixes. Soon you will need to use the Setup Manager Wizard that is included in the Windows 2000 Professional Resource Kit. The Setup Manager Wizard helps automate the installation of Windows 2000 Professional on multiple computers. After completing this lab, you will be able to:

➤ Install the Windows 2000 Professional Resource Kit on your workstation.

➤ Identify major components and their functions.

➤ Start the Setup Manager Wizard.

Estimated completion time: **25 minutes**

ACTIVITY

1. If necessary, start your computer with Windows 2000, and log on as the administrator.

2. If installing from a CD, place a copy of the Windows 2000 Professional Resource Kit in the CD-ROM drive. Skip to Step 4 if the CD does not self-start. If the CD self-starts, click the **Install Resource Kit** option and skip to Step 5.

3. If installing from the network, perform the following:

   a. Obtain the workgroup, server, and share name of the Resource Kit and record them on your Lab 2.3 Student Answer Sheet.

   b. Right-click **My Network Places** and click the **Map Network Drive** option.

   c. Click the **Browse** button to display existing workgroups.

   d. Expand the workgroup and server identified in Step 3 a. above.

   e. Click the share name of the Resource Kit, and click **OK**.

2

   f. Remove the check mark from the Reconnect at Logon box.

   g. Select any available drive letter, and click **Finish**.

 4. Start the Windows 2000 Professional Resource Kit installation.

   a. Click **Start**, click **Run**, and click the **Browse** button.

   b. In the Look in box, select the drive letter containing the Resource Kit.

   c. Double-click the **Setup** program, and return to the Run window.

   d. Click **OK** to start the Windows 2000 Professional Resource Kit installation.

 5. A welcome to the Windows 2000 Professional Resource Kit wizard is shown. Click **Next** to start the installation wizard.

 6. Click **I Agree** to the License agreement, and click **Next** to continue.

 7. Your default user name and organization are shown. Click **Next** to accept the name and organization.

 8. When the Installation Type window is visible, click **Custom** and then click **Next** to view the Resource Kit components and space required. Record the Resource Kit components, the size (space required), and the total space required on the Lab 2.3 Student Answer Sheet.

 9. To prevent installation of the Scripting tools, click the down arrow to the left of the **Scripting Tools** option, and then select the **Entire feature will not be available** option. Notice the red X to the left of the Scripting Tools component indicating it will not be installed.

10. Click **Next** to advance to the **Begin Installation** window.

11. Click **Next** to start the installation process, and copy the necessary files to your computer.

12. After all files are copied, click **Finish** and close the 2000 Resource Kit CD window to complete the installation and return to the Windows 2000 desktop.

13. Create a shortcut to start the Setup Manager wizard.

   a. Double-click **My Computer** and then open your Windows 2000 drive by double-clicking it.

   b. Open the **Program Files** folder by double-clicking it, and then click **Show Files**.

   c. Open the **Resource Pro Kit** folder by double-clicking it.

   d. Scroll down to the **setupmgr** program and right-click it.

   e. Select the **Send to** option, and then click the **Desktop (create shortcut)** option.

   f. Close the Resource Pro Kit window.

   g. Notice that a Shortcut to setupmgr icon has been added to your desktop.

14. Start Setup Manager from the desktop shortcut.

15. After verifying that the Welcome to Setup Manager wizard window appears, click **Cancel** and respond with **Yes** and then click **Finish** to return to the Windows 2000 Professional desktop.

16. Remove the Resource Kit CD-ROM.

LAB 2.4 CREATING AN UNATTENDED INSTALLATION FILE

Objective

The Universal Aerospace Corporation has purchased five new workstations from your company for use in their Accounting Department. Kellie Thiele, the network administrator, is upgrading their NetWare server, so they have contracted with you to install Windows 2000 on the new computers. Rather than install each computer separately, you decide to create and use an unattended installation file to automate the Windows 2000 installation. To create an unattended installation file for Universal Aerospace, you first need to identify how Kellie wants the systems to be configured. Use the Lab 2.4 Installation Planing Worksheet to gather the information you need to build the unattended installation file. After completing this lab, you will be able to:

➤ Identify the information needed to create an unattended answer file.

➤ Use the Setup Manager Wizard to create both an unattended answer file and a uniqueness database file.

➤ View and print the contents of the unattended installation files, and identify the purpose of each file.

Estimated completion time: **25 minutes**

ACTIVITY

Before beginning this activity, your instructor may provide you with information you need to fill out the Lab 2.4 Installation Planning Worksheet that follows this lab.

1. Using the information supplied by your instructor, fill in the Lab 2.4 Installation Planning Worksheet. If manual IP addressing is used, be sure that the IP address and subnet mask are compatible with other computers on your network.

2

2. If necessary, start your computer with Windows 2000, and log on as the administrator.

3. Start Setup Manager Wizard from the desktop shortcut you created in Lab 2.3; when the Welcome screen appears, click **Next**.

4. Select the **Create a new answer file** option, and click **Next** to display the Product to Install window. Record the platform options on the Lab 2.4 Installation Planning Worksheet.

5. Verify that the Windows 2000 Unattended Installation option is selected, and then click **Next** to display the Platform window.

6. Verify that the Windows 2000 Professional platform is selected, and then click **Next** to display the User Interaction Level window.

7. The User Interaction Level lets you control what choices the operator on the computer being set up will have. Identify the default option on the Lab 2.4 Student Answer Sheet and describe its use. Because you want the installation to proceed without your involvement, click the **Fully automated** option, and then click **Next** to display the License Agreement window.

8. Click the **I accept the terms of the License Agreement** check box, and then click **Next** to display the Customize the Software window.

9. In the Customize the Software window, enter the user and organization information specified on your Installation Planning Worksheet, and click **Next** to display the Computer Names window.

10. The Computer Names window provides the Windows 2000 installation program with a unique name for the computer being installed. Enter the name of a computer specified on the Installation Planning Worksheet in the Computer Name field, and then click the **Add** button. Repeat this process for each computer specified on your worksheet. When all computer names have been added, click **Next** to continue.

11. Enter the initial password for the administrator you specified on the Installation Planning Worksheet. This password should be changed after the system is operational. (Because passwords are case-sensitive, be sure to check your Caps Lock key.) After entering the password in both the Password and Confirm password fields, click **Next** to display the Display Settings window.

12. Enter the Colors, Screen area, and Refresh frequency specified on your Lab 2.4 Installation Planning Worksheet, and click **Next** to display the Network Settings window.

13. Click the **Custom settings** option, and click **Next** to display the Number of Network Adapters window.

14. Verify that **One network adapter** is selected, and then click **Next** to display the Networking Components window.

15. To add the Novell Client:

    ■ Click the **Add** button to display the Select Network Component Type window.

    ■ Click **Client** and then click **Add** to display the Select Network Client window.

    ■ Verify that the **Client Service for NetWare** is selected, and click **OK** to return to the Networking Components window.

16. To manually specify an IP address and subnet mask for each computer:

    ■ Click **Internet Protocol (TCP/IP)** and then click **Properties** to display the Internet Protocol (TCP/IP) Properties window.

    ■ Click **Use the following IP address** option, and then enter the IP address and subnet mask specified on your Lab 2.4 Installation Planning Worksheet.

    ■ Click **OK** to return to the Networking Components window.

17. Click **Next** to display the Workgroup or Domain window.

18. Enter the Workgroup name specified on your Lab 2.4 Installation Planning Worksheet, and click **Next** to display the Time Zone window.

19. Use the scroll button to select your time zone, and then click **Next** to display the Additional Settings window.

20. To change the default settings, click **Yes, edit the additional settings** option, and click **Next** to display the Telephony window.

21. Enter your area code, and click **Next** to display the Regional Settings window.

22. On your Lab 2.4 Installation Planning Worksheet, record the default Regional Settings language and other options, if you have not already done so.

23. Explore the Regional Settings window:

    ■ Click the **Specify regional setting in the answer file** option, and on your Student Answer Sheet, record the default language.

    ■ Click the **Customize the default language settings** check box.

    ■ Click the **Custom** button and on your Student Answer Sheet, record the three language options.

    ■ Click **Cancel** and then select the Regional Settings options you identified on your Installation Planning Worksheet.

    ■ Click **Next** to display the Browser and Shell Settings window.

2

24. Unless special proxy values are specified on your Installation Planning sheet (in which case you would enter them), click **Next** to use the default Internet Explorer settings and display the Installation Folder window.

25. Click **Next** to accept the default Winnt folder name and display the Install Printers window.

26. If you have a network printer, enter the name of the printer specified on your Lab 2.4 Installation Planning Worksheet, using the format *servername**printer*. Click **Next** to display the Run Once window.

27. The Run Once window specifies the name of a script file or program you want to run when a user logs on to this workstation. Add any commands specified on your Lab 2.4 Installation Planning Worksheet, and click **Next** to display the Distribution Folder window.

28. The Distribution Folder windows are used to create a network share that contains the files needed to perform the unattended installation. Because you will test the unattended installation by installing from a CD, click **No, this answer file will be used to install from a CD**, and click **Next**. You might receive a message saying you need to create a distribution file for the IE Branding you chose. Click **Yes** to display the Answer File Name window.

29. Click the **Browse** button and perform the following steps to create an answer file named Unattend.txt in a folder named Install on your C: drive.

    a. Use the scroll button to select your C: drive in the "Save in" text box.

    b. Click the **Create New Folder** icon.

    c. Type **Install** for the folder name and press **Enter**.

    d. Double-click the newly created **Install** folder and enter **Unattend.txt** in the Filename field; then click **Save** and **Next** to continue.

30. Click **Finish** to exit the Setup Manager Wizard.

31. Use Notepad to retrieve and print the following files from your C:\Install folder.

    - Unattend.txt
    - Unattend.udf
    - Unattend.bat

32. In the Unattend.bat file identify the following commands:

    - The command used to provide the path to your Windows 2000 Professional installation source files
    - The commands used to specify the name of the unattend files

33. Given the information in the batch file, record (in the Lab 2.4 Student Answer Sheet) the Winnt32 command that results when you issue the following batch command:

    UNATTEND.BAT Acct1

34. In the Unattend.txt file, identify the following information:
    - Locate the AutoPartition=1 command, and then use the Unattend.doc file to record the purpose of the AutoPartition command on your Student Answer Sheet.
    - Locate the workgroup name and verify that it is correct.
    - If you manually assigned an IP Address, locate the IP Address and Subnet numbers.
    - Locate and identify the DHCP setting.
    - Locate the [UserData] heading, and record its contents on your Student Answer Sheet.

35. In the Unattend.udf file, identify the following information:
    - Identify the Unattend.txt headings and record them on your Student Answer Sheet.
    - On your Student Answer Sheet, record the value that would be substituted into the Unattend.txt file when using the following command:

      Winnt32 /unattend:unattend.txt /udf:Acct2,unattend.udf

LAB 2.4 CREATING AN UNATTENDED INSTALLATION FILE

Installation Planning Worksheet

Name: _____ Computer ID: _____

Windows 2000 platform options:

_____ Windows 2000 Professional _____ Windows 2000 Server

User: _____ Organization: _____

When using the unattended installation file to install multiple computers, the Setup Manager Wizard creates a uniqueness database that allows you use the same unattended installation file for multiple computers. In the table below, enter the names of computers you plan to install with the unattended answer files. If assigning manual IP addresses, include each computer's IP address and subnet mask.

Computer Name	IP Address or DHCP	Subnet Mask

Temporary administrator password: _____

Color, screen area, resolution, and refresh frequency to be used:

_____

_____

Include Novell client?   _____ Yes   _____ No

Workgroup/domain name: _____

Time zone: _____   Area code: _____

Regional Settings: _____

   Default Regional Settings options for the Windows version you are installing:

   _____

   Default language setting: _____

Internet Explorer Proxy Settings (if any):

   Address: _____ . _____ . _____ . _____   Port: _____

Network printer name: _____

Run Once command: _____

When performing an unattended installation, you can identify a network share or local CD-ROM as the location for the Windows 2000 installation files. If you want the wizard to copy files to a share, record it below:

Network distribution folder or CD-ROM folder: _____

LAB 2.5 MODIFYING UNATTENDED INSTALLATION FILES

Objective

After the unattended answer file and uniqueness database files have been created and printed, the next step is to make any modifications needed to support or enhance the installation process. One addition you might want to make to either the answer file or uniqueness database file is Microsoft product identification. Placing the product identification in the UserData section of either the answer file or uniqueness database eliminates having to enter it for each computer. If each computer has a separate identification, the ProductID entry should be placed in each computer's section of the uniqueness database file. If you manually assign IP addresses to each computer, you need to create a section in the uniqueness database file that contains each computer's IP address and subnet mask. After completing this lab, you will be able to:

➤ Modify the AutoPartition settings in the unattended answer file.

➤ Modify the uniqueness database to include product identification and an IP address.

➤ Use the WINNT32 utility to start an unattended installation of Windows 2000 Professional.

➤ Verify your installation.

Estimated completion time: **10–15 minutes**

ACTIVITY

1. If necessary, start your computer and log on as administrator.

2. Double-click **My Computer** and navigate to the C:\Install folder.

3. Use Notepad to remove the AutoPartition setting in the Unattend.txt file as follows:

   a. Double-click the **Unattend.txt** file to open it with Notepad.

   b. To manually select a partition for the Windows 2000 installation, remove the AutoPartition setting line.

4. Add the ProductId setting to the Unattend.txt file as follows:

   a. Locate the UserData section heading.

   b. Add the following line after the Computer Name in the UserData section:

   ProductID="xxxxx-xxxxx-xxxxx-xxxxx-xxxxx"

   (Replace all "x"s with the correct CD Key or Product ID.)

   c. Save and print the Unattend.txt file. Close the file.

5. Use Notepad to add ProductID and IP Address settings to your Unattend.udf file.

   a. Right-click the **Unattend.udf** file, and click **Open With** to display the Open With window. Double-click **Notepad** to edit the Unattend.udf file.

   b. Add the following statement to include each computer's ProductID in the UserData section:

   ProductID="xxxxx-xxxxx-xxxxx-xxxxx-xxxxx"

   (Replace all "x"s with the correct CD Key or Product ID.)

   c. If you are manually assigning IP addresses, add the following section after each computer's UserData section:

   [*computername*:params.MS_TCPIP.Adapter1]

   > **DHCP=NO**
   >
   > **IPAddress=192.168.1.5**
   >
   > **Subnetmask=255.255.255.0**

   d. Save and print the unattend.udf file, then close the file.

6. If necessary, use Notepad to change the CD-ROM drive letter in the unattend.bat file as follows:

   a. Right-click the **Unattend.bat** file, and click **Edit**.

   b. If necessary, modify the letter corresponding to your CD-ROM drive, so it matches the drive letter used by Windows 95/98.

   c. Save and print the **Unattend.bat** file.

7. Have your instructor check your file modifications.

LAB 2.6 PERFORMING AN UNATTENDED INSTALLATION

Objective

After the unattended answer file and uniqueness database files have been created and modified, your next step is to test the unattended installation process by using these files to install Windows 2000 Professional on your computer. After completing this lab, you will be able to:

➤ Use the WINNT32 utility to start an unattended installation of Windows 2000 Professional.

➤ Verify your installation.

Estimated completion time: **40–50 minutes**

ACTIVITY

1. Obtain your four Windows 2000 installation floppy disks and then perform the steps outlined in Lab 2.1 to remove the existing Windows 2000 partition and restart your computer with Windows 95/98.

2. Insert the Windows 2000 Professional CD-ROM.

3. Click **No** when asked if you want to upgrade to Windows 2000.

4. Exit the Windows 2000 Professional CD window.

5. Start the unattended installation batch file.

   a. Click **Start, Run** and enter the command **C:\Install\Unattend.bat** *your-computer-name* in the Run window (replace *your-computer-name* with the name of the computer you specified on the Installation Planning Worksheet following Lab 2.2) to install Windows 2000 using the computer information you saved in the unattended installation file in Lab 2.5.

   b. Click **OK** to start the unattended installation.

c. If your system has virus protection software installed, you may receive a message indicating a suspected virus activity has occurred when the setup program writes to the boot sector of the C: drive. Click the option to ignore any virus activity and continue the unattended installation.

d. Initial setup files will now be copied to your computer. After all the necessary files are copied, your computer will automatically restart with the Windows 2000 setup program.

6. By default, the Windows 2000 setup program will attempt to load the Windows 2000 operating system files in your primary Windows 95/98 partition. Because you do not have the necessary 763 MB of free space on drive C:, you will receive a "Partition too full" message. Press **Enter** to go back and then perform the following process to create and format a new partition for Windows 2000.

a. Highlight the **Unpartitioned space** option from the partition window and press C to create a new partition.

b. Enter a partition size of approximately 1 GB (1000 MB) leaving at least 50–100 MB of unpartitioned space for use in later lab projects.

c. Press **Enter** to create the new partition.

d. Highlight the New (Unformatted) partition and press **Enter** to display the format options.

e. Be sure that the **Format the partition using the NTFS file system** is highlighted and press **Enter** to start the formatting process.

7. Sit back and relax while Windows 2000 Professional is installed on your system. If your system has virus protection software installed, you might receive a message indicating a suspected virus activity when the installation program writes to the boot sector of the C: drive. Ignore any virus message and continue the installation.

8. After installation is complete, restart your computer to Windows 2000 Professional and log on as Administrator. If you receive a NetWare login dialog box, click **Cancel** and then click **Yes** to continue logging on without connecting to a NetWare server. Click **Exit** when you see the Windows 2000 "Getting Started" window. Congratulations, your new Windows 2000 Professional system is now up and running!

9. Have your instructor verify your installation by checking the following:

- Verify IP address settings.
- Verify computer name and workgroup name.

Using MMC, Task Scheduler, and Control Panel

Labs included in this chapter

➤ Lab 3.1 Customizing a Microsoft Management Console

➤ Lab 3.2 Creating Local Users

➤ Lab 3.3 Configuring Accessibility Services

➤ Lab 3.4 Configuring Other Services

➤ Lab 3.5 Configuring Hardware Profiles and Power Management

Microsoft MCSE Exam #70-210 Objectives	
Objective	Lab
Configure and troubleshoot desktop settings	3.1
Implement, configure, manage, and troubleshoot a security configuration	3.1
Create and manage local users and groups	3.2, 3.5
Configure and troubleshoot accessibility services	3.3
Configure and troubleshoot fax support	3.4
Update drivers	3.4

Student Answer Sheets to accompany the labs in this chapter can be downloaded from the Online Companion for this manual at *www.course.com*.

LAB 3.1 CUSTOMIZING A MICROSOFT MANAGEMENT CONSOLE

Objective

Dennis Geisler, the owner of the Animal Care Center, wants one of the users to perform limited administrative functions on the Windows 2000 Professional system when he is out of the office. These clerical functions include viewing user connection information, defragmenting the hard drive, viewing event messages, and monitoring logical drive usage. These functions can be performed using the Windows 2000 Administrative tools, but Dennis wants you to create a special console that allows only a specified user to perform these limited functions. The limited tools should then be added to the Start menu to make them easy for users to access. After completing this lab, you will be able to:

➤ Create a Microsoft Management Console (MMC) with specific snap-ins and extensions.

➤ Create multiple windows containing specific functions.

➤ Limit users to only the windows you have configured.

➤ Save the console on the Start menu.

Requirements

➤ Windows 2000 Professional installed as per Lab 2.6.

Estimated completion time: **15–20 minutes**

ACTIVITY

1. Start your computer with Windows 2000 Professional, and log on as an administrator.

2. Create a folder named **Consoles** off the root of your Windows 2000 drive. Use the folder to store your customized management console files.

3. Open a new Microsoft Management Console window.

   a. Click **Start**, **Run**.

   b. Enter **mmc** in the Open text box, and click **OK**.

   c. A new console window with only the Console Root will be visible, as shown in Figure 3-1.

   d. Maximize the MMC Console window.

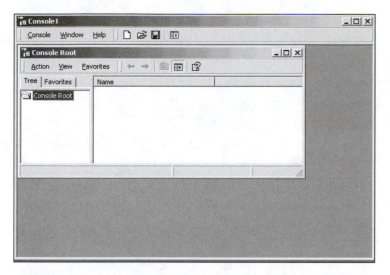

Figure 3-1   New MMC

4. Add the Event Viewer Snap-in.

   a. Click the **Add/Remove Snap-in** option from the Console menu to display the Add/Remove Snap-in window.

   b. Click the **Add** button to display the Add Standalone Snap-in window, as shown in Figure 3-2.

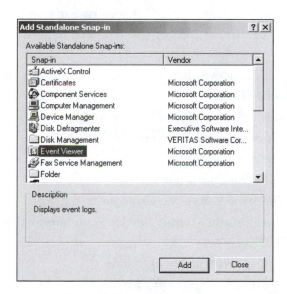

Figure 3-2   Add Standalone Snap-in

   c. Double-click the **Event Viewer** snap-in to display the Select Computer window.

d. Verify that the **Local computer** option is selected, and then click **Finish** to add the Event View snap-in.

e. Click **Close** to return to the Add/Remove Snap-in window.

5. Repeat steps 4a through 4e to add the following snap-ins:

a. Computer Management

b. Shared Folders

c. Disk Defragmenter (When you select Disk Defragmenter it will not display the Select Computer window. This is because the Disk Defragmenter program can be run only on the local computer.)

6. After all four snap-ins are added, return to the Microsoft Management Console main window.

a. If necessary, click **Close** to return to the Add/Remove Snap-in window. Verify that the four snap-ins have been added.

b. Click **OK** to return to the MMC console window.

7. Create a separate Event Viewer window.

a. Right-click the **Event Viewer** option from the console tree.

b. Click the **New Window from Here** option.

c. Remove the console tree from the 2:Event Viewer window:

- Click **Customize** from the View menu.
- Remove the check mark from the **Console tree** option.
- Click **OK**. Notice that the console tree has been removed from the 2:Event Viewer window.

8. Create a separate Sessions windows from the Shared Folders Snap-in.

a. Expand the **Shared Folders** Snap-in.

b. Right-click the **Sessions** option from Shared Folders.

c. Click the **New Window from Here** option.

d. Remove the console tree from the Sessions window:

- Click **Customize** from the **View** menu.
- Remove the check mark from the **Console tree** option.
- Click **OK**. Notice that the console tree has been removed from the 3:Sessions window.

9. Create a separate Logical Drives window as follows:

a. Expand the **Computer Management** Snap-in.

b. Expand the **Storage** extension.

c. Right-click **Logical Drives** and click the **New Window from Here** option.

d. Remove the console tree from the Logical Drives window:

- Click **Customize** from the **View** menu.
- Remove the check mark from the **Console tree** option.
- Click **OK** to close the Customize View window. Notice that the console tree has been removed from the 4:Logical Drives window.

10. Create a separate Disk Defragmenter window.

a. Right-click **Disk Defragmenter** and click the **New Window from Here** option.

b. Click **Customize** from the **View** menu, and remove the check mark from the **Console Tree** option.

c. Click **OK** to close the Customize View window.

11. Close the 1:Console Root window.

12. Tile the windows.

a. Click the **Tile Horizontally** option from the **Window** menu.

b. All four snap-in windows should now appear in the MMC main Console1 window similar to Figure 3-3.

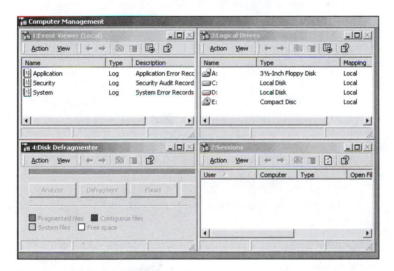

Figure 3-3 Tiled user console

13. Save in Author mode as follows. Saving in Author mode allows you to make changes to this management console in the future.

    a. Click the **Console** menu, **Options** option.

    b. Verify that the Console mode is set to Author mode. On your Lab 3.1 Student Answer Sheet record the description of the Author mode.

    c. Click **OK** to return to the management console.

    d. Click the **Console** menu, **Save As** option.

    e. Select your **Consoles** folder, and save the console using the name **Lab3-1**.

14. Selected User limited mode:

    a. Click the Console menu, **Options** option.

    b. Describe each user mode console and its possible use.

    c. Select **User mode – limited access, multiple window**.

    d. Remove the check mark from the **Allow the user to customize views** option.

    e. Click **OK** to return to the main Console window.

15. Save the console on the Start Menu.

    a. Click the Console menu, **Save As** option.

    b. Navigate to the root of the drive containing Windows 2000 Professional.

    c. Navigate to the \Documents and Settings\All Users\Start Menu\ Programs folder:

       - Double-click the **Documents and Settings** folder.
       - Double-click the **All Users** folder.
       - Double-click the **Start Menu** folder.
       - Double-click the **Programs** folder.

    d. Enter the name **Computer Management** and click **Save**.

16. Test the console you created:

    a. Close the Computer Management console.

    b. Click **Start**, **Programs**, **Computer Management**.

    c. The new Computer Management console you created should be shown along with the windows. Notice that the user is limited to the windows and snap-ins you assigned.

    d. Open the Author mode version of the console:

       - Click **Start**, **Run**.
       - Use the Browse button and select your **Lab3-1** console file from the Consoles folder.

- If you receive an error message saying that Disk Defrag does not support more than one instance running at a time, click **OK** to continue.

- Click **OK** to start your author mode version of the console.

e. Flip back and forth between the two consoles and, on the Student Answer Sheet, identify at least two differences or limitations when running the user version of the management console, as compared to the author version.

f. Have your instructor or lab assistant check your console and sign off on your Student Answer Sheet.

g. Close all console windows and log off.

LAB 3.2 CREATING LOCAL USERS

Objective

To reduce operator errors affecting the operation of the Windows 2000 Professional computer at the Animal Care Center, Dennis wants you to create two user accounts to eliminate the need for users logging on as Administrator. You will set up one user account named AppUser that is limited to running applications, and another account named SysOp that can use the Management Console you created in Lab 3.1, but that does not have full administrative authority to the system. After completing this lab, you will be able to:

➤ Create a restricted local user account.

➤ Create a power-user account.

➤ Verify user account restrictions.

Estimated completion time: **20–30 minutes**

ACTIVITY

1. If necessary, start your computer with Windows 2000 Professional, and log on as an administrator.

2. Display the Control Panel window by clicking **Start**, pointing to **Settings**, and clicking **Control Panel**.

3. Double-click the **Users and Passwords** icon to start the Users and Passwords application.

4. Create a restricted user named AppUser.

    a. Click the **Add** button to start the Add New User wizard, as shown in Figure 3–4.

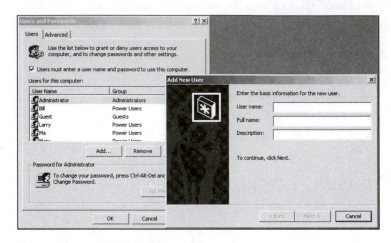

Figure 3-4   Add New User

    b. Enter the following information:

- User name: **AppUser**
- Full name: **Application User**
- Description: **Application user account**

    c. Click **Next** to display the password window.

    d. Enter **password** in both the Password and Confirm password fields, and click **Next** to display the level of access window.

    e. Record the access options on your Lab 3.2 Student Answer Sheet.

    f. Click **Restricted user** and click **Finish**.

    g. Notice that the new user has been added to the Users tab.

5. Create a Power User named SysOp.

    a. Click the **Add** button to start the Add New User wizard.

    b. Enter the following information:

- User name: **SysOp**
- Full name: **System Operator**
- Description: **Computer operator user account**

    c. Click **Next** to display the password window.

    d. Enter **password** in both the Password and Confirm password fields, and click **Next** to display the level of access window.

    e. Record the access options on your Student Answer Sheet.

    f. Click **Standard user** and click **Finish**.

    g. Notice that the new user has been added to the Users tab.

6. Add the requirement that the Ctrl+Alt+Delete key sequence be used to log on to the computer, as follows:

   a. Click the **Advanced** tab.

   b. Check the **Require users to press Ctrl-Alt-Delete before logging on** option. On your Student Answer Sheet, record how requiring users to press Ctrl+Alt+Delete before logging on increases security.

7. Group objects may contain one or more users and are often used to organize users. Windows 2000 contains a number of predefined system groups that are used to provide rights and permissions to multiple users. In this step you document default group membership for your newly created user.

   a. Click the **Advanced** button in the Advanced User Management area to display the Local Users and Groups window.

   b. Double-click the **Groups** folder, and record the predefined groups on your Student Answer Sheet.

   c. Double-click the **Power Users** group, and list the members on your Student Answer Sheet.

   d. Click **OK** and then close the Local Users and Groups window and return to the Users and Passwords window.

8. Click **OK** to close the Users and Passwords windows and return to Control Panel.

9. Close the Control Panel window.

10. Click **Start**, **Shut Down** and select the **Log off Administrator** option. Notice that the Press Ctrl+Alt+Delete to begin window is shown.

11. Now you want to set the computer to automatically launch the Management Console at logon. Start by logging on as Administrator.

12. Use Scheduler to automatically launch the Management Console at logon.

   a. Open the **Control Panel**.

   b. Double-click the **Scheduled Tasks** icon.

   c. Double-click the **Add Scheduled Task** icon, and click **Next** to start the Scheduled Task Wizard.

   d. Click **Browse** and navigate to the \Documents and Settings\ All Users\Start Menu\Programs folder.

   e. Double-click **Computer Management**.

   f. Click the **When I log on** option, and click **Next**.

   g. In the Enter the user name: text box, replace Administrator with **SysOp**.

   h. Enter the password in both fields, and then click **Next**.

   i. Click **Finish** to save the task.

13. Test the AppUser account.

   a. Log off the Administrator user.

   b. Press **Ctrl+Alt+Delete** and log on as **AppUser**. If necessary, click **OK** in the NetWare dialog box and close the Getting Started with Windows 2000 window.

   c. Verify that you can run applications such as Microsoft Office or WordPad.

   d. Start the Computer Management console.

   e. On the Student Answer Sheet, record any error messages you receive.

   f. On the Student Answer Sheet, record what Event Viewer logs you can view.

   g. On the Student Answer Sheet, record the results of viewing Logical Drive information.

   h. On the Student Answer Sheet, record the results of clicking the Analyze button in the Disk Defragmenter window.

   i. Close the Computer Management console and log off.

14. Test the SysOp account.

   a. Press **Ctrl+Alt+Delete** and log on as **SysOp**. If necessary, click **OK** in the NetWare dialog and close the Getting Started with Windows 2000 window.

   b. Verify that you can run applications such as WordPad.

   c. If necessary, start the Computer Management console.

   d. On the Student Answer Sheet, record any error messages you receive.

   e. On the Student Answer Sheet, record what Event Viewer logs you can view.

   f. On the Student Answer Sheet, record the results of viewing Logical Drive information.

   g. On the Student Answer Sheet, record the results of clicking the Analyze button in the Disk Defragmenter window.

15. Log off.

LAB 3.3 CONFIGURING ACCESSIBILITY SERVICES

Objective

You have just visited the Animal Care Center and learned that a new employee has a disability that often causes repeated keystrokes. This person also has a difficult time viewing smaller print on the screen. In this lab, you simulate making the system easier for this employee to use. You will configure and test the accessibility options available with Windows 2000 Professional. After completing this lab, you will be able to:

➤ Use the Control Panel to configure and troubleshoot accessibility services.

Estimated completion time: **10–15 minutes**

ACTIVITY

1. If necessary, start your computer with Windows 2000, and log on as an administrator.

2. Open **Control Panel**.

3. Follow Step 4 in Lab 3.2 to create a new restricted user named Special.

4. Log off, and then log on as the user named Special.

5. Open **Control Panel**, and double-click the **Accessibility Options** icon to display the window shown in Figure 3-5.

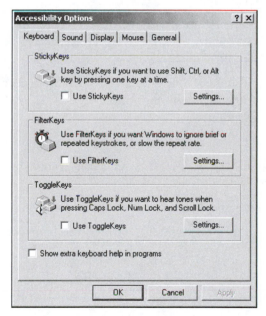

Figure 3-5 Accessibility Options

6. In the FilterKeys area, check the **Use FilterKeys** box, and click the **Settings** button. On the Lab 3.3 Student Answer Sheet, record the keyboard shortcut for FilterKeys.

7. The user seems to be having a problem with a letter repeating when a key is accidentally pressed multiple times. Click the **Settings** button, and on your Student Answer Sheet, record the default amount of time a key must be held down (repeat time).

8. Try typing in the Test Area. Notice how long you need to hold down a key before it repeats.

9. Use the Short – Long bar to change the time keys must be held down in order to repeat. On your Student Answer sheet, record the shortest (non-zero) time a key must be held down. Try typing in the Test Area, and notice the difference between different time settings.

10. Set the keyboard repeat rate to **.30** seconds and click **OK**.

11. In the Keyboard shortcut box, remove the check mark from the Use shortcut option.

12. Click **OK** to save your settings.

13. Click the **Sound** tab, and on your Student Answer Sheet, record the sound setting.

14. Click the **Use SoundSentry** option.

15. The high contrast option is helpful for users who are visually challenged. To enable the high contrast option, click the **Display** tab, and click the **Use High Contrast** check box.

16. Click the **Settings** button, and on your Student Answer Sheet, record the shortcut key sequence for the high contrast option. Click **OK** or **Cancel** to return to Accessibility Options.

17. Click the **Mouse** tab, and on your Student Answer Sheet, record the options.

18. Click the **General** tab. On your Student Answer Sheet, record the default notification settings.

19. Click **OK** to save the settings and exit.

20. Use the shortcut keys you recorded in Step 16 to test the high-contrast display option.

21. Use the same shortcut keys to turn off the high-contrast option.

22. Start **Notepad** and notice how long you have to hold down each key to type.

23. Exit Notepad and do not save any documents.

24. Log off and then log on as **AppUser**.

25. On your Student Answer Sheet, record whether or not the accessibility options apply to other users.

26. Log off.

LAB 3.4 CONFIGURING OTHER SERVICES

3

Objective

The Windows 2000 Professional systems at the Melendres and Associates law firm are working well. However, Mr. Melendres wants you to stop by and do the following:

- Disable the modems on computers that are not connected to the phone line.
- Change the screen resolution to support a new application.
- Configure faxing from Mr. Melendres's computer.
- Install an updated video driver and set video resolution.
- Allow users to view hidden files on all folders.
- Configure an Internet Explorer default home page.

After completing this lab, you will be able to use the Control Panel to:

➤ Unplug hardware devices.

➤ Configure and troubleshoot fax support.

➤ Configure folder options.

➤ Configure Internet Explorer.

This lab involves changing system configuration settings that could affect system operation. You might need to obtain permission before proceeding. As an alternative, the objectives in this lab can be accomplished through participating in a classroom demonstration.

Estimated completion time: **50–60 minutes**

ACTIVITY 1

All of the new computers at the Melendres and Associates law firm came with built-in modems. However, only two computers are actually plugged into a phone. In this activity, you use the Add/Remove hardware feature to simulate how to disable the modems on the computers that are not attached to a phone line. If you do not have a modem attached to your computer, you can use the Printer (LPT1) port to simulate the process.

1. If necessary, start your computer and log on as Administrator.

2. Open the **Control Panel**.

3. Double-click **Add/Remove Hardware**, and then click **OK** to start the Wizard.

4. Click the **Uninstall/Unplug a device** option, and click **Next** to choose a removal task.

5. Click the **Uninstall a device** option, and click **Next** to display a list of hardware devices.

6. Select the **Modem** (or **Printer Port (LPT1)** device, and click **Next** to display the Confirm Device window.

7. Click **Yes**, and then click **Next** to uninstall the device.

8. Click **Finish** to complete the removal process.

9. On your Student Answer Sheet, record your results along with any helpful notes.

10. Close Control Panel.

ACTIVITY 2

Mr. Melendres wants you to configure faxing support on his computer. In this activity, you simulate this process by reinstalling either the modem device or printer port that you uninstalled in Activity 1.

1. Open **Control Panel**.

2. Double-click **Add/Remove Hardware** and click **Next** to display the Choose a Hardware Task window.

3. Verify that **Add/Troubleshoot a device** is selected, and click **Next** to automatically detect your hardware.

4. If you are reinstalling the modem, double-click the modem device and click **Finish** to return to the Control Panel. If you are reinstalling the printer port, follow the steps below:

    a. Double-click the **Add a new device** option.

    b. Select **No, I want to select the hardware from a list** and then click **Next** to display a Hardware types window.

    c. Double-click **Ports (COM & LPT)** to display the Select a Device Driver window.

    d. Click **Printer Port** and click **Next**. Because the printer port is not a plug-and-play device, you might receive a warning telling you that Windows cannot detect the hardware settings. Click **OK** to accept this warning message.

    e. Select **Input/Output Range** under Resource Type.

    f. Click the **Change Settings** button, and then click **OK** to accept the current settings.

g. Click **OK** to close the Resources tab and return to the setup wizard.

h. Click **Next** to display a summary window indicating that the printer port was installed.

5. Click **Finish** to return to the Control Panel, and then click **Yes** to restart your computer. On your Student Answer Sheet, record your results along with any helpful notes.

ACTIVITY 3

Configure fax services.

1. If necessary, start your computer with Windows 2000 Professional, and log on as an administrator.

2. Open **Control Panel**.

3. Double-click the **Fax** icon to display the Fax Properties window shown in Figure 3-6.

Figure 3-6 Fax configuration

4. Fill in the User Information screen. On your Lab 3.4 Student Answer Sheet, record the information you enter.

5. Click the **Status Monitor** tab, and on your Student Answer Sheet, record the default settings.

6. Click the **Advanced Options** tab. On your Student Answer Sheet, record the modem device type along with the default log options.

7. Click **OK** to close the Fax Properties window.

8. Close Control Panel.

Activity 4

Mr. Melendres recently purchased a computer for his home from your company. He wants you to help him provide better Internet security and content control, along with a default home page. In this activity, you use the Control Panel to manage Internet security and provide some content control.

1. If necessary, log on using your administrator account.

2. Open **Control Panel**.

3. Double-click **Internet Options** to display the Internet Properties window.

4. On the General tab, change the Address to **http://www.lawyers.com**.

5. Mr. Melendres wants to know the amount of disk space used by temporary Internet files, as well as where the files are kept. To access this information:

   a. In the Temporary Internet files box, click the **Settings** button.

   b. On your Student Answer Sheet, record the path to the Internet temporary files, along with the default disk space.

   c. Reduce the amount of disk space to **15** MB.

   d. Click **OK** to return to the General page.

   e. Reduce the Days to keep pages in history to **15**.

6. Mr. Melendres wants to apply the most restrictive Internet content setting to his computer because his children sometimes use the machine. To change these settings:

   a. Click the **Content** tab.

   b. In the Content Advisor box, click the **Enable** button to display the Content Advisor window shown in Figure 3-7.

   c. On your Student Answer Sheet, record the five levels for each category.

   d. Be sure the most restrictive setting is applied to each category.

   e. To change the password to "secret," click the **General** tab and then click **Change Password**. Leave the "Old password" field blank, and enter **secret** in both the "New password" and "Confirm new password" text boxes.

   f. Click **OK** to save your settings.

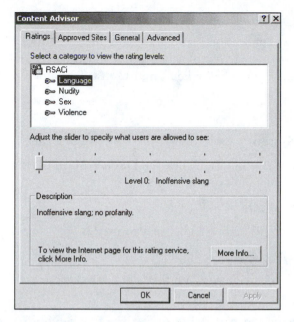

Figure 3-7   Internet Content Advisor

7. Mr. Melendres recently learned that certain Internet Web sites record information called cookies on local computers. He is concerned about these Internet cookies, and wants to be notified before a cookie is written to his system. Secure Socket Layers (SSL) provides a means to help secure data transmitted across the Internet. Because security is very important when transmitting legal documents, Mr. Melendres wants the highest level of SSL set on his system.

   a. Click the **Advanced** tab, and scroll down to find the highest SSL level. On your Student Answer Sheet, record the highest SSL setting.

   b. On your Student Answer Sheet, record any cookie settings that you can configure from the Advanced tab.

   c. Click the **Security** tab.

   d. Click the **Custom Level** button.

   e. On your Student Answer Sheet, record any cookie settings that you can configure from the Security tab.

   f. Click **OK** to return to the Internet Properties window.

8. Click **OK** to close the Internet Properties window and return to Control Panel.

9. Close the Control Panel window.

ACTIVITY 5

Mr. Melendres has a new application that requires a higher resolution than his current video driver supports. He has obtained a new video driver and wants you to install it for him. In this activity, you simulate installing a new video device driver and setting the display resolution.

1. Open **Control Panel**.

2. Double-click the **System** icon to display the System Properties window.

3. Click the **Hardware** tab, and then click the **Device Manager** button to display a window showing all system devices.

4. Expand **Display adapters**.

5. Right-click your display adapter, and click **Properties.**

6. Click the **Driver** tab.

7. Click the **Update Driver** button, and then click **Next** to start the Upgrade Driver wizard.

8. Verify that the **Search for a suitable driver for my device (recommended)** is selected, and then click **Next** to display the Locate Driver Files window shown in Figure 3-8.

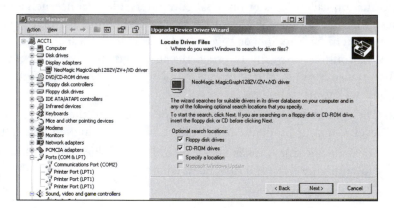

Figure 3-8 Locate Driver Files

9. If Mr. Melendres has the new drivers on a floppy disk, you remove the check mark from the CD-ROM option, click the **Specify a location** option, and then click **Next** to specify the path to the driver files.

10. Click **Cancel** twice to return to the Device Manager window.

11. Close the Device Manager, and click **Cancel** to exit the System Properties windows.

12. To change the display resolution, you can either select the **Display** icon from Control Panel, or right-click in any empty space on the desktop and click **Properties**.

13. Click the **Settings** tab.

14. Use the slide bar to change the display resolution to 800 × 600 pixels, and then click **Apply**.

15. A message indicating that Windows will now apply your settings is shown. Click **OK** to apply the settings. To keep the settings, click **Yes**. Respond within 15 seconds, or the settings will be not be changed.

16. Click **OK** to close the Display Properties window.

17. On your Student Answer Sheet, record your results along with any helpful notes.

18. Close Control Panel.

ACTIVITY 6

Mr. Melendres wants to be able to view any hidden files, as well as see all file extensions when he opens a folder on his office computer. In this activity, you use the Folder Options of Control Panel to view hidden files and file extensions.

1. Open **Control Panel**.

2. Double-click the **Folder Options** icon.

3. Click the **View** tab.

4. Click the **Show hidden files and folders** option.

5. Click to remove the check mark from the **Hide file extensions for known file types** option.

6. Click **OK** to save your settings and return to Control Panel.

7. Close the Control Panel window.

8. Test folder options.

   a. Use My Computer to open the **Consoles** folder you created in Lab 3.1.

   b. Verify that you can view the .msc extension on the Lab3-1 console file.

   c. Right-click the **Lab3-1.msc** file, and click **Properties**.

   d. Click the **Hidden** attribute.

   e. Click **OK** to return to the Consoles folder.

   f. On the Lab 3.4 Student Answer Sheet, describe how hiding the Lab3-1.msc file changed your view.

   g. Close all windows and log off.

ACTIVITY 7

Mr. Melendres has some special fonts on one of his computers that he wants to install on his office computer. In this activity, you simulate installing a new font by first copying a font file to a floppy disk, then deleting the font from the hard drive, and then installing the font back into your computer.

1. If necessary, start your computer with Windows 2000, and log on as an administrator.

2. Obtain and format a floppy disk. (If you do not have access to a floppy disk, create a folder named **Floppy** on your local C: drive.)

3. Copy a font file to the floppy disk or folder as follows:

   a. Navigate to the WINNT\Fonts folder.

   b. Click the **Arial** font, and click **Copy** from the **Edit** menu.

   c. Open a window to your floppy disk or folder.

   d. Click **Paste** from the **Edit** menu. The Arial font file should appear on the disk or in the folder.

   e. Close all windows.

4. Remove the font from Windows 2000.

   a. Open **Control Panel**.

   b. Double-click the **Fonts** icon.

   c. Right-click **Arial** and click **Delete**.

   d. Click **Yes** to confirm the deletion.

5. Install a font from the floppy disk or folder.

   a. Click the **File** menu, then click **Install New Font**.

   b. Navigate to your floppy disk or folder.

   c. From the List of fonts window, click the **Arial** font you copied, and then click the **OK** button to install the font.

   d. The new font (Arial) should now appear in the Fonts window.

   e. Close the Fonts window.

   f. If necessary, close Control Panel.

   g. On your Student Answer Sheet, record your results along with any helpful notes.

   h. Log off.

LAB 3.5 CONFIGURING HARDWARE PROFILES AND POWER MANAGEMENT

Objective

Mr. Melendres has recently purchased a notebook computer that he plans to use on the road or in the courtroom. He wants to be able to plug the notebook into his network when at the office, but does not want to receive network error messages when he is working offline. In addition, he wants to conserve battery power when using the notebook on the road. After completing this lab, you will be able to:

➤ Configure hardware profiles that allow a user to select either network or offline options.

➤ Configure Windows 2000 Professional power management features.

Estimated completion time: **20–25 minutes**

ACTIVITY

1. If necessary, start your computer with Windows 2000, and log on as an administrator.

2. Open **Control Panel**.

3. Double-click the **System** icon to display the System Properties window.

4. Click the **Hardware** tab.

5. Click the **Hardware Profiles** button to display the Hardware Profiles window shown in Figure 3-9.

6. Configure a new hardware profile for office use.

   a. Highlight the current profile, and click the **Copy** button.

   b. Enter **Office** in the To field, and click **OK**.

   c. Click the **Office** profile and click the **Properties** button.

   d. Click the **Always include this profile as an option when Windows starts** option.

   e. Click **OK** to save.

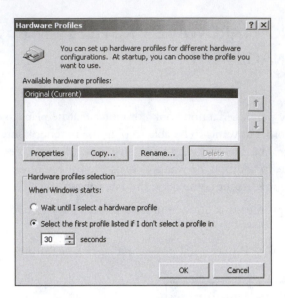

Figure 3-9 Hardware Profiles

7. Configure a new hardware profile for on the road.

 a. Highlight the current profile, and click the **Copy** button.

 b. Enter **On the road** in the To field, and click **OK**.

 c. Click the **On the road** profile, and click the **Properties** button.

 d. Click the **This is a portable computer** check box.

 e. Click the **The computer is undocked** option.

 f. Click the **Always include this profile as an option when Windows starts** option.

 g. Click **OK** to save.

8. Rename the current profile.

 a. Click the current profile and click the **Rename** button.

 b. Enter **Original** in the To field, and click **OK**.

9. Make Office the default profile, and the On the road profile the second choice.

 a. Click the **Office** profile.

 b. Click the **up arrow** until the Office profile is the first profile listed.

 c. Click **On the road** and then click the **up arrow** until it is the second profile listed.

3

10. Click **OK** to save your profiles and return to the System Properties window.

11. Click **OK** to return to Control Panel.

12. Set the power options. Double-click the **Power Options** icon.

13. In the Power Schemes window, select **Portable/Laptop**.

14. Change the settings to turn off the monitor after **10** minutes, and turn off the hard disks after **20** minutes.

15. Click the **Hibernate** tab and click **Enable hibernate support**. On your Lab 3.5 Student Answer Sheet, record the description of the hibernate mode.

16. Click **OK** to save your power settings and return to Control Panel.

17. To disable the network adapter in your On the road profile:

   a. Restart the computer, log on as Administrator, and select the **On the road** profile from the startup hardware profiles you created in Step 7.

   b. Open **Control Panel**.

   c. Double-click the **System** icon, and click the **Hardware** tab.

   d. Click the **Device Manager** button.

   e. Expand the **Network adapters** category.

   f. Right-click your adapter and click **Properties**.

   g. In the Device usage field, select the **Do not use this device in the current hardware profile (disable)** option, and click **OK** to return to the Device Manager window.

   h. Close all windows.

18. Test your profiles.

   a. Restart your computer.

   b. Select the **Office** profile and press **Enter**.

   c. Log on as an administrator and verify that you can access the network.

   d. Restart your computer.

   e. Select the **On the road** profile and press **Enter**.

   f. Log on as an administrator and verify that the network is unavailable. On the Lab 3.5 Student Answer Sheet, record how you were able to determine that this profile disabled network access.

   g. Restart the computer and select the **Office** profile.

19. Remove the Office and On the road profiles.

   a. Restart your computer and log on as the administrator.

   b. Open **Control Panel** and double-click the **System** icon.

   c. Click the **Hardware** tab and then click the **Hardware Profiles** button.

   d. Click the **Office** profile to highlight it.

e. Click the **Delete** button and click **Yes** to confirm the deletion.

f. If necessary, click the **On the road** profile to highlight it.

g. Click the **Delete** button and click **Yes** to confirm the deletion.

h. Click **OK** twice to close the System window.

i. Close the Control Panel window.

j. Restart your computer and verify that the extra profiles have been removed.

MANAGING WINDOWS 2000 FILE SYSTEMS AND STORAGE

Labs included in this chapter

➤ Lab 4.1 Creating and Managing Drives and Folders

➤ Lab 4.2 Managing Disk Storage and Mount Points

➤ Lab 4.3 Managing Dynamic Disk Storage

➤ Lab 4.4 Securing the File System

➤ Lab 4.5 Auditing File System Activity

➤ Lab 4.6 Sharing Folders

Microsoft MCSE Exam #70-210 Objectives	
Objective	**Lab**
Monitor and configure disks	4.1, 4.2, 4.3
Configure and manage file systems	
Convert from one file system to another	4.1
Monitor, configure, and troubleshoot volumes	4.3
Monitor, manage, and troubleshoot access to files and folders	
Control access to files and folders by using permissions	4.4, 4.5
Configure, manage, and troubleshoot file compression	4.2, 4.4
Manage and troubleshoot access to shared folders	
Create and remove shared folders	4.6
Control access to shared folders by using permissions	4.6

Student Answer Sheets to accompany the labs in this chapter can be downloaded from the Online Companion for this manual at *www.course.com*.

LAB 4.1 CREATING AND MANAGING DRIVES AND FOLDERS

Objective

Your company's policy when installing Windows 2000 is to separate the Windows 2000 operating system from application data and shared data by leaving unallocated disk space. Keeping application data on a separate volume or volumes from the Windows 2000 operating system facilitates backup and recovery operations. In addition, leaving unallocated disk space allows the flexibility of assigning the extra space as one or more volumes when needed. The Animal Care Center wants to transfer shared data from the Novell server to the Windows 2000 Professional system. To do this, you need to establish another volume and create some shared folders. New volumes can be formatted using FAT16, FAT32, or the NTFS file system. Although any of these file systems can be used to store shared folders, NTFS volumes provide more security and reliability. FAT volumes have the advantage of being accessible from DOS or Windows 95 in the event Windows 2000 will not start. In this lab, you learn how to create FAT volumes and convert them to the NTFS file system. After completing this lab, you will be able to:

➤ Create and format a new disk partition.

➤ Identify the limitations of Basic disk storage.

➤ Change a drive letter on a volume or partition.

➤ Convert a FAT file system to NTFS.

This lab involves working with disk partitions. Therefore, errors made in the lab could corrupt or delete the existing operating system or files. If the computer you use is used for other purposes or classes, you should have a removable disk or an image of the existing partitions, as described in the Introduction to this lab manual, before you continue.

Requirements

➤ At least 50 MB of unallocated space on your primary disk drive

Estimated completion time: **20–25 minutes**

ACTIVITY

1. If necessary, start your computer with Windows 2000, and log on as an administrator.

2. Create a Microsoft Management Console (MMC) for disk management.

   a. Click **Start**, click **Run**, type **mmc** in the Open text box, and press **Enter**.

   b. Click **OK** to open an empty console window.

   c. From the **Console** menu, click **Add/Remove Snap-in** to display the Add/Remove Snap-in window.

   d. Click the **Add** button to display the Add Standalone Snap-in window.

   e. Click **Disk Management** and then click the **Add** button.

   f. Verify that the **Local computer** option button is selected, and then click **Finish** to return to the Add Standalone Snap-in window.

   g. Click **Close** and then click **OK** to return to the console window. Notice that the Console Root now includes the Disk Management tool.

   h. Save this console to make it available in the Programs menu for all users:

      - From the **Console** menu, click **Save As**.
      - Navigate up to, and double-click the **Documents and Settings** folder.
      - Double-click **All Users**.
      - Double-click **Start Menu**.
      - Double-click **Programs**.
      - Enter the name **Disk Management** in the File Name text box.
      - Click **Save**.
      - Exit the Disk Management console.

3. Identify the disk type of your disk drive.

   a. Start the Disk Management tool by clicking **Start**, pointing to **Programs**, and clicking **Disk Management**.

   b. Click **Disk Management (Local)** to display a Disk Management window similar to the one shown in Figure 4-1. (Depending upon your Windows 95/98 installation, the file system for your C: partition might be either FAT or FAT32.)

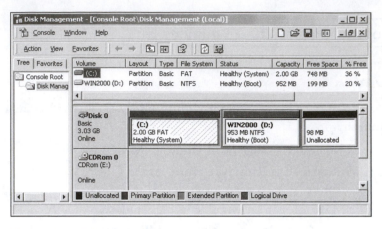

Figure 4-1 Disk Management window

    c. Right-click **Disk 0** and click the **Properties** option. On the Lab 4.1
Student Answer Sheet, enter the information for your disk 0.

4. Creating new partitions or logical drives changes letters assigned to existing
drives, causing software problems. To prevent this, you can assign each
volume or logical drive the letter you want it to have. In this step of the
lab you assign a drive letter to each drive, and to the CD-ROM. To assign a
drive letter to each partition and to the CD-ROM drive:

    a. Right-click the drive containing your Windows 2000 operating
system. If you are unsure which drive contains your operating system,
do the following:

- Open **Control Panel**.
- Double-click the **System** icon.
- Click the **Advanced** tab.
- Click the **Environment Variables** button.
- The drive letter specified in the Path variable is the boot drive
containing your Windows 2000 operating system.
- Close Control Panel.

    b. Click the **Change Drive Letter and Path** option.

    c. Click the **Edit** button, and on your Student Answer Sheet, record the
message you see.

    d. Right-click your **CD-ROM** drive.

    e. Click the **Change Drive Letter and Path** option.

    f. Click the **Edit** button to display the Edit Drive Letter or Path window.

    g. Click the list arrow to display available drive letters.

    h. Click **R** (for ROM) and click **OK**. A warning message is shown.

i. Click **Yes** to confirm the change.

j. Notice that your CD-ROM drive has been change to "R:".

k. Close all windows.

5. Create a new logical drive consisting of half your existing free space.

a. Right-click the free space.

b. Click **Create Logical Drive** and click **Next** to launch the Create Logical Drive wizard.

c. Verify that the **Logical drive** option button is selected and then click **Next** to display the Specify Partition Size window.

d. Enter a partition size that will leave at least 25 MB of free space after the drive is created. (To format the new drive with the FAT32 file system, the drive must be at least 50 MB.)

e. Click **Next** to accept the default drive letter and display the Format Partition window.

f. If your new drive is at least 50 MB, use the scroll button in the "File system to use" text box to select the **FAT32** file system. If your drive is less than 50 MB, select the **FAT** file system.

g. Enter the name **SHARED DATA** in the Volume label text box and click **Next** to display the summary window. On your Student Answer Sheet, record the summary information.

h. Click **Finish** to create and format the new logical drive. If you receive an error message indicating that the volume is in use, click **OK** to continue and then right-click the new logical drive and click the **Format** option. Enter the volume name **SHARED DATA**, and depending upon the drive size, format the drive using FAT (less than 50 MB) or FAT32 (50 MB or larger).

i. Exit Disk Management.

6. Create the following folder structure on your new drive, using Windows Explorer and the File, New, Folder menu options. Select the drive and create the Forms, Projects, and Inventory folders; then select the Projects folder and create the Ads, Docs, Images, and Website folders.

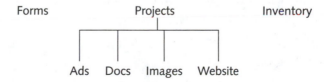

7. To simulate storage use, copy to your Images folder three .bmp files from the WINNT folder located on your Windows 2000 drive. Copy all files that have the extension .txt from the WINNT folder to your Docs folder.

8. Find and record FAT or FAT32 folder information.

   a. Double-click **My Computer**.

   b. Double-click your new drive to open the **Shared Data** window.

   c. Right-click your **Projects** folder, and click **Properties** to display the General properties tab for your Projects folder.

   d. On your Student Answer Sheet, record FAT or FAT32 folder information.

   e. Click **Cancel** to return to the Shared Data window.

   f. Close all windows.

9. To take advantage of the security and reliability features of Windows 2000, you need to convert the drive to NTFS.

   a. Make sure all Windows Explorer windows to the drive you want to format are closed, otherwise the drive cannot be formatted or converted.

   b. Windows 2000 does not contain a GUI function in Disk Manager to convert file system formats. As a result, to convert to NTFS, you need to open a Command Prompt window. Click **Start**, point to **Programs**, point to **Accessories**, and then click **Command Prompt**.

   c. From the Command Prompt window, enter the command:

   Convert *drive*: /fs:NTFS

   Replace ***drive*:** with the drive letter of the FAT32 drive you want converted to NTFS, and press **Enter**.

   d. Enter **SHARED DATA** as the current volume label, and press **Enter** to perform the conversion.

   e. Type **Exit** and press **Enter** to exit the Command prompt and return to the Windows 2000 desktop.

10. Record NTFS folder information.

    a. Double-click **My Computer**.

    b. Double-click your new drive to open the **Shared Data** window.

    c. Right-click your **Projects** folder, and click **Properties** to display the General properties tab for your Projects folder.

    d. On your Student Answer Sheet, record the NTFS folder information.

    e. Click **Cancel** to return to the Shared Data window.

    f. Close the Shared Data window.

    g. Close My Computer.

    h. Log off.

LAB 4.2   MANAGING DISK STORAGE AND MOUNT POINTS

Objective

The number of scanned images stored on the shared Animal Care Center computer located in Dennis's office is filling up the Shared Data volume. Dennis has called you and wants you to make more disk space available to the Projects folder. After completing this lab, you will be able to:

➤ Configure file compression.

➤ Identify limitations of Basic disk storage.

➤ Identify the steps necessary to extend a volume.

➤ Identify the steps necessary to convert a Basic disk to Dynamic storage.

➤ Mount a volume to an empty directory.

Requirements

➤ At least 25 MB of unallocated space on your primary disk drive

This lab involves working with disk partitions. Therefore, errors made in the lab could corrupt or delete the existing operating system or files. If the computer you use is used for other purposes or classes, you should have a removable disk or an image of the existing partitions, as described in the Introduction to this lab manual, before you continue.

Estimated completion time: **15–20 minutes**

ACTIVITY

1. If necessary, start your computer with Windows 2000, and log on as an administrator.

2. One way to make more disk storage available is to compress the files. Because of the large number of repeated bit strings in scanned images, compressing scanned image files can free up a lot of disk space. In this step, you compress the Images folder and determine the amount of disk space saved.

   a. Open **My Computer** and navigate to your **Projects** folder.

   b. Right-click the **Images** folder, and click the **Properties** option.

   c. On your Lab 4.2 Student Answer Sheet, record the Size on disk value (folder size before compression).

   d. From the General tab, click the **Advanced** button.

   e. Click the **Compress contents to save disk space** check box, and then click **OK** to return to the Images Properties window.

   f. Click the **Apply** button.

   g. On the Confirm Attribute Changes window, click the **Apply changes to this folder, subfolders, and files** option button, and then click **OK**.

   h. On your Student Answer Sheet, record the Size on disk value (folder size after compression).

3. Although compressing the files has provided temporary relief to the disk storage problem, to provide a more long-term solution, you take some of the unallocated disk space and use it to extend the Projects folder. To attempt to extend the existing drive, do the following:

   a. In the Disk Management window, click the drive containing the Projects folder.

   b. Click the **Action** menu, **All Tasks** selection.

   c. On your Student Answer Sheet, list the tasks you can perform on a Basic disk partition.

   d. On your Student Answer Sheet, record why the Extend a volume option is not available.

   e. Press **Esc** twice to return to the Disk Management console.

4. Dynamic storage drives support spanned, mirrored, striped, and RAID-5 volumes. As a result, a possible solution to extending a drive is to convert the existing drive to Dynamic storage. To determine the feasibility of converting drive 0 to Dynamic storage, do the following:

   a. Right-click **Disk 0**.

   b. Click the **Upgrade to Dynamic Disk** option to display the Upgrade to Dynamic Disk window.

   c. Verify that Disk 0 is selected, and then click **OK** to upgrade disk 0.

   d. Click **Yes** to confirm the upgrade, and display the Disks to Upgrade window.

   e. Click the **Upgrade** button.

   f. On your Student Answer Sheet, record the message you receive.

   g. Click **No** to abort the upgrade.

5. Another alternative to extending a partition is to create a new partition, and then mount that partition within an empty folder on the drive you want to extend. For example, in this step you provide more disk space for the Images folder by creating a new partition, moving the files from the Images folder to the new partition, and then mounting the new partition in the empty Folder directory.

a. If necessary, start the Disk Management console.

b. Follow the procedure in Lab 4.1, Step 5 to create another partition using the remainder of the unallocated disk space. On your Student Answer Sheet, record the drive letter of the new partition.

c. Follow the procedure in Lab 4.1, Step 6 to change the partition number in the Boot.ini file.

d. Use My Computer to move all the files from the Images folder to the new drive.

e. From the Disk Management console, right-click the new volume and click the **Change Drive Letter and Path** option to display the Change Drive Letter and Path window.

f. To mount the drive in an NTFS folder, you first need to remove the drive letter. Click the **Remove** button, and then click **Yes** to confirm the action and return to the Disk Management console.

g. From the Disk Management console, right-click the new volume, and click the **Change Drive Letter and Path** option to display the Change Drive Letter and Path window.

h. Click the **Add** button to display the Add new Drive Letter or Path window.

i. Click the **Mount in this NTFS folder** option button.

j. Click the **Browse** button, and navigate to your Images folder.

k. Click your **Images** folder, and click **OK** to display the path to the mount point, as shown in Figure 4-2.

l. Click **OK** to mount the drive in the Images folder.

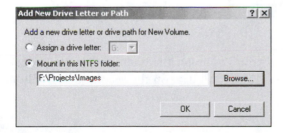

Figure 4-2   Add New Drive Letter or Path window

6. View and record folder statistics.

    a. Double-click **My Computer**.

    b. Open your **Shared Data** drive.

    c. Right-click your **Projects** folder, click **Properties**, and on your Student Answer Sheet, record the storage space used.

    d. Open your **Projects** folder. On your Student Answer Sheet, describe the appearance of the Images folder.

    e. Right-click the **Images** volume, click **Properties**, and on your Student Answer Sheet, record the NTFS mounted volume information.

    f. Click the **Properties** button, and on your Student Answer Sheet, record the space utilization statistics.

    g. Click **Cancel** twice to close the Images windows.

    h. Double-click the **Images** volume object, and verify that all image files are accessible.

7. Close all windows and log off.

LAB 4.3 MANAGING DYNAMIC DISK STORAGE

Objective

The Melendres and Associates law firm recently purchased a new hard drive from your company. Mr. Melendres wants you to install the drive on his Windows 2000 system and set up some shared storage areas. If possible, he wants the option of reserving space on the drive that can be used later to either add on to the existing shared area, or can be used as a separate volume. After completing this lab, you will be able to:

➤ Allocate a new drive as Basic storage.

➤ Create and delete partitions on Dynamic storage.

➤ Convert a drive to Dynamic storage.

➤ Extend an existing partition.

Requirements

➤ A second disk drive on your computer that you can use to practice working with Dynamic disk storage. All data on the second drive will be erased during this lab.

This lab involves working with disk partitions. Therefore, errors made in the lab could corrupt or delete the existing operating system or files. If the computer you use is used for other purposes or classes, you should have a removable disk or an image of the existing partitions, as described in the Introduction to this lab manual, before you continue.

4

Estimated completion time: **20–30 minutes**

ACTIVITY

1. If necessary, start your computer with Windows 2000, and log on as an administrator.

2. Start the Disk Management console to display a window showing both drives, as shown in Figure 4-3.

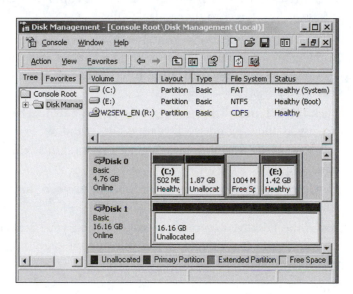

Figure 4-3   Disk Management console for two disks

3. If necessary, allocate the new drive as Basic storage. If you are installing a new drive that has not been previously partitioned or formatted, you need to allocate the drive as Basic storage by doing the following:

   a. Right-click **Disk 1**.

   b. If necessary, select the disk type as **Basic** and click **OK**.

4. Create a partition consisting of half the available disk space.

   a. Right-click in the **unallocated** disk area.

b. Click the **Create Partition** option, and then click **Next** to start the New Partition wizard.

c. Verify that the **Primary Partition** option button is selected, and then click **Next** to display the Specify Partition Size window.

d. Enter a partition size equal to approximately one-half the available space, and then click **Next** to display the Assign Drive Letter or Path window.

e. Click **Next** to accept the default drive letter and display the Format Partition window.

f. Verify that NTFS format is selected, and then enter the name **Legal Docs** in the Volume label text box. Click the **Enable file and folder compression** check box, and click **Next** to display the summary window.

g. On your Lab 4.3 Student Answer Sheet, record the summary information.

h. Click **Finish**.

i. Right-click the **Legal Docs** partition, and click **Properties**. On your Student Answer Sheet, record the available tabs.

5. As you learned in Lab 4.1, partitions created on Basic drives cannot be extended. In this step, you convert the drive to Dynamic storage and then attempt to extend the Legal Docs partition. To convert disk 1 to Dynamic storage, do the following:

a. Right-click **Disk 1** and click the **Upgrade to Dynamic Disk** option to display the Upgrade to Dynamic Disk window.

b. Verify that Disk 1 is checked, and then click **OK** to display the Disks to Upgrade window.

c. Click the **Upgrade** button, and on your Student Answer Sheet, record the warning message.

d. Click **Yes** to the Disk Management message, and on your Student Answer Sheet, record the Upgrade Disks warning message.

e. Click **Yes** to continue the operation.

f. Disk 1 should now be labeled as Dynamic storage on the Disk Management console.

6. Attempt to extend the partition created in Step 4.

a. Click the drive you want to extend.

b. Click the **Action** menu, **All Tasks** option.

c. On your Student Answer Sheet, list the tasks you can perform on a partition that was originally created on a Basic disk.

      d. On your Student Answer Sheet, record why the Extend Volume option is available but not executable.

      e. Press **Esc** twice to return to the Disk Management console.

7. To extend a partition, the partition initially must be created on a Dynamic disk. In this step, you delete the existing partition, and then create a new partition on the Dynamic disk drive.

      a. Right-click the **Legal Docs** partition, and then click **Delete Volume**. On your Student Answer Sheet, record the warning message.

      b. Click **Yes** to delete the partition.

      c. Right-click in the **unallocated** area of disk 1 to display an option menu.

      d. Click the **Create Volume** option and click **Next** to launch the Create Volume Wizard.

      e. On your Student Answer Sheet, record the Volume type options, along with the default option.

      f. Click **Next** to display the Select Disks window.

      g. Verify that Disk 1 is selected. Enter approximately half of the unallocated disk capacity in the Size For selected disk text box.

      h. Click **Next** to display the Assign drive letter or Path window.

      i. Click **Next** to display the Format Volume window. Verify that the NTFS file system is selected, and then enter **Legal Docs** in the Volume label text box.

      j. Click the **Enable file and folder compression** option, and then click **Next** to display the Create Volume Wizard summary window.

      k. Click **Finish** to create and format the volume.

8. Extend the Dynamic disk volume.

      a. Click the newly created **Legal Docs** volume.

      b. Click the **Action** menu, **All Tasks** option.

      c. Click the **Extend Volume** option, and click **Next** to start the Extend Volume wizard.

      d. In the Size for all selected disks text box of the Select Disks window, enter half of the available disk space, and then click **Next** to display the Extend Volume wizard summary window.

      e. Click **Finish** to extend the volume.

      f. Right-click the first segment of the **Legal Docs** volume and click **Properties**. On your Student Answer Sheet, record the available tabs.

      g. Click **Cancel** to return to the Disk Management console.

      h. Close the Disk Management console and log off.

4

Lab 4.4 Securing the File System

Objective

Mr. Melendres wants his legal assistants and secretaries to have access to case and client information on his computer, but he is concerned about securing information to prevent unauthorized access or changes to sensitive files. To provide access for the assistants and secretaries, you need to create user accounts and storage folders, and then use NTFS permissions to provide the required access permissions. After completing this lab, you will be able to:

➤ Create restricted user accounts and groups.

➤ Secure the file system using NTFS permissions.

➤ Use inheritable permissions to set default permissions to subfolders.

➤ Predict NTFS permission changes when copying or moving an object.

Estimated completion time: **30 minutes**

Activity

1. If necessary, start your computer with Windows 2000, and log on as an administrator.

2. Create the following folder structure on your Windows 2000 boot partition. The Cases folder contains a subfolder for cases currently in progress. Within this folder Mr. Melendres creates an In-Progress folder for each case he is currently working on. When a case is completed, Mr. Melendres moves the folder to the Completed folder. The Clients folder contains a Microsoft Access database containing name, address, e-mail address, phone number and notes for each client who has contacted the Melendres and Associates law firm.

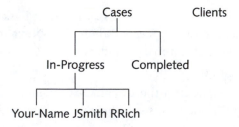

3. Use Notepad to create the following files:

    a. A text file named **Claim1** in the Your–Name folder.

    b. A text file named **Lawsuit** in the JSmith folder.

    c. A text file named **Corp** in the RRich folder.

4. Create a user named LegalSec1 as follows:

    a. Open Control Panel.

    b. Double–click **Users and Passwords**.

    c. Click **Add** and enter the following user information:

       User name: **LegalSec1**
       Full name: **Legal Secretary 1**
       Description: **Legal secretary**

    d. Click **Next**.

    e. Enter and confirm a password of **win2000** and click **Next**. (In an actual network, a password should consist of both letters and numbers. For this lab, be sure you can remember the password you enter.)

    f. Click the **Restricted user** option button, and then click **Finish**.

5. Create a group named Assistants.

    a. Click the **Advanced** tab.

    b. In the Advanced User Management box, click the **Advanced** button to display the Local Users and Groups Window. Click the **Groups** folder to display the window shown in Figure 4-4.

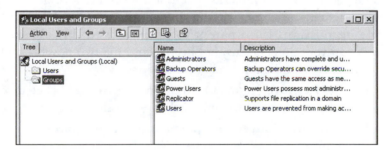

Figure 4-4   Local Users and Groups

    c. Click the **Action** menu, **New Group** option.

    d. Enter **Assistants** in the Group name text box, and **Legal Assistants** in the Description text box.

    e. Click the **Add** button to display the Select Users or Groups window.

      f. Scroll down and double-click the **LegalSec1** user.

      g. Click **Add**, then click **OK** to add the user to the group and return to the New Group window.

      h. Click the **Create** button to create the group and return to the New Group window.

      i. Click **Close** to return to the Local Users and Groups window. Verify that the new group is shown.

      j. Close the Local Users and Groups window.

      k. Click **OK** to close the Users and Passwords window.

      l. Close the Control Panel window.

6. Check default permissions.

      a. Open **My Computer**.

      b. Right-click your **Windows 2000 boot drive**, and click the **Properties** option.

      c. Click the **Security** tab. On your Lab 4.4 Student Answer Sheet, record the default permissions.

      d. Click **Cancel** to close the Properties window.

      e. Double-click your Windows 2000 boot drive.

      f. Right-click the **Cases** folder, and click the **Properties** option.

      g. Click the **Security** tab. On your Student Answer Sheet, record the default permissions.

      h. The group Everyone inherits permissions from the root of the drive. To stop the inheritance, remove the check mark from the **Allow inheritable permissions from parent to propagate to this object** check box. On your Student Answer Sheet, record the two possible options for dealing with the inheritable permissions.

      i. Click the **Remove** button. On your Student Answer Sheet, describe the results of removing the inheritable permissions option.

      j. Click the **Allow inheritable permissions from parent to propagate to this object** check box.

      k. Click the **Apply** button. On your Student Answer Sheet, record the results.

7. Provide the Assistants group with permissions to maintain the Clients database.

      a. Double-click **My Computer** and open your Windows 2000 boot drive.

      b. Right-click the **Clients** folder you created in Step 2, and click the **Properties** option.

c. Click the **Security** tab. On your Student Answer Sheet, record the default user permissions assigned to the Clients folder.

d. Turn off inheritable permissions by clicking the **Allow inheritable permissions from parent to propagate to this object** check box.

e. Click the **Remove** option to remove the group Everyone from the security list.

f. Click the **Add** button to display the Select Users, Computers, or Groups window.

g. Double-click the **Administrators** group.

h. Double-click the **Assistants** group.

i. Click **OK** to return to the Clients Properties window. Verify that both the Administrators and Assistants groups have been added to the Security window, as shown in Figure 4-5.

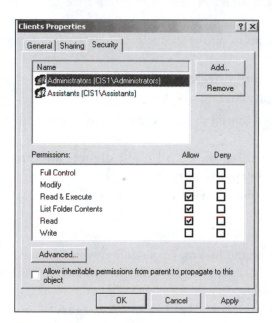

Figure 4-5   NTFS Security tab

j. Grant the Administrators group Full Control:

  ■ Click the **Administrators** group in the upper Name window.

  ■ Click the **Allow** box for **Full Control** in the Permissions window.

k. To allow the legal assistants to update the client database files, grant the Assistants group the Modify right:

- Click the **Assistants** group in the upper Name window.
- Click the **Allow** box for **Modify** in the Permissions window.

l. Click **OK** to save your permission changes.

8. Provide the Administrators group with Full Control to the Cases folder and all subfolders.

a. Right-click the **Cases** folder, and click the **Properties** button.

b. Click the **Security** tab.

c. To turn off inheritable permissions, click to remove the check mark from the **Allow inheritable permissions from parent to propagate to this object** check box.

d. Click the **Remove** option to remove the group Everyone from the security list.

e. Click the **Add** button to display the Select Users, Computers, or Groups window.

f. Double-click the **Administrators** group, and click **OK**.

g. Click the Allow **Full Control** check box.

h. Click the **Advanced** button to display the Access Control Settings for Cases window.

i. Click the **Reset permissions on all child objects and enable propagation of inheritable permissions** check box.

j. Click **OK**. Describe the Security message on your Student Answer Sheet.

k. Click **Yes** to return to the Cases Properties window.

l. To allow users to find the In-Progress and Completed folders, you need to provide the Assistants group with the List Folder Contents right to the Cases folder:

- Click the **Add** button, double-click the **Assistants** group, and click **OK** to add Assistants to the Security window with default rights.
- Remove all rights except List Folder Contents.

m. Click **OK** to save your changes and return to My Computer.

9. Provide the Assistants group with the default of Read only access to the Completed folder and all its subfolders.

a. Open the **Cases** folder from My Computer.

b. Right-click the **Completed** folder, and click the **Properties** option.

    c. Click the **Security** tab. On your Student Answer Sheet, record the default security settings.

    d. Click the **Add** button to display the Select Users, Computers, or Groups window.

    e. Double-click the **Assistants** group and click **OK**. On your Student Answer Sheet, record the default permissions granted to the Assistants group.

    f. Click **OK** to accept the default permissions.

10. Provide the Assistants group with the permissions needed to change documents in the In-Progress folder.

    a. Right-click the **In-Progress** folder, and click the **Properties** option.

    b. Click the **Security** tab. On your Student Answer Sheet, record the default security settings.

    c. Click the **Add** button to display the Select Users, Computers, or Groups window.

    d. Double-click the **Assistants** group, and click **OK**.

    e. Be sure Assistants is highlighted, and then click the Allow **Modify** permissions check box.

    f. Click **OK** to save the permission settings.

11. Check subfolder permissions.

    a. Double-click the **In-Progress** folder to display its subfolders.

    b. Right-click the **JSmith** folder, and click the **Properties** option.

    c. Click the **Security** tab. On your Student Answer Sheet, record the permissions for the JSmith folder.

    d. Click **Cancel** and then click the **Back** button.

    e. Double-click the **Completed** folder to display its subfolders.

    f. Right-click the **RRich** folder, and click the **Properties** button.

    g. Click the **Security** tab. On your Student Answer Sheet, record the permissions for the RRich folder.

    h. Click **Cancel** and then click the **Back** button.

12. Move the JSmith folder from the In-Progress folder to the Completed folder, and check permissions.

    a. Use My Computer to open the **Cases** folder.

    b. Double-click the **In-Progress** folder to open it.

    c. Right-click the **JSmith** folder, and click the **Cut** option.

    d. Click the **Up Button** to move back to the Cases folder window.

    e. Double-click the **Completed** folder to open it.

    f. Click the **Edit** menu, **Paste** option.

    g. Right-click the **JSmith** folder, and click **Properties**.

    h. Click the **Security** tab. On your Student Answer Sheet, record the permissions for the Assistants group.

    i. Remove the check marks from all permissions except Read, Execute, and List.

    j. Click **OK** to save your changes.

    k. Click the **Up Button** to return to the Cases folder window.

13. Copy the **Your-name** folder from the In-Progress folder to the Completed folder and check its permissions.

    a. Double-click the **In-Progress** folder to open it.

    b. Right-click the **Your-name** folder, and click the **Copy** option.

    c. Click the **Up Button** to return to the Cases folder window.

    d. Double-click the **Completed** folder to open it.

    e. Click the **Edit** menu, **Paste** option.

    f. Right-click the **Your-name** folder, and click the **Properties** option.

    g. Click the **Security** tab. On your Student Answer Sheet, record the rights for the Assistants group.

    h. On your Student Answer Sheet, describe why the permissions obtained when copying the Your-name folder were different from the permissions obtained when moving the JSmith folder.

    i. Click **Cancel** to return to the Completed folder window.

    j. Close all windows and log off.

Lab 4.5 Auditing File System Activity

Objective

Windows 2000 provides the capability to audit resources and services for either successful or failed access attempts. Auditing is useful to monitor resource usage, locate intruder activity, or track changes made to files and folders. For example, assume that in order to track any changes made to the Cases/In-Progress folder, Mr. Melendres wants you to enable auditing on the In-Progress folder and all its subfolders. After completing this lab, you will be able to:

➤ Turn on a local audit policy.

➤ Configure auditing for files and folders.

Estimated completion time: **10 minutes**

ACTIVITY

1. The first step to configuring auditing for the Melendres and Associates firm is to enable the local audit policy on the computer. Follow the procedure described below:

   a. Open **Control Panel** and double-click the **Administrative Tools** icon.

   b. Double-click the **Local Security Policy** icon and expand the **Local Policies** folder.

   c. Click the **Audit Policy** folder to list all audit policy options, as shown in Figure 4-6.

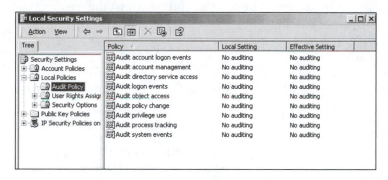

Figure 4-6   Local Audit Policy options

   d. To audit changes to files, double-click the **Audit object access** option to display the Local Security Policy Settings—Audit object access window.

   e. Click both the **Success** and **Failure** check boxes.

   f. Click **OK** to enable object access auditing.

   g. Close the Local Security Settings window.

   h. Close the Administrative Tools window.

2. After enabling object access auditing, you next need to specify which objects, such as files or folders, you want to audit. Follow the procedure listed below to audit any changes made to files in the In-Progress folder and in all its subfolders.

   a. If necessary, use My Computer to open the **Cases** folder.

   b. Right-click the **In-Progress** folder, and click the **Properties** button.

   c. Click the **Security** tab, and then click the **Advanced** button.

   d. Click the **Auditing** tab to display the Auditing Entries window.

   e. Click the **Add** button to display the Select User, Computer, or Group window.

   f. To audit for changes made by any user, double-click **Everyone**.

   g. In the Object tab window, click **auditing** for successful completion of the following access events:

- Create Files/Write Data
- Create Folders/Append Data
- Delete Subfolders and Files
- Delete

   h. Click **OK** to add this auditing entry to the Audit window.

   i. Click **OK** to save your changes and return to the In-Progress Properties window.

   j. Click **OK** to return to My Computer.

   k. Log off.

3. Log on as LegalSec1 and modify the file in the JSmith folder to indicate that the case is completed.

4. Log on as administrator and check the audit file.

   a. Launch the Computer Management console you created in Lab 3.1. Click **Start**, point to **Programs**, and click **Computer Management**. (If you no longer have the Computer Management console, open **Control Panel** and double-click the **Administrative Tools** icon.)

   b. Open **Event Viewer** and double-click the **Security** log.

   c. On your Lab 4.5 Student Answer Sheet, record the security message information.

   d. Exit Event Viewer.

LAB 4.6 SHARING FOLDERS

Objective

The Animal Care Center wants to share and secure the Projects, Forms, Website, and Images folders you created in Lab 4.1. The owner, Dennis Geisler, wants users to be able to access files, but have the ability to change only those files that they have created in the Docs folder. The SysOp user should be able to update files in any of the shared folders. In addition, because users will be able to create files in the Docs subfolder, Dennis is concerned about the Docs subfolder taking up too much disk space. Dennis wants you to limit the amount of disk space that can be used by Docs. When the space in Docs is used, users will be encouraged to remove old and unwanted files. After completing this lab, you will be able to:

➤ Share folders.

➤ Manage shared folder permissions.

➤ Access shared folders.

➤ Set disk quotas.

Estimated completion time: **40-45 minutes**

ACTIVITY 1

Share the Forms folder, set and test permissions for the folder.

1. If necessary, start your computer with Windows 2000, and log on as an administrator.

2. If necessary, follow the procedure in Lab 3.2 to create users named **AppUser** and **SysOp**.

3. Share the Forms folder with the share name Office Forms. Provide all users with Read permission, Administrators with Full Control, and the SysOp user with Change permission.

   a. Double-click My Computer and open the drive containing your Projects, Forms, and Inventory folders.

   b. Right-click the **Forms** folder and click **Properties**.

   c. Click the **Sharing** tab to display the window shown in Figure 4-7.

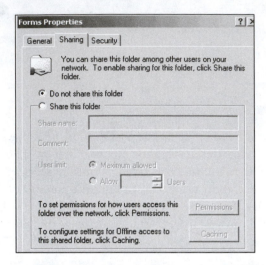

Figure 4-7   Folder Properties, Sharing tab

    d. Click the **Share this folder** option button.

    e. In the Share name text box, enter **Office Forms**.

    f. Verify that the User limit is set to **Maximum allowed**.

    g. Click the **Permissions** button. On your Lab 4.6 Student Answer Sheet, record the default permissions.

    h. Highlight the group **Everyone** and then click the **Remove** button to remove the group Everyone from the Permissions window.

    i. Click the **Add** button. Add the Administrators and Users groups by double-clicking the group **Administrators** and double-clicking the group **Users**.

    j. Click **OK** to return to the Share Permissions window.

    k. On your Student Answer Sheet, record the default permissions for the Users group.

    l. Highlight the **Administrators** group, and click the Allow **Full Control** permission.

    m. Click the **Add** button, and double-click the **SysOp** user. Click **OK** to return to the Shared Permissions window.

    n. Verify that the **SysOp** user is selected, and then click the Allow **Change** permission.

    o. Click **OK** to save the permissions and return to the Forms folder Sharing tab.

    p. Click **OK** to complete sharing your Forms folder.

    q. Close all windows and log off.

4. Assume you are the SysOp user located on another computer and you need to edit the Office Forms shared folder. Proceed as follows:

    a. Log on as the **SysOp** user.

    b. Double-click **My Network Places** and double-click the **Computers Near Me** option to display all computers in your workgroup. Your computer name should appear on the screen.

    c. Double-click your computer name to display a window showing shared folders and printers.

    d. Double-click the **Office Forms** share.

    e. Create two text document files, one named **Travel.txt** and the other named **PO.txt**.

    f. Use Notepad to enter the line **Use this form to report travel expenses** in the Travel.txt file.

    g. Save the Travel.txt file and exit Notepad.

    h. Close all windows and log off.

5. Test the Office Forms share as a user.

    a. Log on using your **AppUser** user name.

    b. Use **My Network Places** to navigate to the Office Forms shared folder.

    c. Double-click the **Travel.txt** form to open it, and verify its contents.

    d. Add a line that says **$100.00 mileage expense for Joe Smith**.

    e. Attempt to save the form. On the Student Answer Sheet, record what happens.

    f. Exit Notepad without saving the document, and close all windows.

6. Try accessing and changing the file using My Computer.

    a. Double-click **My Computer** and open the drive containing your Forms folder.

    b. Open the **Forms** folder, and double-click the **Travel.txt** document to start **Notepad**.

    c. Add a line that says **$100.00 mileage expense for Joe Smith**.

    d. Save the Travel.txt document. On the Student Answer Sheet, record what happens.

    e. Exit Notepad and log off.

    f. On the Student Answer Sheet, explain why you were able to save the Travel.txt file through My Computer, but not through My Network places.

7. To prevent users that are logged on the local computer from modifying data, you need to set NTFS permissions on the folders you want to secure. To secure the Forms folder with NTFS permissions, use the following procedure:

a. Log on as an administrator.

b. Double-click **My Computer** and open the drive containing your Forms folder.

c. Right-click your **Forms** folder, and click the **Properties** button.

d. Click the **Security** tab to display the default security permissions. Note that by default Everyone has Full Control.

e. Follow the procedure in Lab 4.4, Step 6 to remove the Everyone group, and add the following security permissions:

- Give the group Administrators: Full Control.
- Give the group Users: Read, Execute, and List permissions.
- Give the SysOp user: Write permission only. (Note that the SysOp user also will obtain read, execute, and list permissions from being a member of the Users group.)

f. Click **OK** to save your permissions and return to the My Computer window.

8. Repeat Steps 4 and 5 to test SysOp and AppUser permissions.

ACTIVITY 2

Share the Projects Folder, provide and then test the following access permissions.

➤ Administrator has Full Control to all folders and subfolders.

➤ SysOp has Modify permissions to all folders and subfolders.

➤ Users have Read permissions to the Images and Website folders.

➤ Users have the ability to create and manage their own documents in the Docs folder, but can only read other user documents.

1. Log on as an administrator.

2. Share the Projects folder.

3. Provide Users with the Change permission, and Administrators with Full Control permissions. Provide Administrators with Full Control to all folders and subfolders, SysOp with Modify permissions to all folders and subfolders, and Users with Read permissions as follows:

a. If necessary, use My Computer to navigate to the drive containing your Projects folder.

b. Right-click the **Projects** folder, and click the **Properties** option.

c. Click the **Security** tab. Remove the check from the **Allow inheritable permissions from parent to propagate to this object** check box. Click **Yes** to confirm the action.

d. Click the **Add** button and double-click **Administrators**, **Users**, and **SysOp**.

e. Click **OK** to return to the Properties window.

f. Highlight **Administrators** and click **Full Control**.

g. Highlight **SysOp** and click **Modify**.

h. Verify that Users have only Read, Execute, and List permissions.

i. Click the **Advanced** button, and check the **Reset permissions on all child objects and enable propagation of inheritable permissions** check box. Click **Yes** to confirm the action.

j. Click **OK** twice to return to the My Computer window.

4. Provide the Users group with permissions to create and manage only their own documents in the Docs folder.

a. Double-click the **Projects** folder to open it.

b. Right-click the **Docs** folder, and click the **Properties** option.

c. Click the **Security** tab. On your Lab 4.6 Student Answer Sheet, record the default permissions.

d. Click the **Advanced** button to display the Access Control Settings for the Docs window shown in Figure 4-8.

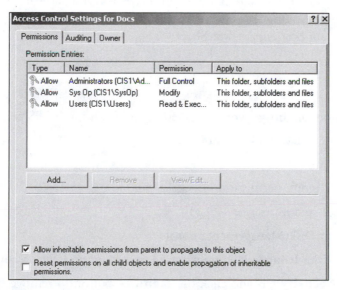

Figure 4-8   Access Control Settings window

    e. Highlight the **Users** group and click the **View/Edit** button.

    f. Click the **Create Files/Write Data** permission, and then click **OK** to return to the Access Control Settings for Docs window. Notice that another entry has been added for the Users group.

    g. Click **OK** twice to return to the Docs Properties window.

    h. Click the **Add** button, and then double-click the **CREATOR OWNER** group. Creator Owner is a special group whose rights apply only on a file-by-file basis to the creator or owner of that file. By assigning this group the Full Control permission, you allow the owner or creator of a file to manage that file, yet prevent them from modifying or deleting other files in the folder.

    i. Click **OK**. Highlight the **CREATOR OWNER** object, and click the **Full Control** permission.

    j. Click **OK** to return to the My Computer window.

5. Close all windows and log off.

6. Test access to your Projects folder by logging on as the AppUser. Then create and access documents in the Docs folder using both My Network Places and My Computer. Record your results on the Student Answer Sheet.

7. From My Network Places, browse to the Website folder. Attempt to create a file in the Website folder. Record the results on your Student Answer Sheet.

8. From My Network Places, browse to the Images volume. Notice that while this folder is located on a different drive, it is still accessible from the Projects share. Attempt to create a file in the Images volume. Record the results on your Student Answer Sheet.

9. Log off.

ACTIVITY 3

Restrict users from the Images volume by setting the following NTFS permissions.

➤ Administrators have Full Control.

➤ Users have only Read, Execute, and List permissions.

➤ SysOp has Modify permission.

1. Log on as an administrator.

2. Launch your Disk Management console.

3. Right-click the **Images** volume named Legal Docs, and click **Properties**.

4. Click the **Security** tab, and click the **Remove** button to remove the group **Everyone**.

5. Click the **Add** button, and double-click **SysOp**, **Administrators**, and **Users**.

6. Click **OK** to return to the Images Legal Docs Properties window.

7. Highlight **Administrators** and click the **Full Control** permission.

8. Highlight **SysOp** and click the **Modify** permission.

9. Verify that the Users group has only Read, Execute, and List permissions.

10. Click **OK** to save your changes.

11. Exit the Disk Management console.

12. Close all windows and log off.

13. Repeat Activity 2, Step 8 to test permissions to the Images volume.

ACTIVITY 4

Set disk quotas on the disk containing the Projects folder.

1. Log on as an administrator.

2. Open **My Computer**.

3. Right-click the drive containing your Projects folder, and click the **Properties** option.

4. Click the **Quota** tab, and click the **Enable quota management** and **Deny disk space to user exceeding quota limit** check boxes.

5. Set the disk limit to **10 KB** and the warning level to **8 KB**.

6. Click the **Log event when a user exceeds their quota limit** check box.

7. Click **OK** to save the quota configuration. Click **OK** again.

8. Log off.

9. Log on as the **AppUser**.

10. Use My Computer to navigate to the Docs folder.

11. Use Notepad to create documents until you receive a warning. Record the message on your Student Answer Sheet.

12. Create additional files until you have exceeded your quota.

13. Log off.

14. Log on as Administrator, and start **Event Viewer**.

15. On your Student Answer Sheet, record the security log quota message.

16. Close all windows and log off.

USERS, GROUPS, PROFILES, AND POLICIES

Labs included in this chapter

➤ Lab 5.1 Creating Local Users and Groups

➤ Lab 5.2 Assigning Group and User Permissions

➤ Lab 5.3 Configuring and Managing User Profiles

➤ Lab 5.4 Applying Account Policies

➤ Lab 5.5 Applying Policies for Auditing and User Rights

Microsoft MCSE Exam #70-210 Objectives	
Objective	Lab
Implement, configure, manage, and troubleshoot local user accounts	
Create and manage local users and groups	5.1
Implement, configure, and troubleshoot account settings	5.4, 5.5
Implement, configure, and troubleshoot account policy	5.4, 5.5
Implement, configure, manage, and troubleshoot local user authentication	
Configure and troubleshoot local user accounts	5.2
Configure and manage user profiles	5.3

Student Answer Sheets to accompany the labs in this chapter can be downloaded from the Online Companion for this manual at *www.course.com*.

LAB 5.1 CREATING LOCAL USERS AND GROUPS

Objective

The Melendres and Associates law firm wants to set up a Windows 2000 Professional computer as a server for sharing case and billing information. Currently each attorney and a legal assistant share a Windows 2000 computer to enter ongoing legal information on current cases and to archive completed cases for future reference. The administrative assistant's computer is used to enter and print client bills. Mr. Melendres wants to combine each attorney's case information with the billing system on a single Windows 2000 Professional system. He then wants to create user and group accounts to allow the following access to the system:

➤ Allow only Mr. Melendres and his legal assistant, Meme Rodregus, to update the Melendres case information.

➤ Allow only Ms. Damrau and her legal assistant, Rose Wiggerts, to update the Damrau case information.

➤ Allow all employees to read the case information from any attorney.

➤ Allow only the administrative assistant, Jan Cunningham, and Mr. Melendres to maintain the billing system files.

➤ Allow Jan Cunningham to back up and restore network files.

After completing this lab you will be able to:

➤ Define a naming convention and use it to name users and groups.

➤ Identify default and system groups.

➤ Create local groups.

➤ Create local users and assign them to one or more groups.

➤ Use default groups to provide backup rights.

Estimated completion time: **30 minutes**

ACTIVITY 1

Define a user naming convention and identify default Windows 2000 system and local groups.

1. If necessary, start your computer with Windows 2000, and log on as an administrator.

2. On the Lab 5.1 User and Group Planning sheet that follows this lab, define a user naming convention and use it to define logon names for all

users. (Refer to *MCSE Guide to Windows 2000 Professional*, Course Technology, ISBN 0-619-01513-6, Chapter 5, for information on defining a naming convention.) The attorneys should be set up as power users.

3. On your Student Answer Sheet, identify the Windows 2000 default groups.

   a. Open **Control Panel** and double-click the **Users and Passwords** applet.

   b. Click the **Advanced** tab, and then click the **Advanced** button to display the Local Users and Groups window.

   c. Click the **Groups** folder to display all group names.

   d. Record the default groups on your Lab 5.1 Student Answer Sheet. From your Student Answer Sheet, identify any of the default groups that can be used on your User and Group Planning Sheet.

   e. Resize the Local Users and Groups window so it uses about half the screen.

   f. Minimize the Local Users and Groups window, close the Users and Passwords window, and close the Control Panel window.

4. Identify the Windows 2000 system groups.

   a. Double-click **My Computer**, right-click the drive containing your Windows 2000 operating system, and click the **Properties** option.

   b. Click the **Security** tab, and then click the **Add** button to display the Select Users, Computers, or Groups window.

   c. Compare the groups listed in the Select Users, Computers, or Groups windows to the groups in your Local Users and Groups window. The system groups are the groups listed in the Select Users, Computers, or Groups window, and not listed in the Local Users and Groups windows.

   d. Record the system groups on your Student Answer Sheet. From a reference book (such as *MCSE Guide to Microsoft Windows 2000 Professional*, Course Technology, ISBN 0-619-01513-6) briefly record the purpose of each system group along with its default member(s).

   e. Close all windows.

ACTIVITY 2

Create the file system, create local users and groups, and add a user to a group.

1. Create the file system.

   a. Double-click **My Computer** and open the drive containing your Windows 2000 operating system.

   b. Create a folder named **Lab5**.

c. Create the following folders and subfolders within the Lab5 folder.

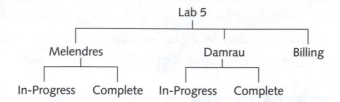

2. According to the recommended Microsoft procedure, you should assign folder permissions to local groups. Then, users who need access to the folders are made members of the appropriate local groups. On the User and Group Planning sheet, define the local groups you will need to assign permissions to the folders you created in Step 1.

3. Create local users.

   a. Open **Control Panel** and double-click the **Users and Passwords** applet.

   b. Click the **Advanced** tab to display the Advanced User Management dialog box.

   c. Click the **Advanced** button within the Advanced User Management box to display the Local Users and Groups window shown in Figure 5-1.

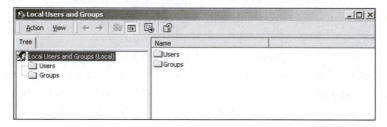

Figure 5-1   Local Users and Groups window

   d. Click the **Users** folder in the left-side tree window to display all existing users in the right-side results window.

   e. On your Lab 5.1 Student Answer Sheet, record any user names that are marked as disabled.

   f. Click the **Action** menu, **New User** option to display the New User window.

   g. In the User name text box, enter the Logon name of a user from your Lab 5.1 User and Group Planning Sheet.

   h. Enter the user's full name and description in the Full name and Description text boxes.

i. Enter an initial password and remove the check mark from the **User must change password at next logon** option.

j. Click the **Create** button.

k. Repeat steps (f) through (j) to create all the users on your User and Group Planning Sheet. Click **Close** to return to the Local Users and Groups window.

4. Create local groups and assign users.

   a. Click the **Groups** folder in the left-side tree window to display all groups in the right-side results window.

   b. Click the **Action** menu, **New Group** option to display the New Group window.

   c. Enter a group name and description from your User and Group Planning Sheet.

   d. To add group members, click the **Add** button to display the Select Users or Groups window.

   e. Use the scroll bar to find the first user's name and click it.

   f. Ctrl+click each additional user name until all users for the group are highlighted.

   g. Click the **Add** button to insert the names in the bottom window.

   h. After all group members are included, click the **OK** button to return to the New Group window.

   i. Click the **Create** button.

   j. Repeat steps (b) through (i) until all four groups are created.

   k. Click the **Close** button to return to the Local Users and Groups window.

5. Add Jan Cunningham to the Backup Operators group.

   a. Click the **Users** folder to display the existing user accounts.

   b. Double-click Jan Cunningham's account to display the Properties page.

   c. Click the **Member Of** tab to display current group memberships.

   d. Click the **Add** button, and double-click the **Backup Operators** group.

   e. Click **OK** to add Backup Operators to the list of groups Jan belongs to.

   f. Click **OK** to return to the Local Users and Groups window.

   g. Close the Local Users and Groups window.

   h. Click **OK** to close the Users and Passwords applet.

   i. Close the Control Panel window.

6. Close all windows and Log off.

5

LAB 5.1 CREATING LOCAL USERS AND GROUPS

User and Group Planning Sheet

Name: _____   Computer ID: _____

User/Group Naming Convention:

User Names

Logon name	Full Name	Description	Password
	Sebastian Melendres	Head Attorney ❑ Power user ❑ Restricted User ❑ Other	❑ Change at logon ❑ Cannot change ❑ Never expires
	Julie Damrau	Attorney ❑ Power user ❑ Restricted User ❑ Other	❑ Change at logon ❑ Cannot change ❑ Never expires
	Meme Rodregus	Legal assistant for Mr. Melendres ❑ Power user ❑ Restricted User ❑ Other	❑ Change at logon ❑ Cannot change ❑ Never expires
	Rosemary Wiggerts	Legal assistant for Ms. Damrau ❑ Power user ❑ Restricted User ❑ Other	❑ Change at logon ❑ Cannot change ❑ Never expires
	Jan Cunningham	Administrative Assistant ❑ Power user ❑ Restricted User ❑ Other	❑ Change at logon ❑ Cannot change ❑ Never expires

Local Groups

Group Name	Resource Managed	Description/Department	Members
	Sebastian Melendres cases		
	Julie Damrau cases		
	Client billing system		
	Read all case information		
	Back up/restore the system		

LAB 5.2 ASSIGNING GROUP AND USER PERMISSIONS

Objective

In this lab you complete the process of securing the Melendres and Associates server. You will assign permissions to the groups and users to accomplish the access needs defined in Lab 5.1. In addition, Mr. Melendres has a folder with certain files that he cannot let anyone access. Because support people, such as yourself, need to log on as administrator, he wants to secure the folder so that it cannot be accessed by anyone with administrator privileges. After completing this lab you will be able to:

➤ Provide NTFS permissions to groups and users.

➤ Secure a folder from administrator access by taking ownership.

➤ Test security permissions.

> Estimated completion time: **30 minutes**

ACTIVITY

1. On the Lab 5.2 Permissions Planning Sheet, determine the permissions to be granted to each group. Be sure to include the Administrators group with Full Control.

2. If necessary, start your computer with Windows 2000, and log on as an administrator.

3. Secure the Billing folder.

    a. If necessary, double-click **My Computer** and navigate to your newly created Lab5 folder.

    b. Right-click the **Billing** folder and click the **Properties** option.

    c. Click the **Security** tab to display the security window shown in Figure 5-2.

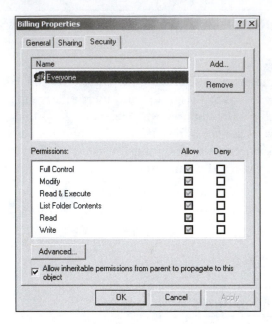

Figure 5-2   Folder Security window

    d. Remove the check mark from the **Allow inheritable permissions from parent to propagate to this object** check box.

    e. Click the **Remove** button to remove the group Everyone from the name list.

    f. Add the groups and permissions identified on your Lab 5.2 Permissions Planning Sheet.

    g. Click **OK** to close the Billing properties window.

4. Secure the Melendres folder.

    a. Right-click the **Melendres** folder and click the **Properties** option.

    b. Click the **Security** tab, and remove the check from the **Allow inheritable permissions from parent to propagate to this object** check box.

    c. Click the **Remove** button to remove the group Everyone from the name list.

    d. Add the groups and permissions identified on your Permissions Planning Sheet.

    e. Click **OK** to close the Melendres properties window.

5. Secure the Damrau folder.

    a. Right-click the **Damrau** folder and click the **Properties** option.

b. Click the **Security** tab, and remove the check mark from the **Allow inheritable permissions from parent to propagate to this object** check box.

c. Click the **Remove** button to remove the group Everyone from the name list.

d. Add the groups and permissions identified on your Permissions Planning Sheet.

e. Click **OK** to close the **Damrau** properties window.

f. Use the **UP** button to navigate back to your Lab5 folder.

6. If necessary, on your Permissions Planning Sheet, make any additional permission assignments indicated.

7. Each attorney needs a private area that only that attorney has access to. This can be accomplished by creating a "Private" subfolder for each attorney, and giving only the attorney full control of the folder. The attorney can then log on and take ownership of his or her Private folder. After doing this, all users are locked out, including the Administrator. The only way the Administrator can gain control is by taking ownership and adding the Administrators group to the security permissions list. Follow the procedure below to setup a Private folder for Mr. Melendres.

a. Double-click the **Melendres** folder to open it.

b. Create a subfolder named **Private**.

c. Right-click the **Private** folder and click **Properties**.

d. Click the **Security** tab, and remove the check mark from the **Allow inheritable permissions from parent to propagate to this object** check box.

e. Click the **Remove** button to remove all objects from the security window.

f. Click the **Add** button and double-click the user name you assigned to Mr. Melendres.

g. Click **OK** to return to the Private Properties window, and then click **Full Control** in the Allow column for the Melendres user.

5

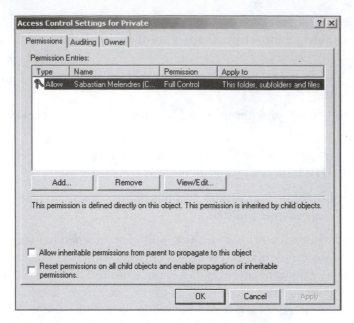

Figure 5-3   Access Control Settings window

h. Try to give ownership to Mr. Melendres:

- Click the **Advanced** button to display the Access Control Settings for Private window, as shown in Figure 5-3.
- Click the **Owner** tab, and record the current owner of this folder.
- On your Lab 5.2 Student Answer Sheet, record the results of attempting to give ownership to Mr. Melendres.
- Click **OK** to return to the Private Properties window.

i. Click **OK** to save the permission changes and return to the My Computer window.

j. Close all windows and log off.

k. Log on as the Melendres user. If necessary, click **Cancel** and then click **Yes** to bypass the NetWare login process.

l. Use My Computer to navigate to the Lab5\Melendres folder.

m. Right-click the **Private** subfolder and click the **Properties** option.

n. Click the **Security** tab, and then click the **Advanced** button to display the Access Control Settings for Private.

o. Click the **Owner** tab.

p. On your Student Answer Sheet, record the names of users you can select as owners.

q. Click the Melendres user, and then click **OK** to make Mr. Melendres the owner of the folder.

r. Click **OK** to save your changes and return to My Computer.

s. Close all windows and log off.

8. On your Permissions Planning Sheet, make an entry for each attorney's Private folder. Include path, whether to inherit parent permissions, owner, and permissions.

9. Repeat Step 7 to establish a Private folder for Ms. Damrau.

10. Share the Melendres, Damrau, and Billing folders.

a. Share each of the following folders, and change the shared permissions by removing the group Everyone, and adding the group Users with Full Control:

- Melendres
- Damrau
- Billing

b. On your Student Answer Sheet, describe why it is not necessary to provide specific groups and users with shared permissions.

c. Close all windows and log off.

11. Test and debug the system.

a. Log on as the Melendres user.

b. Use My Network Places to browse to the Melendres In-Progress folder.

c. Create a subfolder named **BMeulner**.

d. Within the BMeulner subfolder, use Notepad to create a text file named **CaseLog**. Place the following line in the CaseLog file: **Case opened on mm/dd/yyyy**.

e. Close Notepad and navigate to the Melendres Private folder.

f. Create two text files named **GoodGuys** and **BadGuys** in the Private folder.

g. Close all windows and log out.

h. Log on as Rose Wiggerts and use My Network Places to navigate to the Melendres In-Progress folder. Attempt to access the CaseLog file in the BMeulner folder.

i. On your Student Answer Sheet, record the results of your attempt to access the file.

j. On your Student Answer Sheet, record the results of your attempt to change the file and save it.

k. Close all windows and log off.

l. Log on as Administrator.

     m. Use My Computer to navigate to the Melendres folder.

     n. On your Student Answer Sheet, record the results of attempting to access the Private subfolder.

     o. To view the contents of the Private folder, the administrator must be an owner of the folder, and the Administrators local group must be given Full Control permissions to the Private folder. On your Student Answer Sheet, record the steps you take to make the administrator an owner of the Private folder with Full Control permissions.

     p. On your Student Answer Sheet, describe how Mr. Melendres could learn that you have accessed the Private folder.

12. Close all windows and log off.

LAB 5.2 CREATING LOCAL USERS AND GROUPS

Permissions Planning Sheet

Name: _____   Computer ID: _____

Use this table to identify each folder name in the "Folder Path" column, along with whether this folder is to inherit permissions from its parent. Record group and user names across the top row, and then place the permissions for each group or user in the corresponding folder's row.

Folder Path	Inherit Parent Permissions	Owner	Group1	Group2	Group3	Group/User	Group/User	Group/User
	❏ Yes ❏ No							
	❏ Yes ❏ No							
	❏ Yes ❏ No							
	❏ Yes ❏ No							
	❏ Yes ❏ No							
	❏ Yes ❏ No							
	❏ Yes ❏ No							
	❏ Yes ❏ No							
	❏ Yes ❏ No							

LAB 5.3 CONFIGURING AND MANAGING USER PROFILES

Objective

At the Animal Care Center, several people share the Windows 2000 Professional computer in Dennis' office by logging on with either the AppUser or SysOp user name. The problem is that sometimes a user accidentally deletes a program icon, or makes changes to the desktop wallpaper or color scheme. Dennis wants you to configure a standard desktop for the SysOp and AppUsers that cannot be changed. After completing this lab, you will be able to:

➤ Configure a desired user profile.

➤ Access user profile information.

➤ Create mandatory profiles.

➤ Test user profile configurations.

Requirements

➤ A Microsoft Management Console as created in Lab 3.1.

➤ The following user accounts as created in Lab 3.2:

-AppUser (Restricted user)

-SysOp (power user)

Estimated completion time: **15–20 minutes**

ACTIVITY

1. View default user profile information.

   a. Log on as AppUser.

   b. Double-click **My Computer** and open the drive containing your Windows 2000 boot files.

   c. Navigate to the Documents and Settings folder and double-click the **AppUser** subfolder.

   d. Double-click the **Desktop** folder, and record its contents on your Lab 5.3 Student Answer Sheet.

   e. Close all windows.

2. Configure a profile for the AppUser.

   a. Create desktop shortcuts to the WordPad and Calculator programs.

   b. Set a unique desktop wallpaper and screen saver.

    c. View profile information:

- Double-click **My Computer** and open the drive containing your Windows 2000 boot files.
- Navigate to the Documents and Settings folder, and double-click the **AppUser** subfolder.
- Double-click the **Desktop** folder, and record its contents on your Student Answer Sheet.
- Close all windows and log off.

3. Configure a profile for the SysOp user.

    a. Log on as the SysOp user.

    b. Create a desktop shortcut to the Microsoft Management console.

    c. Set the desktop background and the screen saver as follows:

- Right-click on any unused area of the desktop and click **Properties**.
- Use the scroll bar to select the **Ocean Wave** background.
- Click the **Screen Saver** tab, and select the **Starfield Simulation** screen saver.
- Click **OK** to save and apply your changes.
- If necessary, click **Yes** to enable Active Desktop.

    d. Close all windows and log off.

4. Make the SysOp profile mandatory.

    a. Log on as Administrator.

    b. Double-click **My Computer** and navigate to the Documents and Settings folder.

    c. Right-click the **SysOp** folder and click **Properties**.

    d. Click the **Security** tab, and click the **SysOp** user in the name list window.

    e. In the Permissions window, reduce SysOp to only Read, Execute, and List Folder permissions.

    f. Click **OK** to save changes, and return to the My Computer window.

    g. Double-click the **SysOp** folder, and change the name of the NTUSER.DAT file to **NTUSER.MAN**. (It may be necessary to perform the following to view protected system and hidden files: from the **View** menu, click **Folder Options**, then click the **View** tab. Click the **Show hidden files and folders** option. Remove the check from **Hide protected operating system files (Recommended)**. Click **OK**.)

    h. Close all windows and log off.

    i. To ensure that the settings are saved, log on as SysOp and then log back off.

5. Repeat Step 4 to make the AppUser profile mandatory.

6. Test the user profiles.

   a. Log on as SysOp.

   b. Attempt to delete the Management console from the desktop, and record the results on your Student Answer Sheet.

   c. Right-click your desktop and use the **Properties** option to change your background to **Gone Fishing**. Record the results on your Student Answer Sheet.

   d. Log off.

   e. Log on as AppUser.

   f. Attempt to change the desktop or background settings. Record the results on your Student Answer Sheet.

   g. Log off.

LAB 5.4 APPLYING ACCOUNT POLICIES

Objective

Because of an increase in its number of cases, the Melendres and Associates law firm has added another attorney, and plans to hire three temporary employees to help enter documents into a shared directory. With the three new employees in the office, Mr. Melendres wants to tighten up security to prevent unauthorized access to files. After completing this lab, you will be able to:

➤ Configure a password policy.

➤ Configure an account lockout policy.

➤ Configure an audit policy.

➤ Configure user rights.

➤ Identify common rights and their default users or groups.

> Estimated completion time: **15–20 minutes**

ACTIVITY

1. If necessary, start your computer with Windows 2000, and log on as an administrator.

2. Using the following steps, create three new local user accounts named Temp1, Temp2, and Temp3. Set up the accounts so the users cannot change their password.

   a. Double-click the **Users and Passwords** applet from Control Panel.

b. Click the **Advanced** tab, and then click the **Advanced** button to display the Local Users and Groups window.

c. Click the **Users** folder, and then use the **New User** option of the Action menu to create the temporary users named **Temp1**, **Temp2**, and **Temp3**.

3. Create a local group named Temps, and make the three new user accounts members.

a. Click the **Groups** folder to display all existing groups.

b. Click the **Action** menu, **New Group** option, and enter the group name **Temps**.

c. Click the **Add** button and double-click each of the Temp users you created in Step 2.

d. Click the **Create** button to create the Temps group.

e. Click **Close** to return to the Local Users and Groups window.

4. Change the temporary user names to T_Assist1, T_Assist2, and T_Assist3.

a. Click the **Users** tab to display all users.

b. Right-click **Temp1** and then click the **Rename** option.

c. Type the new **T_Assist1** username, and press **Enter**.

d. Repeat this process for the temporary users 2 and 3.

e. Click the **Groups** tab, and double-click the **Temps** groups. Verify that the user names have been changed.

f. Click **Cancel** and close all windows.

5. Within the Lab5 folder, create a subfolder named **Shared**.

6. Follow the procedure below to use the CREATER OWNER system group to provide all users with permissions to create and manage their own files in the Shared folder, but to only read files created by other users.

a. Right-click the **Shared** group and click the **Properties** option.

b. Click the **Security** tab, and remove the check from the **Allow inheritable permissions from parent to propagate to this object** check box. Click the **Remove** button to complete the operation.

c. Click the **Add** button, and double-click **CREATER OWNER**, **Administrators**, **Power Users**, and **User** groups.

d. Click **OK** to return to the Shared Properties window.

e. Grant the following permissions:

- Administrators – Full Control
- CREATER OWNER – Full Control
- Power Users – Full Control
- Users – Read, Execute, and List

    f. To allow users to create files, you need to perform the following substeps:

- Click the **Advanced** button to display the Access Control Settings for Shared.
- Highlight the **Users** group, and click the **View/Edit** button.
- Click to **Allow** the **Create Files/Write Data** permission, and click **OK**.
- Click **OK** to save the permissions and return to the Shared Properties window.

    g. Click **OK** to close the Shared Properties window.

    h. Close all windows.

7. Configure a password policy that forces users to enter a different password consisting of at least 6 characters every 90 days:

    a. Open **Control Panel** and double-click the **Administrative Tools** applet.

    b. Double-click the **Local Security Policy** applet to display the Local Security Settings window (Figure 5-4).

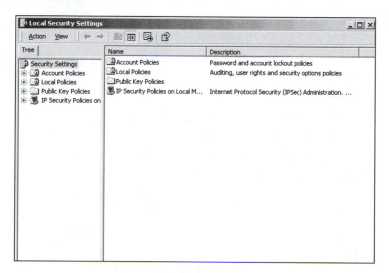

Figure 5-4   Local Security Settings window

    c. Expand the **Account Policies** folder, and click the **Password Policy** subfolder.

    d. Double-click the **Enforce password history** policy, and set passwords remembered to **10**. Click **OK** to return to the Local Security Settings window.

    e. Double-click **Maximum password age** and set the days to **90**. Click **OK** to return to the Local Security Settings window.

    f. To prevent users from rapidly making several password changes, double-click the **Minimum password age** policy, and set the days to **1**. Click **OK** to return to the Local Security Settings window.

    g. Double-click the **Minimum password length** policy, and set the number of characters to **6**. Record the maximum password length on your Lab 5.4 Student Answer Sheet. Click **OK** to return to the Local Security Settings window.

    h. Double-click the **Passwords must meet complexity requirements** policy, and record the default setting on your Student Answer Sheet. Click **Cancel** to return to the Local Security Settings window.

    i. Double-click the **Store passwords using reversible encryption for all users in the domain** policy, and record the default setting on your Student Answer Sheet. Click **Cancel** to return to the Local Security Settings window.

    j. Close all windows and log off.

8. Test the password policy.

    a. Log on as the Meme Rodregus user.

    b. Press the **Ctrl+Alt+Delete** key combination to display the Windows Security window.

    c. Click the **Change Password** button.

    d. Enter the old password in the Current password box, and enter a new password of **pass** in both the New password and Confirm new password text boxes, and then click **OK**.

    e. Record the message you receive on your Student Answer Sheet.

    f. Enter **password** for the password, and click **OK**.

    g. Click the **Change Password** button again, and try to change the password to **theboss**.

    h. Record the message you receive, along with the reason for the message, on your Student Answer Sheet.

    i. Click **Cancel** and close the Windows Security window.

    j. Log off.

9. Configure a lockout policy that will lock a user's account for 20 minutes if five unsuccessful logon attempts are made within a 10-minute period.

    a. Log on as an administrator.

    b. Open **Control Panel** and double-click the **Administrative Tools** applet.

    c. Double-click the **Local Security Policy** applet to display the Local Security Settings window.

d. If necessary, expand the Account Policies folder, then click the **Account Lockout Policy** in the left-side tree window.

e. Double-click the **Account lockout duration** policy. Record the default lockout minutes on your Student Answer Sheet. Change the duration to **20** minutes, and click the **OK** button to save your change.

f. Record the Suggested Value Changes on your Student Answer Sheet, and click **OK** to accept.

g. Double-click the **Account lockout threshold** option, and record the default setting on your Student Answer Sheet. If necessary, change the value to **5** and click the **OK** button to save your change.

h. Double-click the **Reset account lockout counter after** policy, and change the minutes to **10**. Click **OK** to save the change, and return to the Local Security Settings window.

i. Log off.

10. Test the lockout policy.

a. Attempt to log on as the Melendres user, and use incorrect passwords until the account is locked out.

b. Record the lockout error message, along with the number of logon attempts, on your Student Answer Sheet.

c. Log on as administrator.

d. Start the **Users and Passwords** applet from Control Panel.

e. Click the **Advanced** button, and then click the **Users** folder.

f. Double-click the **Melendres** account.

g. On your Student Answer Sheet, describe the action you need to take to unlock the Melendres account.

h. Close all windows.

LAB 5.5 APPLYING POLICIES FOR AUDITING AND USER RIGHTS

Objective

In addition to securing existing accounts and providing access permissions, Mr. Melendres wants to monitor any changes made to the In-Progress case files, as well as learn of any failed attempts to access unauthorized files. Mr. Melendres wants to prevent the temporary employees from logging on locally to the shared Windows 2000 Professional system. Only valid users should be allowed to access the computer from the network. In addition, he currently cannot access the security log when logged in with his user name. He wants to be able to access the security log information, as well as have a list of rights he has as a power user. After completing this lab, you will be able to:

➤ Configure an audit policy.

➤ Configure user rights.

➤ Identify common rights and their default users or groups.

Estimated completion time: **15–20 minutes**

ACTIVITY

1. If necessary, start your computer with Windows 2000, and log on as an administrator.

2. If necessary, start the **Administrative Tools** applet from Control Panel, and double-click **Local Security Policy**.

3. Configure audit polices that will audit unsuccessful attempts to log on, changes to file system objects, and system events.

   a. If necessary, expand the Local Policies folder.

   b. Click the **Audit Policy**. Enable each of the following auditing policies:

      ■ Audit **failure** of **account logon events**.

      ■ Audit **success** or **failure** of **object access**.

      ■ Audit **success** or **failure** of **system events**.

4. Disable the ability to shut down the system without logging on.

   a. Click the **Security Options** policy.

   b. On your Lab 5.5 Student Answer Sheet, record each enabled security policy.

   c. To prevent the Windows 2000 system from being shut down before an authorized user logs on, double-click the **Allow system to be shut down without having to log on** policy, then select **Disabled**, then click **OK**.

5. Close the Local Security Settings window.

6. Close the Administrative Tools window.

7. Configure an audit policy that will record any failed attempts made by members of the Temps group to access information in either of the attorney folders.

   a. Double-click **My Computer** and navigate to your **Lab5** folder.

   b. Right-click the **Melendres** folder and click the **Properties** option.

   c. Click the **Security** tab, and then click the **Advanced** button to display the Access Control Settings for Melendres window.

d. Click the **Auditing** tab, and click **Add** to display the Select User, Computer, or Group window.

e. Click the **Temps** group, and click **OK** to display the Auditing Entry for Melendres window shown in Figure 5-5.

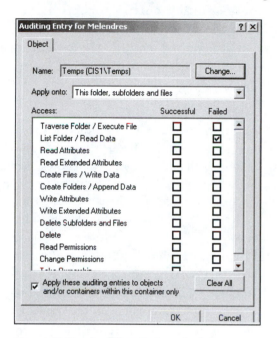

Figure 5-5   Auditing Entry window

f. Click the **Failed** check box on List Folder/Read Data access.

g. Click the **Apply these auditing entries to objects and/or containers within this container only** check box, and then click the **OK** button to save your entry in the auditing window.

h. Click **OK** to return to the Melendres Properties window.

i. Click **OK** to return to My Computer.

j. Repeat steps (a) through (i) to audit failed attempts to access the Damrau folder.

8. Configure an audit policy that will record any successful update information to each attorney's In-Progress folder:

a. Double-click the **Melendres** folder to display the In-Progress and Complete subfolders.

b. Right-click the **In-Progress** folder and click the **Properties** option.

c. Click the **Security** tab and click the **Advanced** button.

d. Click the **Auditing** tab, and record any existing audit entries for the In-Progress folder on your Student Answer Sheet.

    e. Click the **Add** button, and then double-click the **Everyone** system group to display the Auditing Entry for In-Progress window.

    f. In the **Successful** column, click the **Create Files/Write Data** and **Create Folders/Append Data** check boxes.

    g. Click the **Apply these auditing entries to objects and/or containers within this container only** check box.

    h. Click **OK** to save your changes and return to the Auditing window.

    i. Click **OK** to return to the In-Progress properties window.

    j. Click **OK** to return to My Computer.

    k. Close all windows.

9. Mr. Melendres does not want the temporary employees to have the right to log on locally to his computer; only valid users should be able to access the computer from the network. In addition, Mr. Melendres currently cannot access the security log when logged in with his user name. He wants to be able to access the security log information as well as have a list of rights he has as a power user. Follow the procedure described below to configure the user rights policy.

    a. Double-click **Local Security Policy** from the Administrative Tools applet of Control Panel.

    b. Expand the **Local Policies** folder, and double-click the **User Rights Assignment** subfolder to display user rights in the results window.

    c. Double-click the **Access this computer from the network** option, and remove the check mark for this right from the Everyone system group. Click **OK** to return to the Local Security Settings window.

    d. Double-click the **Deny logon locally** right, and click the **Add** button.

    e. Double-click the **Temps** group, and click **OK** twice to save your change and return to the Local Security Settings window.

    f. Double-click **Manage auditing and security log** and click the **Add** button.

    g. Double-click the **Melendres** user, and click **OK** twice to save your change and return to the Local Security Settings window.

    h. Double-click each right, and on your Student Answer Sheet, record the rights that a power user has.

10. Close all windows and log off.

11. Test your audit policy by logging on as a temporary employee, and attempting to access the In-Progress folder. Record your results on the Student Answer Sheet.

12. Log on using the Melendres account, and start **Event Viewer.** Document the security messages on your Student Answer Sheet.

13. After recording any security messages, close Event Viewer and log off.

CHAPTER SIX

WINDOWS 2000 SECURITY AND ACCESS CONTROLS

Labs included in this chapter

➤ Lab 6.1 Working with Local Computer Policies

➤ Lab 6.2 Applying User Configuration Policies

➤ Lab 6.3 Customizing the Logon Process

➤ Lab 6.4 Working with Encryption

➤ Lab 6.5 Automating the Logon System

Microsoft MCSE Exam #70-210 Objectives	
Objective	Lab
Implement, configure, and troubleshoot local Group policy	6.1, 6.2, 6.5
Implement, configure, manage, and troubleshoot a security configuration	6.1
Configure and troubleshoot desktop settings	6.2
Implement, configure, manage, and troubleshoot a security configuration	6.3
Implement, configure, manage, and troubleshoot local user authentication Configure and troubleshoot local user accounts	6.3
Encrypt data on a hard disk by using the Encrypting File System (EPS)	6.4

Student Answer Sheets to accompany the labs in this chapter can be downloaded from the Online Companion for this manual at *www.course.com*.

Lab 6.1 Working with Local Computer Policies

Objective

The Superior Technical College has recently upgraded all of their administrative computers to Windows 2000 Professional. They have called Computer Technology Services, and you have been asked to assist Brenda Bohle, the network administrator, in securing these systems from intruders. Because some of the systems are used to access information on state servers across the Internet, the college wants to provide maximum security for data transmitted. In addition, to prevent excessive use of disk space, the management wants to place a limit of 200 MB on each user. After completing this lab, you will be able to:

➤ Create a Microsoft Management console for the local computer policy.

➤ Identify components of the Computer Configuration settings.

➤ Setup an IP Security policy.

➤ Configure Windows file protection scanning.

➤ Configure a Disk Quota policy.

Estimated completion time: **15–20 minutes**

Activity

1. If necessary, start your computer with Windows 2000, and log on as an administrator.

2. Create a Microsoft Management Console to manage the local group policy and users.

   a. Click the **Start** button, **Run** option, enter the command **MMC**, and click **OK** to open a console root window.

   b. Click the **Console** menu, **Add/Remove Snap-in** option.

   c. Click the **Add** button to display the Add Standalone Snap-in window.

   d. Scroll down and double-click the **Group Policy** option.

   e. Verify that the **Local Computer** object is selected, and click **Finish** to return to the Add Standalone Snap-in window.

   f. Scroll down and double-click the **Local Users and Groups** snap-in.

   g. Verify that the **Local Computer and Groups** object is selected, and click **Finish** to return to the Add Standalone Snap-in window.

h. Click **Close**. Verify that both Local Computer Policy and Local Users and Groups Snap-ins are shown in the Add/Remove Snap-in window.

i. Click **OK** to close the Add/Remove Snap-in window, and return to the MMC Console Root.

j. Click **Save as** from the Console menu, and enter the name **Computer Policy Management** in the File name text box.

k. Click the **Save** button to save the console in the Administrative Tools folder.

3. In the left-side Tree window, expand the **Computer Configuration** folder of the Local Computer Policy, and record the three subfolders (Computer Configuration policies) on your Lab 6.1 Student Answer Sheet.

4. Expand each subfolder, and on your Student Answer Sheet, record the path to the Password Policy settings subfolder.

5. On your Student Answer Sheet, record the path to the Audit Policy subfolder.

6. Click the **IP Security Policies** folder to view the security options shown in Figure 6-1.

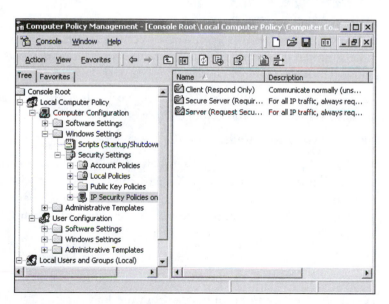

Figure 6-1   IP Security Policies

7. Turn on the IP Security policy that requires the use of Kerberos security, and that does not allow unsecured communication with clients who do not respond to the security request. Record the security policy you select on your Student Answer Sheet.

    a. Double-click an IP Security option from the right-side results window.

    b. Click the **General** tab and read the description for this security setting.

    c. If the description reads that it will not allow unsecured communications with clients, record that security policy name on your Student Answer Sheet.

    d. If the description reads that it allows communications with clients, repeat Step 7, selecting a different IP Security policy. Click **Cancel** to return to the console window.

8. Click the **Administrative Templates** subfolder within the Computer Configuration branch of Local Computer Policy, and on your Student Answer Sheet, list the three subfolders contained within the Administrative Templates folder.

9. Expand each **Administrative Template** subfolder, and on your Student Answer Sheet, identify which of the three Administrative Template subfolders contains the Windows File Protection subfolder.

10. Within the Windows File Protection folder, double-click the **Set Windows File Protection scanning** option, and click the **Explain** tab. List the scanning frequency options on your Student Answer Sheet. Which scanning frequency is the default?

11. Select the option that will scan files at each startup. Record the scanning frequency you select on your Student Answer Sheet.

12. Click the **Disk Quota** folder from the Tree window.

13. Assume you want to enable disk quotas on all NTFS volumes so that when a user reaches the default of 200 MB, the system responds as though the physical space on the volume is exhausted, and logs the event on the Application log. On your Student Answer Sheet, identify which Disk Quota policies you would enable.

14. Enable the 200 MB Disk Quota policies identified in Step 3.

    a. Double-click one of the policies you identified in Step 3.

    b. Click the **Enabled** option button from the Policy tab.

    c. Click **OK** to save the setting.

    d. Repeat steps a. through c. for the other quota policies you identified in Step 13.

15. Close the Computer Policy Management console and log off.

LAB 6.2 APPLYING USER CONFIGURATION POLICIES

Objective

The Superior Technical College recently purchased several new Windows 2000 Professional-based systems from your company for use in their desktop publishing program. Brenda Bohle, the network administrator, wants you to help her secure these systems to prevent students from browsing the network or changing desktop settings. In addition, she wants to protect the Administrator account from unauthorized access by renaming the account to Admin, and then creating a dummy administrator account. After completing this lab, you will be able to:

➤ Configure local user configuration policies to restrict user functions on a Windows 2000 workstation.

➤ Rename the Administrator account, create a fake administrator user, and audit any access to this account.

Estimated completion time: **20 minutes**

ACTIVITY

1. If necessary, start your computer with Windows 2000, and log on as an administrator.

2. Click the **Start** button and record the Start menu options on your Lab 6.2 Student Answer Sheet.

3. Start the Computer Policy Management console from **Programs, Administrative Tools**.

4. Expand the **User Configuration** policy to display the three policy folders within the User Configuration policy.

5. List the contents of the **Software Settings** policy folder on your Student Answer Sheet.

6. List the contents of the **Windows Settings** policy on your Student Answer Sheet.

7. List the six subfolders in the Administrative Templates policy on your Student Answer Sheet.

8. Click the **Start Menu & Taskbar** policy folder to display the options shown in Figure 6-2.

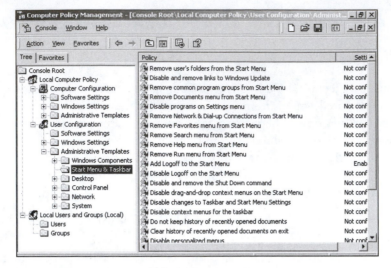

Figure 6-2 Start Menu & Taskbar options

9. Implement the following Start Menu & Taskbar policies.

a. Prevent students from making changes to Taskbar and Start Menu Settings:

- Double-click **Disable changes to Taskbar and Start Menu Settings**:
- Click the **Enabled** option button, and then click **OK**.

b. Remove the Run command from the Start Menu:

- Double-click **Remove Run for the Start Menu**.
- Click the **Enabled** option button, and then click **OK**.

c. Add a Log off option to the Start Menu:

- Double-click **Add Logoff to the Start Menu**.
- Click the **Enabled** option button and then click **OK**.

10. Click the **Desktop** policy, and implement the following policies.

a. Prohibit students from changing the default My Documents path:

- Double-click **Prohibit user from changing My Documents path**.
- Click the **Enabled** option button and then click **OK**.

b. Prevent the students from saving settings at exit:

- Double-click **Don't save settings at exit**.
- Click the **Enabled** option button and then click **OK**.

11. Click the **Control Panel** policy to implement the following policies.
    a. Prevent students from adding or removing programs:
       - Open the **Add/Remove Programs** folder.
       - Double-click **Disable the Add/Remove programs**.
       - Click the **Enabled** option button, and click **OK**.
    b. Prevent students from changing the display configuration from Control Panel:
       - Open the **Add/Remove Programs** folder.
       - Double-click **Disable Display in Control Panel**.
       - Click the **Enabled** button, and click **OK**.
    c. Prevent students from setting a password on screen savers:
       - Open the **Add/Remove Programs** folder.
       - Double-click **Password protect the screen saver**.
       - Click the **Enabled** option button, and then click **OK**.

12. Click the **System** policy, and disable use of the command prompt. Record the policy and option button you use on your Student Answer Sheet.

13. Close the Computer Management console. The policy settings you've changed should take effect immediately.

14. Test the effects of the User Configuration Policy on the Administrator user.
    a. Right-click anywhere on the **taskbar**, and click the **Properties** option. Record the message you receive on the Student Answer Sheet.
    b. Click the **Start** button. On your Student Answer Sheet, record new or removed options, compared to the list you created in Step 2.
    c. Create a folder named **Documents** on the root of your Windows 2000 drive. Right-click **My Documents** and click **Properties**. On your Student Answer Sheet, record the results of changing the target path to the Documents folder.
    d. Open Control Panel, and double-click **Add/Remove Programs**. Record the message you receive on your Student Answer Sheet.
    e. Double-click the **Display** icon. Record the message you receive on your Student Answer Sheet.
    f. Click **Start, Programs, Accessories, Command Prompt**. Record the message you receive on your Student Answer Sheet.

15. Verify that the restrictions apply to all users as follows:
    a. Log off as the administrator.
    b. Log on as another user.

    c. Try to change the taskbar, and open a command prompt. Record the results on your Student Answer Sheet.

    d. Log off.

16. Follow the steps below to remove the User Configuration restrictions.

    a. Log on as administrator, and start the **Computer Policy Management** console.

    b. Expand the **User Configuration** folder.

    c. Use the **Start Menu & Taskbar** policy to do the following:

       ■ Double-click **Disable changes to taskbar and Start menu** settings, click the **Disabled** option button, and click **OK**.

       ■ Double-click **Remove Run from the Start Menu**, click the **Disabled** option button, and click **OK**.

    d. Use the **Desktop** policy to perform the following:

       ■ Double-click **Prohibit user from changing My Documents path**, click the **Disabled** option button, and click **OK**.

       ■ Double-click **Don't save settings at exit**, click the **Disabled** option button, and click **OK**.

    e. Use the **Control Panel** policy to perform the following actions. On your Student Answer Sheet, record the policy and setting you use.

       ■ Enable the Add/Remove programs icon.

       ■ Enable access to the display settings.

       ■ Enable the password protection option on screen savers.

    f. Use the **System** policy to enable the command prompt. On your Student Answer Sheet, record the policy and setting you use.

    g. Exit the Computer Policy Management console.

17. Verify that you can now open a command prompt window, access the Run command from the Start menu, change the taskbar, access the Add/Remove programs option, and change display settings.

18. Close all windows and log off.

LAB 6.3 CUSTOMIZING THE LOGON PROCESS

Objective

Melendres and Associates is concerned about the legal ramifications of prosecuting an intruder for unauthorized access to their computer system. According to Mr. Melendres, legally an intruder should be warned prior to attempting to log on that unauthorized access is prohibited. In addition, Mr. Melendres thinks that displaying the last user's name on the logon window makes it easier for an intruder to attempt to log on. Therefore, he wants the user name field to be blank by default at logon. He is also concerned that, at present, anyone who accesses the logon screen can shut down the shared Windows 2000 system without logging in. He wants only himself and the administrator to have the right to shut down the system. After completing this lab, you will be able to:

➤ Remove the name of the last user who logged on from the Windows 2000 logon window.

➤ Display a warning message about illegal logons prior to the logon prompt.

➤ Disable the Shut Down button from the logon window.

➤ Provide a user with the right to shut down the system.

6

Estimated completion time: **15–20 minutes**

ACTIVITY

1. If necessary, start your computer with Windows 2000, and log on as an administrator.

2. Start your **Computer Policy Management** console.

3. If necessary, create the following users.

   - Logon name: **SMelendres**, Full Name: **Sebastian Melendres**.
   - Logon name: **MRodregus**, Full Name: **Meme Rodegus**.

4. Modify the computer configuration policy to remove the name of the last user from the logon screen as follows.

   a. Expand the **Computer Configuration** policy tree.

   b. Browse the **Windows Settings** tree until you find the **Do not display the last user name in logon window** policy. On your Lab 6.3 Student Answer Sheet, record the path to the policy.

   c. Double-click the **Do not display last user name in logon screen** policy, and click the **Enabled** option button.

   d. Click **OK** to return to the Computer Policy Management console.

5. Require the Ctrl+Alt+Del key combination to be pressed to log on.

   a. Double-click the option to disable the "Disable CTRL+ALT+DEL requirement for logon" option as shown in Figure 6-3. On your Student Answer Sheet, record the local policy setting you select to require the user to press the Ctrl+Alt+Del keys to log on.

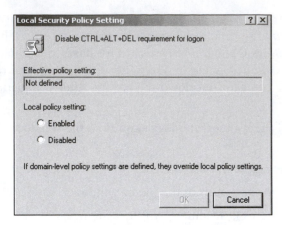

Figure 6-3 Enabling the Ctrl+Alt+Del logon sequence

6. To display a legal warning message prior to logging on, you need to supply a title along with the message text.

   a. On your Student Answer Sheet, record the two message policies you need to enable.

   b. Enter the following title and message text:

      ■ Double click the **Message title** policy, and enter: **Unauthorized access to this system is illegal** in the Local policy setting text box. Click **OK** to save your changes.

      ■ Double-click the **Message text** policy, and in the Local policy setting text box enter: **The information on this computer is the property of the Melendres and Associates law firm and is protected by intellectual property law. You must have legitimate access to an assigned account on this computer to access any information. Your activities may be monitored, and any unauthorized access will be punished to the full extent of the law.** Click **OK** to save your changes.

7. To prevent the network from being shut down by users, you can disable the Shutdown button from the logon window. On your Student Answer Sheet, record the policy along with the setting you would use to prevent shutdown prior to logging on.

8. Provide the Melendres user with rights to shut down the system.

   a. Click the **User Rights Assignment** policy folder.

   b. Double-click the **Shut down the system** right, and on your Student Answer Sheet, record default groups to which this right is assigned.

c. Remove the check mark from the **Local Policy Setting** check box for the **Users** group.

d. Click the **Add** button, and double-click the **Melendres** user from the Select Users or Groups window.

e. Click **OK** to return to the Local Security Policy Setting window.

f. Verify that your Melendres user has been added, and then click **OK** to return to the Computer Policy Management console.

g. Close the Computer Policy Management console and log off.

9. Test the policies you have enabled by logging on as the Rodregus user and attempting to shut down the system from the logon screen.

a. Log on as the Rodegus user.

b. On your Student Answer Sheet, record the logon information requested.

c. Attempt to shut down the computer system using the Start menu, Shut Down option, and record the results on your Student Answer Sheet.

d. Log off.

10. Log on as the Melendres user, and attempt to shut down the system.

a. Log on as the Melendres user.

b. Attempt to shut down the computer system and on your Student Answer Sheet, record the results.

LAB 6.4 WORKING WITH ENCRYPTION

Objective

Mr. Melendres wants to have a shared public folder in which users can store sensitive files in an encrypted format that only they or other selected users can access. Windows 2000 allows this level of security through file and folder encryption. After completing this lab, you will be able to:

➤ Create a folder to store encyrpted files.

➤ Create files in the encrypted folder.

➤ Copy files to the encrypted folder.

➤ Move files to the encrypted folder.

➤ Use the CIPHER command to encrypt, decrypt, or view encryption status information.

Estimated completion time: **20–25 minutes**

ACTIVITY

1. If necessary, start your computer with Windows 2000, and log on as Mr. Melendres.

2. If necessary, create a folder named **Public** from the root of your Windows 2000 drive.

3. Launch **WordPad** from the **Start, Programs, Accessories** menu, and create a document file that describes the following options of the CIPHER command.

   CIPHER command options:

   /E – Encrypt files

   /D – Decrypt files

   /F – Force encryption on all files, even if already encrypted

   /S – Encrypt files in all subfolders

4. Save the document in the My Documents folder with the name **CIPHER**.

5. Use WordPad to create a second document named **Suspects** that contains a description of two suspected criminals in one of Mr. Melendres' cases (you provide the description). Save the document in the My Documents folder.

6. Exit WordPad.

7. Double-click **My Documents** from the desktop, and use the **File, New** menu to create a subfolder named **Secured**.

8. Encrypt the Secured folder.

   a. Right-click the **Secured** folder, and click the **Properties** option to display the General properties tab.

   b. Click the **Advanced** button to display the Advanced Attribute window, as shown in Figure 6-4. List the advanced attributes on your Lab 6.4 Student Answer Sheet.

Figure 6-4 Advanced Attributes window

    c. Click the **Encrypt contents to secure data** check box, and then click **OK** to return to the General tab.

    d. Click **OK** to save your changes and return to the My Documents window.

9. Create a file named **Witness** in the Secured folder.

    a. Double-click the **Secured** folder to open it.

    b. Click the **File** menu, **New** option, and click **Text Document**.

    c. Enter the name **Witness** for the file, and press **Enter**.

    d. Double-click the **Witness** file to start the Notepad application.

    e. Enter the names and phone numbers of three fictitious witnesses.

    f. Save the document, and exit Notepad.

10. Check the encryption status of the newly created text file.

    a. Right-click the **Witness** file, and click the **Properties** option.

    b. On the General tab, click the **Advanced** button.

    c. On your Student Answer Sheet, record all attributes that are set.

    d. Click **Cancel** twice to return to the Secured folder window.

    e. Double-click the **Witness** file. Notice how the file appears the same as if it were not encryrpted.

    f. Close Notepad, and click the **Up** button to return to the My Documents window.

11. Copy the Suspects file to the Secured folder.

    a. Right-click the **Suspects** file, and click the Copy option.

    b. Double-click the **Secured** folder, and click the **Edit** menu, **Paste** option.

    c. Right-click the **Suspects** file, and click the **Properties** option.

    d. Click the **Advanced** button from the General tab, and on your Student Answer Sheet, record the encryption status of a file copied to an encrypted folder.

    e. Click the **Cancel** button twice to return to the Secured folder window.

    f. Click the **Up** button to return to the My Documents window.

12. Move the Cipher file to the Secured folder.

    a. Right-click the **Cipher** file, and click the **Cut** option.

    b. Double-click the **Secured** folder, and click the **Paste** option from the Edit menu.

    c. Right-click the **Cipher** file, and click the **Properties** option.

    d. Click the **Advanced** button from the general tab, and on your Student Answer Sheet, record the encryption status of a file moved to an encrypted folder.

    e. Click the **Cancel** button twice to return to the Secured folder window.

13. Determine the encryption status of a file copied from the encrypted folder.

    a. Double-click **My Computer** and open a window to your Public folder.

    b. Arrange and size your windows so you can see both the Public and Secured folders.

    c. Hold down the **Ctrl** key while you click the **Witness** file and drag and drop it into the **Public** folder. Verify that the file is now in both windows.

    d. Right-click the **Witness** file from the Public folder, and click the **Properties** button.

    e. Click the **Advanced** button from the General tab, and on your Student Answer Sheet, record the encryption status of a file copied from an encrypted folder to a nonencrypted folder.

    f. Click **Cancel** twice to return to the desktop.

14. Determine the encryption status of a file moved from the encrypted folder.

    a. Click the **Cipher** file, and drag and drop it into the **Public** folder. Verify that the Cipher file is now only in the Public folder window.

    b. Right-click the **Cipher** file from the Public folder, and click the **Properties** button.

    c. Click the **Advanced** button from the General tab, and on your Student Answer Sheet, record the encryption status of a file moved from an encrypted folder to a nonencrypted folder.

    d. Click **Cancel** twice to return to the desktop.

15. Use the CIPHER command to check the encryption status of files.

    a. Open a Command Prompt window by clicking **Start, Programs, Accessories, Command Prompt**.

    b. Change to the Public folder by entering the following command:

       CD \Public [Enter]

    c. Enter the following CIPHER command and on your Student Answer Sheet, record the status of all files in the Public folder.

       CIPHER *.* [Enter]

    d. Enter the following CIPHER command (including quote marks) and on your Student Answer Sheet, record the encryption status of all files in the Secured folder.

       CIPHER "\Documents and settings\smelendres\ mydocuments\secured*.*" [Enter]

    e. Enter the following CIPHER command to decrypt all files in the Public folder:

       CIPHER *.* /D [Enter]

    f. Enter the following CIPHER command to force encryption on the Witness file in the Public folder:

       CIPHER Witness.doc /E /F [Enter]

    g. Type **Exit** at the command prompt and log off.

16. Log on as administrator, and attempt to access the files in the Secured folder.

    a. Log on as your administrator account.

    b. Use **My Computer** to navigate to the **Documents and Settings\Smelendres\My Documents** folder.

    c. Double-click a file, and record the results on your Student Answer Sheet.

    d. Navigate to the **Secured** folder.

    e. Double-click the **Suspects** file, and record the results on your Student Answer Sheet.

    f. Navigate to the **Public** folder and double-click the **Witness** file. Record the results on your Student Answer Sheet.

    g. On your Student Answer Sheet, describe how Mr. Melendres could prevent the administrator from accessing files in his Secured folder.

    h. Log off.

17. Log on as another user, and attempt to access encrypted files in the Public folder.

    a. Log on as the Rodregus user.

6

b. Navigate to the **Public** folder, and double-click the **Witness** file. Record the results on your Student Answer Sheet.

c. Exit the WordPad application.

d. Double-click the **Cipher** file, and record the results on your Student Answer Sheet.

e. Close all windows and log off.

LAB 6.5 AUTOMATING THE LOGON SYSTEM

Objective

Superior Technical College wants to place a Windows 2000 Professional computer in their learning resource center, and limit the computer to running only Internet Explorer. The learning resource center manager wants you to configure the computer so that it does not require a logon and will start with Windows NT 3.51 Program Manager, and have only the Internet Explorer option on the desktop. After completing this lab, you will be able to:

➤ Provide an automatic logon for public use.

➤ Launch Program Manager as the default desktop shell.

➤ Configure Program Manager to display only Internet Explorer on the desktop.

Estimated completion time: **15 minutes**

ACTIVITY

1. If necessary, start your computer with Windows 2000, and log on as an administrator.

2. Launch the Computer Policy Management console, and create a user named Anyone.

   a. If necessary expand **Local Users and Groups (Local)** policy.

   b. Click the **Users** folder, and then click the **Action** menu, **New User** option.

   c. Enter **Anyone** in the User name and Full name text boxes. Enter a password of at least 6 characters (such as **password**) in both the Password and Confirm password text boxes.

    d. Remove the check mark from the **User must change password at next logon** check box.

    e. Click the **User cannot change password** and **Password never expires** check boxes.

    f. Click the **Create** button to add the new user.

    g. Click the **Close** button to return to the Computer Policy Management console.

    h. Exit the Computer Policy Management console.

3. Configure the Program Manager interface so only Internet Explorer is included on the desktop.

    a. Click the **Start** menu, **Run** option.

    b. Enter the command **Progman.exe** and click **OK**.

    c. Click the **File** menu, **New** option, and click the **Common Program Group** option button.

    d. Click **OK** to create a Common Program Group.

    e. Enter the name **Internet Explorer** and click **OK** to create the program group window.

    f. Click the **File** menu, **New** option, and verify that the Program Item option button is selected.

    g. Click **OK** to display the Program Item Properties window.

    h. Enter **Internet Explorer** in the Description text box, and click the **Browse** button.

    i. Navigate to the **Program Files** folder on your Windows 2000 drive.

    j. Double-click the **Internet Explorer** folder.

    k. Double-click the **IEXPLORE** program.

    l. Click **OK** to save the Internet Explorer icon in your Program Manager window.

    m. Click the **File** menu, **Exit** option to exit the Program Manager application.

4. Modify the Windows 2000 Registry to use Progman.exe as the default shell.

    a. Click the **Start** menu, **Run** option.

    b. Enter the command **regedit** in the Open text box, and click **OK**.

6

c. Select the **HKEY_LOCAL_MACHINE\SOFTWARE\Microsoft** key, as shown in Figure 6-5.

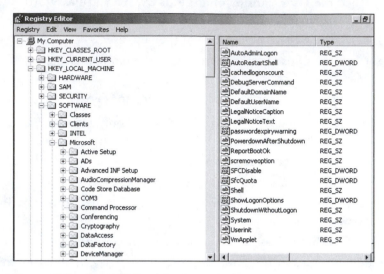

Figure 6-5 Regedit Registry key window

d. Double-click **Microsoft** and navigate down to the **Windows NT/CurrentVersion** key.

e. Click the **Winlogon** folder to display the key values shown in Figure 6-6.

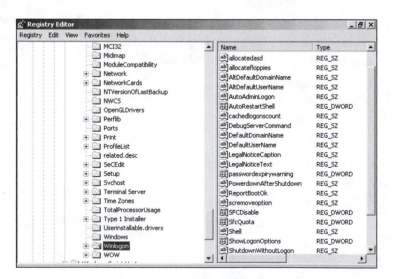

Figure 6-6 Winlogon key values window

f. Double-click the **Shell** value, and on your Lab 6.5 Student Answer Sheet, record the existing value.

g. Change the Value data text box to **Progman.exe**.

h. Click **OK** to save your new setting.

5. Modify the AutoAdminLogon and DefaultUserName registry keys to automatically log on the administrator for testing.

a. Double-click the **AutoAdminLogon** value, and change the 0 to a **1** to enable the auto logon feature.

b. Click **OK** to save your change.

c. Double-click the **DefaultUserName** value, and enter the user name **Anyone** in the key value text box.

d. Click **OK** to save the key value.

6. Add a DefaultPassword registry key value.

a. Click the **Edit** menu, **New** option.

b. Click **String Value** to create a new key value.

c. Type **DefaultPassword** and press **Enter**.

d. Double-click the newly created **DefaultPassword** key value, and enter the password for your Administrator in the Value data text box.

e. Click **OK** to save the new key value.

f. Exit the Registry editor program.

7. Test the automatic logon.

a. Perform a Shutdown and Restart function by clicking **Start**, **Shutdown**, **Restart**.

b. If necessary, respond to the warning message. Describe the results on your Student Answer Sheet.

c. Click the **File** menu, **Logoff** option, and click **OK**.

d. Log on as the Administrator.

8. Return the Shell to Windows Explorer.

a. Click **Run** from the File menu.

b. Enter the command **regedit** in the Command Line text box, and click **OK**.

c. Double-click the **Shell** key value, and change Progman.exe back to **explorer.exe**.

d. Click **OK** to save the key value.

e. Double-click the **AutoAdminLogon** key, and change the 1 back to a **0** to disable the Autologon feature.

f. Right-click the **DefaultPassword** key value, and click the **Delete** option.

g. Click **Yes** to confirm the deletion. On your Student Answer Sheet, describe why it is important to remove this key from the Registry.

h. Close the Registry Editor.

9. Shut down and restart the system to verify that the system is back to manual logon.

a. Click the **File** menu, **Shutdown** option.

b. Click the **Shutdown and Restart** option button, and then click **OK** to restart your computer.

c. Log on as Administrator, and verify that the Windows Explorer window is visible.

d. Log off.

CHAPTER SEVEN

NETWORK PROTOCOLS

Labs included in this chapter

➤ Lab 7.1 Documenting and Removing Network Components

➤ Lab 7.2 Defining an IP Address Scheme

➤ Lab 7.3 Installing and Configuring the TCP/IP Protocol

➤ Lab 7.4 Assigning IP Addresses Automatically

➤ Lab 7.5 Working with IP Protocols

Microsoft MCSE Exam #70-210 Objectives	
Objective	Lab
Install, configure, and troubleshoot network adapters	7.1
Configure and troubleshoot the TCP/IP protocol	7.2, 7.3, 7.4, 7.5

Student Answer Sheets to accompany the labs in this chapter can be downloaded from the Online Companion for this manual at *www.course.com*.

LAB 7.1 DOCUMENTING AND REMOVING NETWORK COMPONENTS

Objective

Prior to changing or adding network components on a computer, it's important to document the existing configuration so that you can return the system to its original state in the event of problems. Because the labs in this chapter require you to change your computer's network configuration, in this first lab you will document your current network settings prior to removing them. After completing this lab, you will be able to:

➤ Use My Network Places to document your current network configuration.

➤ Remove existing network protocols and services.

Estimated completion time: **10 minutes**

ACTIVITY

1. If necessary, start your computer with Windows 2000, and log on as an administrator.

2. In this step you document your existing network components so that you can restore them after completing the labs in this chapter. Follow the steps below to record your network configuration.

   a. Right-click **My Network Places** and click **Properties**.

   b. Double-click **Local Area Connection** and on your Lab 7.1 Student Answer Sheet, record the requested connection information.

   c. Click the **Properties** button to display the Local Area Connection Properties window.

   d. Record the installed network protocols from the Components window on your Student Answer Sheet.

   e. Click the **Configure** button to display network card configuration properties. Use the necessary tabs, and record the network card information requested on your Student Answer Sheet.

   f. Click **Cancel** to return to the Local Area Connection Properties window.

   g. Record any existing clients or services from the Components window on your Student Answer Sheet.

h. Click each network protocol (such as Internet Protocol, NetBEUI, or NWLink), and then use the **Properties** button to find information about that protocol. On your Student Answer Sheet, record the requested information.

3. To install the necessary protocols and services for the lab projects in this chapter, in this step you first remove any existing protocols and services from your Windows 2000 Professional computer.

a. Click a protocol, and then use the **Uninstall** button to remove it. Record the steps you perform on your Student Answer Sheet. Note that you do not need to restart your computer until all components have been removed.

b. Repeat Step 3a to remove all protocols.

c. Click a service, and use the **Uninstall** button to remove it. Record the steps you perform on your Student Answer Sheet.

d. Repeat Step 3c to remove all services.

e. Click a client, and use the **Uninstall** button to remove it. Record the steps you perform on your Student Answer Sheet.

f. Repeat Step 3e to remove all services.

4. Save your changes and click **Close**.

5. Restart your computer after removing all protocols and clients.

LAB 7.2   DEFINING AN IP ADDRESS SCHEME

Objective

The Washington School, a private elementary school, is installing a network consisting of two separate subnets linked together by a Window 2000 server, as shown in Figure 7-1. The computers attached to the Lab 212 subnet consist of four Windows 2000 Professional computers, along with six Windows 98-based systems. The office network consists of four networked Windows 2000 Professional systems used for word processing, desktop publishing, and running specialized school administration software. In addition to accessing shared applications and data files, the school wants computers on both networks to be able to access the Internet using proxy server software running on a Windows 2000 server named LabHost. The school has contracted with your company to set up and configure these computers to use only the TCP/IP protocol. Although the school's Internet Service Provider (ISP) has provided the proxy server with an IP address to attach to the Internet, it is up to you to come up with an IP address scheme for computers in the school office and computer lab.

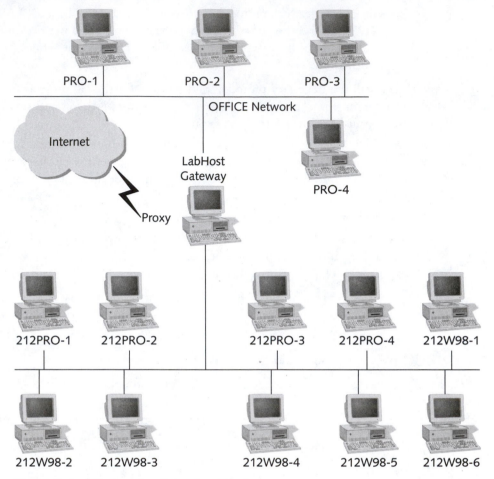

Figure 7-1   Washington School network

After completing this lab, you will be able to:

➤ Define network addresses and subnet masks for a site with multiple subnets.

➤ Define IP addresses for all computers on a Class B network.

➤ Assign IP addresses to network routers.

Estimated completion time: **15 minutes**

ACTIVITY

Note

The Internet Access Board (IAB) has established three main classes of IP addresses. Class A addresses are intended for very large organizations and provide one octet (or byte) for the network address, and three octets for the host (computer) address. Class B addresses are intended for medium-to-large organizations, and provide two octets or bytes for both network and host addresses. Class C addresses are intended for small-to-medium organizations, and provide three octets to identify the network, and only one octet for the computer. Class A networks have numbers ranging between 1 and 127, Class B networks range from 128 through 191, and Class C networks start in the range of 192 to 226.

Use Figure 7–1 to fill out the Lab 7.2 IP Address Planning Sheet with Class B IP addresses for each computer in the office and in Lab 212.

1. Provide a network address and subnet mask for each subnet.

2. Assign an IP address for each network card in the LabHost server.

3. Assign an IP address and default gateway for each computer.

LAB 7.3 INSTALLING AND CONFIGURING THE TCP/IP PROTOCOL

Objective

Now that you have planned the IP configuration for the Washington School, you will simulate installing and configuring TCP/IP on one of the computers in the school office. You will use the IP address information identified in the Requirements section below. After completing this lab, you will be able to:

➤ Install TCP/IP as the only network protocol.

➤ Manually configure an IP address and subnet mask.

➤ Configure TCP/IP settings.

➤ Identify additional IP protocol options.

➤ Configure Internet Explorer to use a proxy server.

➤ Install the Microsoft client along with file and print services.

Requirements

To perform this lab activity, you or your instructor needs to identify the following computer IP addresses. If necessary, the IP address of your server computer can be used for the gateway, Admin_Host, DNS, and Proxy servers.

➤ An IP address for your computer: _____._____. _____._____

➤ Subnet mask: _____._____._____._____

➤ IP address of default gateway computer: _____._____._____._____

➤ IP address of the Admin_Host: _____._____._____._____

➤ IP address of the DNS computer: _____._____. _____._____

➤ IP address of Proxy computer: _____._____._____. _____
   Port #: _____ (80)

➤ DNS suffix: _____
   (for example, Washington.k12.wi.us)

> Estimated completion time: **20–25 minutes**

ACTIVITY 1

After installing network cards and drivers, the next step is to install and configure the TCP/IP protocol. In this activity you manually install and configure the protocol on one computer; in later labs you will use automatic TCP/IP configuration to speed installation on multiple computers.

1. If necessary, start your computer and log on as an administrator.

2. Install the TCP/IP protocol.

   a. Right-click **My Network Places** and click the **Properties** option.

   b. Click **Install** and click the **Protocol** option from the Select Network Component Type window.

   c. Click **Add** and record the possible protocols on your Lab 7.3 Student Answer Sheet.

d. Click the **Internet Protocol (TCP/IP)** protocol, and click **OK** to
add the Internet Protocol (TCP/IP) to the Local Area Connection
Properties Components window.

e. Click on the **Internet Protocol (TCP/IP)** component, and click the
Properties button to display the Internet Protocol (TCP/IP)
Properties window shown in Figure 7-2.

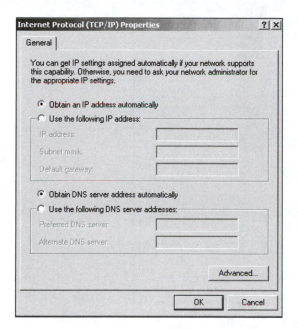

7

Figure 7-2   TCP/IP Properties window

f. Click the **Use the following IP address** option button, and enter
the IP address and subnet mask for your computer that you identified
in the Requirements section.

3. Configure the TCP/IP protocol for default gateway and DNS server.

   a. To set the Internet router as the gateway, click the **Advanced** button to display the Advanced TCP/IP Settings windows shown in Figure 7-3.

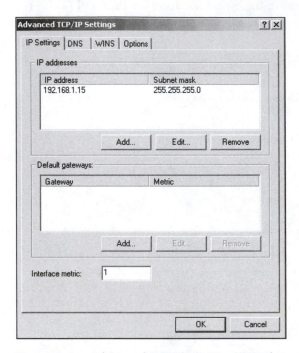

Figure 7-3   Advanced TCP/IP Settings window

   b. To configure a default gateway, click the **Add** button in the Default gateways section, and enter the IP address of the gateway you identified in the Requirements section. The Interface metric setting is used to assign a weight to a gateway when multiple gateways are available. The client computer will then use an available gateway with the lowest metric setting.

   c. Click **Add** to add the gateway to the Default gateways window.

   d. Click the **DNS** tab, and then use the **Add** button to enter the DNS server you identified in the Requirements section.

   e. On your Student Answer Sheet, list the three settings that are applied to all connections with TCP/IP enabled.

   f. Click the **Options** tab, and use the **Properties** button to record the default IP security settings on your Student Answer Sheet.

   g. Click **Cancel** to return to the Advanced TCP/IP Settings window.

   h. Click the **TCP/IP filtering** option, and use the **Properties** button to record the three types of packet filtering you can apply.

i. Click **Cancel** to return to the Advanced TCP/IP Settings window.

j. Click **OK** to save the gateway settings and return to the Internet Protocol (TCP/IP) Properties window.

k. Click **OK** to return to the Local Area Connection Properties window.

ACTIVITY 2

In this activity you install the Microsoft client and then provide the ability for your computer to share resources by adding File and Print services.

1. To communicate with the school's Windows 2000 server, you need to install the Microsoft client service on the computer by following the procedure described below.

   a. Click the **Install** button, and click the **Client** component type.

   b. Click the **Add** button, and record the possible client options on your Student Answer Sheet.

   c. Click the **Client for Microsoft Networks** and click **OK** to add the Microsoft client to your Network Components window.

2. Some of the computers in the administrative office will have printers or folders that need to be shared with other users. To share folders and printers on a Windows 2000 computer, you need to install the File and Printer Sharing service by following the procedure described below.

   a. Click the **Install** button, and click the **Service** option.

   b. Click the **Add** button, and record the possible services on your Student Answer Sheet.

   c. Double-click the **File and Printer Sharing for Microsoft Networks** option to add this service to the network Components window.

   d. Click **Close** to save your network component changes and return to the Network and Dial-up Connections window.

3. View the binding order of protocols on your computer.

   a. Click the **Advanced** option from the menu bar, and then click the **Advanced Settings** option.

   b. Verify that the Internet Protocol (TCP/IP) is bound to both the File and Printer Sharing service and Microsoft Client.

   c. Click the **Provider Order** tab, and record the purpose for this tab on your Student Answer Sheet. In Chapter 8, you will use this tab to change the sequence of providers to make the network more efficient.

   d. Click **Cancel** to return to the Network and Dial-up Connections window.

e. Click the **Advanced** menu, **Optional Networking Components** option to display the Windows Optional Networking Components Wizard shown in Figure 7-4.

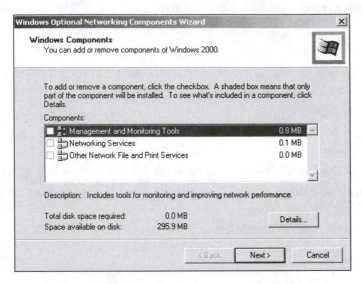

Figure 7-4   Optional Networking Components wizard

f. Click the **Details** button, and record the options for each of the three components on your Student Answer Sheet.

g. Click **Cancel** to return to the Network and Dial-up Connections window.

h. Close the Network and Dial-up Connections window.

4. Configure Internet Explorer to use LabHost as the proxy server.

a. Right-click the **Internet Explorer** icon from your desktop, and click the **Properties** option.

b. Click the **Connections** tab, and then click the **LAN Settings** button.

c. Click the **Use a proxy server** check box, and enter the IP address of the proxy server you identified in the Requirements section.

d. Enter the port number assigned to your proxy server that you identified in the Requirements section (typically 80).

e. Click the **Advanced** button.

f. On your Student Answer Sheet, record the other TCP/IP services that are assigned to the proxy.

g. Click **Cancel** to return to the LAN Settings window.

h. Click the **Bypass proxy server for local address** check box to allow direct access to the Web server attached to the same network as the client.

      i. Click **OK** to save the proxy settings

      j. Click **OK** to save the changes to Internet Explorer and return to the desktop.

5. The school administrator is concerned that students or other users will be able to change the TCP/IP configuration. To dispel her concerns, follow the steps below to create a student account, and then verify that the account does not have rights to change the TCP/IP protocol configurations.

    a. Create a new restricted user named Student (for instructions on creating a new user, see Labs 3.2 and 5.1).

    b. Log off.

    c. Log on as Student.

    d. Right-click **My Network Places** and click **Properties**.

    e. Click the **Properties** button, and double-click **Local Area Connection** to display the Connection Status window.

    f. Record the message you receive on your Student Answer Sheet.

    g. Click the **Install** button. Record the results on your Student Answer Sheet.

    h. Click the **Internet Protocol (TCP/IP)** protocol, and click the **Uninstall** button. Record the results on your Student Answer Sheet.

    i. Click the **Internet Protocol (TCP/IP)** property, and click the **Properties** button. Record the results on your Student Answer Sheet.

    j. Click **Cancel**, then click **Close** twice to exit.

6. Close the Network and Dial-up Connections window and log off.

ACTIVITY 3

The PING command is often used to test communications between computers. The PING command sends a packet to the destination computer and then waits for a reply. When testing the TCP/IP configuration of your computer, it is often a good idea to use the PING command first to send a packet to your own computer address, and then proceed to PING other computers on your subnet. PINGing a computer on another subnet is a good way to test your gateway configuration. In this activity, you use the PING command to test IP communications between your computer and the server you identified in the Requirements section of this lab.

1. Log on as Administrator.

2. Use PING to test the IP configuration of your computer.

    a. Open a Command Prompt window (**Start**, **Programs**, **Accessories**, **Command Prompt**).

7

     b. Enter the command: **PING** *ip_address* (where *ip_address* is the IP address of your Windows 2000 computer), and press **Enter**.

     c. Record the results on your Student Answer Sheet.

3. Use PING to test communications between computers.

     a. Enter the command: **PING** *ip_address* (where *ip_address* is the address of the server computer you identified in the Requirements section), and press **Enter**.

     b. Record the results on your Student Answer Sheet.

4. Type **Exit** and press **Enter** to close the Command prompt.

5. Log off.

Lab 7.4 Assigning IP Addresses Automatically

Objective

As a result of your recommendation, the Washington School has decided to implement a DHCP (Dynamic Host Configuration Protocol) server to automatically assign IP addresses to the computers in Lab 212. The DHCP server will have a range of IP addresses called a scope to be automatically assigned to client computers when they start. A Windows 2000 Professional computer that is configured to obtain an IP address automatically will go through the following process when it starts:

1. The Windows 2000 computer broadcasts a request for a DHCP server.

2. Any DHCP server receiving the request sends out an available IP address offer. (By default, broadcast requests for DHCP servers are not passed by routers.)

3. If no DHCP servers respond to the request, the Windows 2000 Professional computer assigns itself an IP address of 169.254.x.y where x and y represent a unique host number for the subnet.

4. The Windows 2000 computer sends back an acceptance packet.

5. The DHCP server sends back an acknowledgment and reserves the address for that computer for a default of 3 days.

6. The Windows 2000 computer renews the IP address with the DHCP server within the lease period and when it restarts.

To simulate configuring the computers for Lab 212, you need to modify your computer's TCP/IP configuration to obtain IP address information automatically. Using the Windows 2000 automatic address assignment process allows you to test your network settings without a DHCP server. When a DHCP server is available, you can restart the station and verify correct IP address assignment from the DHCP server. After completing this lab, you will be able to:

➤ Configure TCP/IP for automatic address assignment.

➤ Use IPCONFIG to verify the IP address information assigned automatically by Windows 2000 when starting without the DHCP server.

➤ Use IPCONFIG to verify the IP address information assigned when starting with a DHCP server.

➤ Use IPCONFIG to release and renew IP address settings.

Requirements

➤ A Windows NT or Windows 2000 server running the DHCP service. Configure the scope of the DHCP service to assign a default gateway (router), in addition to IP addresses for your network.

7

Estimated completion time: **10–15 minutes**

ACTIVITY 1

Configure TCP/IP to obtain IP address information automatically.

1. If necessary, start your computer with Windows 2000, and log on as an administrator.

2. Modify the TCP/IP configuration to obtain IP address information automatically.

   a. Right-click **My Network Places** and click **Properties**.

   b. Double-click **Local Area Connection** and click the **Properties** button.

   c. Click the **Internet Protocol (TCP/IP)** protocol and click **Properties**.

   d. Click the **Obtain an IP address automatically** option button.

   e. Click the **Advanced** button, and record the IP address setting on your Lab 7.4 Student Answer Sheet.

   f. Click **OK** three times to save your changes and return to the Local Area Connection Status window.

   g. Click **Close** to return to the Network and Dial-up Connections window.

   h. Close all windows and restart your computer.

3. Record the IP address information automatically assigned by Windows 2000.

   a. Log on as the administrator.

   b. Open a Command Prompt (**Start**, **Programs**, **Accessories**, **Command Prompt**).

   c. Type the command **IPCONFIG**, press **Enter**, and record the IP address information on your Student Answer Sheet.

4. To access computers on other subnets, the computer needs to have a default gateway assigned. While the Windows 2000 automatic address assignment assigns an IP address and subnet mask, you still need to manually assign the default gateway and DNS server until the DHCP service is operational. Once DHCP is running, your Windows 2000 Professional computers can obtain their gateway and DNS address automatically. Follow the steps below to manually configure the default gateway for your computer.

   a. Right-click **My Network Places** and click **Properties**.

   b. Double-click **Local Area Connection** and click the **Properties** button.

   c. Click the **Internet Protocol (TCP/IP)** protocol, and click **Properties**.

   d. Click the **Advanced** button, and then click the **Add** button in the Default gateways section.

   e. Enter an IP address of **169.254.1.1** for the default gateway, and click **Add**.

   f. Click **OK** three times to save your settings, and return to the Connection Status window.

   g. Click **Close** to return to the Network and Dial-up Connections window.

   h. Close the Network and Dial-up Connections window.

   i. Open a command prompt, type the command **IPCONFIG**, and press **Enter**.

   j. On your Student Answer Sheet, record the address of the Default gateway.

   k. Type **Exit** and press **Enter** to exit the Command Prompt window.

ACTIVITY 2

Once DHCP is operational, the IPCONFIG command can be used to reassign the TCP/IP configuration settings of a Windows 2000 computer. In this activity you practice using the IPCONFIG command to verify and reassign the TCP/IP settings obtained from the DHCP server. Before starting this activity, the DHCP service must be functioning.

1. Reassign TCP/IP settings obtained from a DHCP server.

   a. Open a Command prompt window.

   b. Enter the command **IPCONFIG/All** and press **Enter**.

   c. Record the IP address information on your Student Answer Sheet.

2. The IPCONFIG command also can be used to have the workstation get a new address from the DHCP server. This is important if you change IP address settings on the DHCP server and do not want to restart the workstation. In this step you use the IPCONFIG command to release its current address and get another.

   a. To release the current IP address, enter the following command at the command prompt: **IPCONFIG/Release**, and press **Enter**.

   b. On your Student Answer Sheet, record the message you receive.

   c. To assign a new IP address, enter the command: **IPCONFIG/Renew**, and press **Enter**.

   d. To record the new address settings, enter the command **IPCONFIG/All**, and record the results on your Student Answer Sheet. Note that your IP address will probably be the same unless you also modify the IP address information in the DHCP server.

5. Type **Exit** and press **Enter** to close the Command Prompt window.

6. Log off.

LAB 7.5 WORKING WITH IP PROTOCOLS

Objective

The Washington School administrator recently informed you that the users on the administration network are unable to access shared resources on computers in Lab 212. You think that this is probably caused because routers do not carry broadcast packets between networks. By default, Microsoft clients find the IP addresses of computer names by broadcasting a request to all computers on the subnet. The computer with the requested name then responds with its IP address. To find the IP address of computers on another subnet, Windows clients need to be configured to use a DNS or WINS server or LMHOSTS file. Creating an LMHOSTS file on each computer that contains the computer names and IP addresses of the computers on the other subnet is often simpler than installing WINS (Windows Internet Service) or DNS (Domain Name Service) on a Windows 2000 Server computer. After completing this lab, you will be able to:

➤ Use the PING and ARP commands to test and troubleshoot TCP/IP communications.

➤ Configure an LMHOSTS file to resolve Windows names to IP addresses.

➤ Configure a HOSTS file to resolve Internet names to IP addresses.

➤ Use the Telnet protocol to connect to another Windows 2000 computer.

Requirements

For this Lab activity, you need the IP address of another Windows computer or Windows 2000 Server computer.

IP address of another Windows computer or Windows 2000 Server:

_____._____._____._____

If you do not have access to a Windows 2000 computer, you can substitute your own Windows 2000 Professional workstation IP address for the server address in this activity.

Estimated completion time: **20–25 minutes**

ACTIVITY

1. If necessary, start your computer, and log on as an administrator.

2. As you learned in Lab 7.4, the IPCONFIG command is useful to check the IP configuration of a computer. Use the IPCONFIG command as shown in Lab 7.4, Step 3 to record the IP configuration of your computer on your Lab 7.5 Student Answer Sheet.

3. Although IP addresses must be assigned to each computer in order to route packets between networks, the IP address must be converted to a network interface card (NIC) address in order for a packet to be sent between computers attached to the same network cable. The Address Resolution Protocol (ARP) handles the process of converting an IP address to a NIC address. In this step, you use the ARP command to determine the NIC address of your workstation and server.

   a. Open a Command Prompt window.

   b. Type the command **ARP a** and press **Enter**.

   c. Record the results of the ARP command on your Student Answer Sheet.

   d. Use the PING command to send test packets to the server address, as shown in Lab 7.3, Activity 2.

   e. At the command prompt, type the command **ARP**, press **Enter**, and on your Student Answer Sheet, record the results of the ARP command after PINGing the server.

   f. Type **Exit** and press **Enter** to exit the Command Prompt window.

4. Using the LMHOSTS file is one way to access Windows computers on other subnets. In this step, you use Notepad to create a LMHOSTS file configured to access your server computer using an alias computer name.

   a. Use Windows Explorer to browse to the following folder: WINNT\system32\drivers\etc

   b. Double-click the **LMHOSTS.SAM** file and, if necessary, select **Notepad** as the editing application.

   c. Enter the following line at the end of the file. Specify the IP address you identified in the Requirements section of this lab with the alias name MyServer.

   ———————.——————.——————.—————— **MyServer**

   d. Save the file as **LMHOSTS** with no extension, and exit Notepad.

5. Although the LMHOSTS file can be used to convert UNC names to IP addresses, the HOSTS file is used by TCP/IP to convert TCP/IP names to IP addresses. In this step, you enter a TCP/IP alias name for your server computer in the HOSTS file, and then PING the server using the TCP/IP alias name.

   a. Use **Windows Explorer** to browse to the following folder: **WINNT\System32\Drivers\ETC**.

   b. Double-click the **HOSTS** file and, if necessary, select **Notepad** as the editing application.

   c. Enter the following lines at the end of the file, specifying the IP address you identified in the Requirements section with the name TelnetHost, and your IP address identified with the name MyTelnet.

   ———————.——————.——————.——————**TelnetHost**

   ———————.——————.——————.—————— **MyTelnet**

   d. Save the HOSTS file, and exit Notepad.

   e. Use the PING command to test the HOSTS file entry by following the steps below:

   - Open a **Command Prompt** window.
   - Use the command **PING** *computer-name* to test each name specified in Step 5c. Record the results on your Student Answer Sheet.

6. The Telnet protocol can be used to access central computers or terminal servers. When using Telnet, your computer becomes a terminal to the other

computer. Windows 2000 allows you to set up a terminal server that accepts Telnet calls from other computers. Windows 2000 Professional includes a Telnet server that allows clients to access a DOS-like command window on the remote computer. One of the teachers at the Washington School wants to access student computers from her workstation in order to check directory contents and copy files. In this step, you use the Telnet protocol to set up a session with both your own and another Windows 2000 Professional computer.

a. Start the Telnet service on your Windows 2000 computer. (If you have a classroom server, your instructor will start the service on the Windows 2000 server.)

- Open the Control Panel by clicking **Start**, **Settings**, **Control Panel**.
- Double-click **Administrative Tools** from the Control Panel window.
- Double-click the **Telnet Server Administration** application to display the menu shown in Figure 7-5.

```
Microsoft (R) Windows 2000 (TM) (Build 2195)
Telnet Server Admin (Build 5.00.99201.1)

Select one of the following options:

0) Quit this application
1) List the current users
2) Terminate a user session ...
3) Display / change registry settings ...
4) Start the service
5) Stop the service

Type an option number [0 - 5] to select that option: _
```

Figure 7-5   Telnet Administration menu

- Enter **4** and press **Enter** to start the service.
- Minimize the Telnet Server Administration window.

b. To test accessing the Telnet service running on your computer, do the following:

- Click **Start**, **Run** and enter the command **TelNet MyTelnet**. (If necessary, replace the name MyTelnet with the name you assigned your computer when you modified the HOSTS file in Step 5c.)
- Click **OK** to start a Telnet session with your computer.
- Describe the contents of the Telnet window on your Student Answer Sheet.
- Type **DIR** and press **Enter** to display the contents of your C: drive.

- Restore the Telnet Server Administration application.
- Use option **1** to record the current user information on your Student Answer Sheet.
- Browse to your **Public** folder on the Windows 2000 system drive (D:), and use the **DIR** command to display its contents.
- Type **Exit** and press **Enter** to exit the Telnet session.

c. If available, repeat Step 6b to access the Telnet service of another computer from your computer.

d. Stop your Telnet service and log off as follows:

- Restore the Telnet Server Administration window.
- Enter option **5** and press **Enter** to stop the Telnet server.
- Enter option **0** and press **Enter** to quit the Telnet application and return to the desktop.
- Log off.

7

INTERNETWORKING WITH NOVELL NETWARE

Labs included in this chapter

➤ Lab 8.1 Installing the NWLink Protocol

➤ Lab 8.2 Configuring NWLink Frame Types

➤ Lab 8.3 Installing Multiple Protocols

➤ Lab 8.4 Testing Network Communications

➤ Lab 8.5 Improving Network Performance

➤ Lab 8.6 Restoring Network Components

Microsoft MCSE Exam #70-210 Objectives	
Objective	Lab
Install, configure, and troubleshoot network adapters	8.1, 8.2, 8.3, 8.6
Configure and troubleshoot the TCP/IP protocol	8.3
Connect to shared resources on a Microsoft network	8.4
Optimize and troubleshoot network performance	8.5

Student Answer Sheets to accompany the labs in this chapter can be downloaded from the Online Companion for this manual at *www.course.com*.

LAB 8.1 INSTALLING THE NWLINK PROTOCOL

Objective

Since receiving a NASA contract to build components for the International Space Station, the Universal Aerospace company has been expanding its engineering department. They recently purchased additional Windows 2000 Professional workstations to be added to the network. Universal Aerospace operates a large Novell NetWare-based network with multiple NetWare servers. While the company plans to eventually convert to TCP/IP, currently all workstations use Novell's IPX/SPX protocol to communicate with the NetWare servers. In addition to communicating with the NetWare servers, the engineers need to use the Windows 2000 Professional workstations to share files and access a plotter attached to one of the Windows 2000 Professional computers. Until the network is converted to TCP/IP, the network administrator, Kellie Thiele, wants to avoid extra network traffic by using only the IPX protocol on the new workstations. In this lab, you will simulate setting up the Windows 2000 Professional computer containing the shared plotter. After completing this lab, you will be able to:

➤ Install NWLink as the only protocol.

➤ Install the Microsoft Client and File and Printer Sharing service.

➤ Use the NWLink protocol to access shared resources on another Windows 2000 Professional workstation.

➤ Install the Client Service for NetWare.

➤ Log on to a NetWare server from a Windows 2000 Professional workstation.

Requirements

If working in a classroom environment, you need a lab partner in order to access a Windows 2000 computer in Activity 2. If working independently, you need to install the NWLink protocol on another Windows 2000 or Windows NT computer.

For Activity 3, you need access to a NetWare 4.x or NetWare 5 server to test the NetWare server on your network login process. The NetWare server should have a user who has access to a directory named Shared on the SYS volume. On the lines below, record the NetWare server name, or Preferred Tree name and context, and user login name and password:

Preferred NetWare server name: _____

Preferred Tree name: _____ User Context: _____

User login name: _____ Password: _____

Estimated completion time: **25–30 minutes**

 ACTIVITY 1

Remove existing network components, and install NWLink as the only protocol.

1. If necessary, start your computer with Windows 2000, and log on as an administrator.

2. Remove existing network components.

   a. Right-click **My Network Places** and click **Properties**.

   b. Double-click **Local Area Connection**, and click the **Properties** button to display the Local Area Connection Properties window.

   c. Click a protocol, and then use the **Uninstall** button to remove it.

   d. Click **No** to the Restart your computer now? message.

   e. Repeat Steps 3c and 3d to remove all protocols.

   f. Click a service and use the **Uninstall** button to remove it.

   g. Click **No** to the Restart your computer now? message.

   h. Repeat Steps 3f and 3g to remove all services.

   i. Click a Client and use the **Uninstall** button to remove it.

   j. Click **No** to the Restart your computer now? message.

   k. Repeat Steps 3i and 3j to remove all clients. After removing the last client, click **Yes** to the Restart your computer now? message.

   l. Click **No** to respond to the There are no protocols installed or enabled message.

3. The NWLink protocol has the advantage of being easy to configure, yet able to access servers on multiple subnets connected by routers. Although the NetBEUI protocol is easy to configure, it will not work across routers. TCP/IP is the best choice for large and diverse intranets, but, as you learned in Chapter 7, it is complex to configure. As a result, NWLink might be the best protocol choice for medium-sized networks, even if they do not contain NetWare servers. Use the following steps to install the NWLink protocol and then use the protocol to access shared folders on other Windows-based computers.

   a. Log on as the administrator.

   b. If necessary, right-click **My Network Places** and click **Properties**.

   c. Right-click **Local Area Connection**, and click the **Properties** option to display the Local Area Connection Properties window.

8

    d. Click the **Install** button to display the Select Network Component Type window.

    e. Click the **Protocol** component, and click the **Add** button to display the Select Network Protocol window.

    f. Double-click the **NWLink IPX/SPX/NetBIOS Compatible Transport Protocol** option.

    g. Record the NWLink network components on your Lab 8.1 Student Answer Sheet.

ACTIVITY 2

Add client components and set up file and printer sharing.

1. To be able to share its plotter, the computer you are configuring must include the Microsoft Client along with the File and Printer sharing services. In this step, you install the Microsoft Client and File and Printer Sharing service on the Windows 2000 Professional computer you are configuring.

    a. Click the **Install** button to display the Select Network Component Type window.

    b. Click the **Client** component, and click **Add** to display network client options.

    c. Click the **Client for Microsoft Networks** and click **OK** to add the Microsoft client to the Components window.

    d. To add the File and Printer Sharing service, click the **Install** button.

    e. Click the **Service** component type, and click **Add** to display the Select Network Component Type window.

    f. Verify that the File and Printer Sharing for Microsoft Networks is selected, and click **OK**. File and Printer Sharing for Microsoft Networks should be added to the Local Area Connections Properties Components window as shown in Figure 8-1.

    g. Click **OK**, then click the **Close** button to return to the Network and Dial-up Connections window.

    h. Close the Network and Dial-up Connections window.

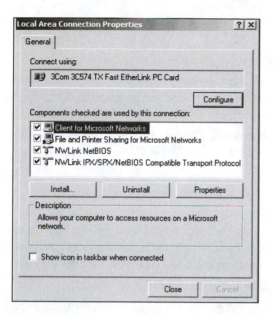

Figure 8-1 Local Area Connection Properties window

2. One of the projects at Universal Aerospace requires engineers to share information about the TransHab international space station. In this step, you simulate setting up this project by creating a shared TransHab folder.

a. Create a shared folder named **Ch8** as follows:

- Use My Computer or Windows Explorer to change to the drive containing your Windows 2000 system files, and create a folder named **Ch8**.

- Right-click the **Ch8** folder, and click **Sharing**.

- Click the **Share this folder as** option button, and click **OK** to accept the share name of Ch8.

- Double-click the newly created **Ch8** folder to open it.

- Create a text document file named **TransHab**.

- Double-click the newly created **TransHab** file, and use Notepad to enter the following description for the TransHab space station module:

TransHab is 23 feet in diameter and is made from lightweight carbon-fiber composite materials. The central core is a hard tunnel with a shell interface that provides three floors and dividers between various compartments. A center passageway runs the length of the module, providing access to all levels. The flooring and dividers are unfolded and extended after the module is inflated.

b. Save the file and exit Notepad.

3. Test your computer's NWLink protocol by accessing the TransHab file on another computer.

   a. Wait until your lab partner completes Step 2, if necessary.

   b. Verify that there is another computer on your network running the NWLink protocol. If necessary, wait for another student to complete Step 5a, and then coordinate this activity with that student.

   c. Double-click **My Network Places** and click the **Search** button from the menu bar to display the Search for Computers pane.

   d. Enter the name of the computer you wish to access in the Computer Name text box, and click **Search Now**.

   e. In the Search Results pane, double-click the computer name to display the shared folders. Note that you might be asked to enter a username and password if the computer you are accessing does not have a username with the same password as the one you used to log on.

   f. Double-click the **Ch8** folder to display its contents.

   g. Double-click the text file to display its contents using Notepad.

   h. Exit Notepad and close all windows.

4. To access services and resources on a NetWare server, you next need to install the Client Service for NetWare.

   a. Right-click **My Network Places** and click **Properties**.

   b. Double-click **Local Area Connections** and click the **Properties** button to display the Components window.

   c. Click **Install**, and then double-click the **Client** component type.

   d. Click the **Client Service for NetWare**, and click **OK**. If a dialog box appears asking if you want to restart your computer, do not respond. Wait for the Select NetWare Logon window shown in Figure 8-2 to be displayed.

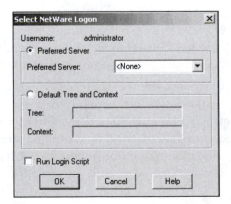

Figure 8-2 Select NetWare Logon window

e. If using a NetWare 3 server, in the Preferred Server text box, enter the name of the default server to be used.

f. If using a NetWare 4 or above server, click the **Default Tree and Context** option button, and enter the name of the Tree along with the default context in the Tree and Context text boxes.

g. If you do not have access to a NetWare server, leave <None> in the Preferred Server text box.

h. On NetWare servers, login scripts are often used to map drive letters to shared folders on the NetWare server. Click the **Run Login Script** check box to enable processing of NetWare login scripts.

i. After specifying a default server, the installation process checks to see if a user exists on the NetWare server with the same name as the one you are currently using on your Windows 2000 system. If the user-name does not exist on the NetWare server, you will receive a message telling you that the specified user does not exist. If this happens, click **Yes** to continue.

j. Click **Yes** to save your changes, and restart the computer.

k. Log on to your Windows 2000 workstation as Administrator.

l. On your Lab 8.1 Student Answer Sheet, record any message you received from the NetWare Authentication process, along with why you received this error message.

m. If you receive an authentication error message, click **No** to select another server or context.

n. Complete the log on process and then log off.

ACTIVITY 3

The engineers at Universal Aerospace need to access files on a NetWare server from their Windows 2000 workstations. In this activity, you log on to and access resources on a NetWare server. (Skip this activity if a NetWare server is not available on your network.)

1. If you have access to a NetWare server on your network, follow the steps below to log on to that server.

    a. If necessary, log on as Administrator.

    b. Create a username on your Windows 2000 computer for the NetWare user identified in the Requirements section of this lab. Use the same password for your Windows 2000 user as the password you used on the NetWare server.

c. Close all windows and log off.

d. Log on using the new user's name and password, and record the results on your Lab 8.1 Student Answer Sheet.

e. If requested, enter the preferred server or tree, and check the **Run login scripts** check box.

f. Log off.

g. Log on using the same username. On your Student Answer Sheet, describe the difference between this logon and the logon in Step 1d.

2. Access resources on the NetWare server.

a. If you selected to run the login scripts from the NetWare server, you should now have drives mapped to your user's home directory and to a shared directory. To verify drive mappings, double-click **My Computer** and on your Student Answer Sheet, record all drive letters mapped to the NetWare server.

b. Double-click **My Network Places** and double-click **Entire Network**.

c. Click the **entire contents** option, and then double-click the **NetWare or Compatible** icon to display your NetWare server.

d. Double-click the NetWare server to display folders to which you have rights. Record the folder names on your Student Answer Sheet.

e. Double-click the Shared folder, and record its contents on your Student Answer Sheet.

f. Close all windows and log off.

LAB 8.2 CONFIGURING NWLINK FRAME TYPES

Objective

The NWLink protocol might use different frame types when sending packets to NetWare servers. The frame type provides the formatting for the bits in the physical frame sent between network cards. Earlier versions of NetWare used a frame type called 802.3, while NetWare versions 4 and later use frame type 802.2. Normally, the NWLink protocol automatically detects the frame type being used on the network, and configures the Windows 2000 computer for that frame type. However, when multiple frame types are in use, you need to manually configure the Windows 2000 computer to accept packets with either frame type. Another consideration with NWLink protocol is that each NetWare server contains an internal network address that must be unique. When configuring multiple frame types or multiple network interface cards on a Windows 2000 system, you need to provide a unique network address for each of the frame types or network cards. For example, the Universal Aerospace network includes a NetWare 3 server that currently uses the 802.3 frame type. Engineers need to access this computer, as well as the main server, which accepts both the 802.2 and 802.3 frame types. On NetWare networks, each network card or frame type must be assigned a unique eight-character hexadecimal network address. After completing this lab, you will be able to:

➤ Configure the NWLink protocol to use multiple frame types.

➤ Configure a frame protocol for a unique network address.

➤ Change the internal network number.

Requirements

➤ At least two Windows 2000-based computers using the NWLink protocol

➤ Configure the NWLink protocol on another computer to use only 803.3 frame types and a network address of 10Ba5e3.

➤ In the space below, record the name of the computer using the 802.3 frame type:

_____

Estimated completion time: **15 minutes**

ACTIVITY

1. If necessary, start your computer with Windows 2000, and log on as an administrator.

2. Change the NWLink frame type to 802.3.

    a. Right-click **My Network Places** and click the **Properties** option.

    b. Double-click **Local Area Connection**, and double-click the **Properties** button from the Status window.

    c. Scroll down and click the **NWLink IPX/SPX/NetBIOS Compatible Transport Protocol** option.

    d. Click the **Properties** button to display the NWLink properties window shown in Figure 8-3.

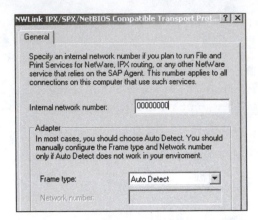

Figure 8-3   NWLink configuration window

    e. On your Lab 8.2 Student Answer Sheet, record three reasons why you would need to specify a unique Internet network number.

    f. Would the Windows 2000 systems in the Universal Aerospace engineering department need to be assigned internal network numbers? Record your answer on the Student Answer Sheet.

    g. Click the **Frame Type** list arrow to display a list of possible frame types. Record the available frame types on your Student Answer Sheet.

    h. Select the **802.3** frame type, and enter **10Ba5e3** for the network number.

    i. Click **OK** to save your changes and return to the Local Area Connection Properties window.

    j. Click **OK** to return to the status window.

    k. Click **Close** to close the status window.

3. Attempt to communicate with another computer using the 802.3 frame type.

    a. Right-click **My Network Places** and click the **Search for Computers** option.

    b. In the left-side Search for Computers pane, enter the name of the 802.3 computer you identified in the Requirements section.

    c. Double-click the computer in the right-side results pane.

    d. List the shared folders on your Student Answer Sheet.

    e. Close all windows.

4. Attempt to communicate with the 802.3 computer using a different network address.

    a. Follow the procedure in Step 2, and change the network address to **10Ba5e**.

b. Follow the procedure in Step 3, and record the results on your Student Answer Sheet.

c. Follow the procedure in Step 2 to change the frame type back to **Auto–detect**.

d. On your Student Answer Sheet, record the network address used in the Auto Detect mode.

5. Close all windows and log off.

LAB 8.3 INSTALLING MULTIPLE PROTOCOLS

Objective

The public library in your area is implementing a micro-lab that will consist of several Windows 2000 computers networked together to access the library's NetWare 4.1 and NT 4.0 servers, along with a shared CD-ROM server and two networked Hewlett-Packard printers. Recently the library's network administrator took a job in another city, leaving the project partially completed. The library has contracted with your firm to continue the project until they can hire another administrator. Your jobs include verifying existing protocols configured by the previous administrator, installing the required protocols and services, and configuring the system to maximize network performance. The NetWare servers and the NT servers are configured to use the NWLink protocol. The CD-ROM server requires the NetBEUI protocol to communicate with its clients. The two HP printers are directly attached to the network using the DLC protocol. Internet access will be provided through the library's proxy server using the TCP/IP protocol. IP address and configuration will be provided by the DHCP service running on the library's NT server. The head librarian wants you to make a master image of one computer that can later be copied to the other computers. In this lab, you will simulate setting up the network protocols for the master image computer. After completing this lab, you will be able to:

➤ Add the NetBEUI protocol.

➤ Add the TCP/IP protocol.

➤ Install the DLC protocol.

➤ Add a printer port using the DLC protocol.

➤ Verify multiple protocol bindings.

Requirements

➤ At least two Windows 2000-based computers with NWLink, NetBEUI, and TCP/IP protocols installed.

➤ Determine if IP addresses will be assigned by DHCP, Windows automatic assignment, or manual assignment.

➤ If manually assigning IP addresses, record the IP address of your computer: ____.____.____.____

Estimated completion time: **15 minutes**

ACTIVITY

1. If necessary, start your computer with Windows 2000, and log on as an administrator.

2. The previous network administrator installed Windows 2000 on the computers in the micro-lab, and configured them to access the NetWare server using the NWLink protocol. In this step, you will verify that the NWLink protocol and Client for NetWare components have been installed, and then add the NetBEUI protocol needed to access the library's CD-ROM tower.

   a. Right-click **My Network Places** and click the **Properties** option.

   b. Double-click the **Local Area Connection** option, and click the **Properties** button.

   c. Record the existing network components on your Lab 8.3 Student Answer Sheet.

   d. Click the **Install** button to display the Select Network Component Type window.

   e. Click on the **Protocol** option and click the **Add** button to display the Select Network Protocol window.

   f. Click on the **NetBEUI Protocol** and click **OK** to add the NetBEUI protocol to the Local Area Connection Properties window.

   g. Click the **Close** button.

3. To access the Internet and communicate with the library's central Windows NT server, the computers in the micro-lab need to have the TCP/IP protocol installed and configured to use the library's Internet router as the gateway. Follow the steps below to install and configure the TCP/IP protocol.

   a. Click **Install** and select the **Protocol** option from the Select Network Component Type window.

b. Click **Add** and select the **Internet Protocol (TCP/IP)** protocol.

c. Click **OK** to add the Internet Protocol to the Components window.

d. Click the **Internet Protocol (TCP/IP)** component, and click the **Properties** button to display the Internet Protocol (TCP/IP) Properties window.

e. If using manually assigned IP addresses, click the **Use the following IP address** option button, and enter the IP address and subnet mask you identified in the Requirements section of this lab.

f. Click **OK** save the TCP/IP configuration and return to the Local Area Connection Properties window.

g. Click **OK** to return to the Local Area Connection Status window.

h. Click **OK** to return to the Network and Dial-up Connections window.

i. Close the Network and Dial-up Connections window.

4. The HP printers in the micro-lab are attached directly to the network using the DLC protocol. In this step, you install the DLC protocol and observe how the Windows 2000 computer can use it to add a printer port.

a. Follow the steps below to record the current printer port options:

- Click **Start**, **Settings**, **Printers** to display the Printers window.
- Double-click **Add Printer** and click **Next** to launch the Add Printer Wizard.
- Verify that the **Local printer** option button is selected, and click **Next** to display the Select the Printer Port window.
- If no local printer is attached, uncheck the **Automatically detect and install my Plug and Play printer box**.
- Click the **Create a new port** option button, and record all existing printer port types on your Student Answer Sheet.
- Click **Cancel** to return to the Printers window.
- Close the Printers window.

b. Follow the steps below to add the DLC protocol:

- Right-click **My Network Places** and click **Properties**.
- Double-click **Local Area Connection** and click the **Properties** button.
- Click **Install**, select the **Protocols** option, and click **Add**.
- Double-click the **DLC Protocol** to add it to the Components window.
- Click **Close** twice to return to the Network and Dial-up Connections window.
- Close the Network and Dial-up Connections window.

8

c. Repeat Step 4a to view the printer port types now available.

d. On your Student Answer Sheet, record the printer port type added as a result of installing the DLC protocol.

e. Close all windows and log off.

LAB 8.4 TESTING NETWORK COMMUNICATIONS

Objective

Prior to installing applications on the library's micro-lab computers, you want to verify that the protocols are configured correctly by testing communications between computers. After completing this lab, you will be able to:

➤ Disable and enable network protocols.

➤ Communicate with a Windows 2000 computer using only the NetBEUI protocol.

➤ Communicate with a Windows 2000 computer using only the TCP/IP protocol.

Requirements

➤ A Windows 2000 server or Windows computer configured for file sharing using the NetBEUI, NWLink, and TCP/IP protocols.

Estimated completion time: **20 minutes**

ACTIVITY

1. If necessary, start your computer, and log on as an administrator.

2. If necessary, share a folder on your Windows-based server computer, and verify that the NWLink, NetBEUI, and TCP/IP protocols are installed on the server computer.

3. Disable all protocols except NetBEUI on your Windows 2000 Professional computer.

    a. Right-click **My Network Places** and click the **Properties** option.

    b. Right-click **Local Area Connection** and click the **Properties** option.

    c. Remove the check mark from the **Internet Protocol (TCP/IP)** check box by clicking the box.

    d. Remove the check mark from the **DLC Protocol** check box by clicking the box.

e. Remove the check marks from both the **NWLink NetBIOS** and **NWLink IPX/SPX/ASPX/NetBIOS Compatible Transport Protocol** check boxes.

f. Verify that only the NetBEUI protocol is enabled.

g. Click **OK** to save your changes and return to the Local Area Connection Status window.

h. Click the **Close** button, and then exit the Network and Dial-up Connections window.

4. Access the shared folder on the server computer using only the NetBEUI protocol.

a. Double-click **My Network Places**.

b. Double-click **Entire Network**, and click the view **entire contents** option.

c. Double-click **Microsoft Windows Network** to display all work-groups and domains.

d. On your Lab 8.4 Student Answer Sheet, record the workgroups and domains you see.

e. Double-click the workgroup or domain name that contains the server sharing the folder specified in Step 2.

f. Double-click the server's computer name to display a list of all shared folders.

g. If accessing an NT or Windows 2000, server you might need to enter a username and password to gain access to the shared resource.

h. Right-click a shared folder, and click the **Create Shortcut** option.

i. Click **Yes** to create the shortcut on your desktop.

j. Close all windows.

k. Double-click the shortcut you created in Step 4h to display the shared folder contents using NetBEUI.

l. Close all windows.

5. Disable the NetBEUI protocol and access the shared folder using only the NWLink protocol.

a. Right-click **My Network Places** and click the **Properties** option.

b. Double-click **Local Area Connection** and click the **Properties** button.

c. Place a check mark in the **NWLink** check box by clicking the box.

d. Remove the check mark from the **NetBEUI Protocol** check box by clicking the box.

e. Verify that only the NWLink protocols are enabled and that the frame type is set to Autodetect.

8

    f. Click **OK** to save your changes and return to the Local Area Connection Status window.

    g. Click the **Close** button, and then exit the Network and Dial-up Connections window.

    h. Double-click the shortcut to the folder you created in Step 4.

    i. Record the results on your Student Answer Sheet.

    j. Close all windows.

6. Enable all protocols on your Windows 2000 Professional computer.

    a. Right-click **My Network Places** and click the **Properties** option.

    b. Double-click **Local Area Connection** and click the **Properties** button.

    c. Place a check mark in the **NetBEUI Protocol** check box by clicking the box.

    d. Place a check mark in the **DLC Protocol** check box by clicking the box.

    e. Verify that all protocols are enabled.

    f. Click **OK** to save your changes and return to the Local Area Connection Status window.

    g. Click the **Close** button, and then exit the Network and Dial-up Connections window.

7. Log off.

LAB 8.5 IMPROVING NETWORK PERFORMANCE

Objective

Having multiple protocols can reduce network performance when bindings for less frequently used protocols are listed prior to the more common protocols. When asked about the micro-lab usage, the library's network administrator thought that the most common use of the micro-lab computers will be using the Microsoft Client to access the shared CD-ROM tower. Although the Microsoft client also is used to access the library server using the TCP/IP protocol, this usage will be less than the CD-ROM tower. Because the library's Windows NT Server uses only the NWLink protocol, the administrator thinks that file and printer sharing on the Windows 2000 Professional computers also should be done using just the NWLink protocol.

One of the reasons why multiple protocols on a client might reduce network performance is because the Multiple Universal naming convention Provider (MUP) sends out requests on protocols according to their bind sequence. If a protocol is unused, it must timeout before the next protocol is attempted. To improve the efficiency of network protocol usage, you need to determine which protocols are to be used for each client and service, and then sequence them in order of usage.

The File and Printer Sharing service also uses up network bandwidth by sending out announcements every 12 minutes. These announcements are used by browser computers to allow you to find network resources through My Network Places. In addition to improving the management of multiple protocols, the library's network administrator also wants the File and Printer Sharing service disabled on all computers except for the two computers that will provide shared folders to the micro-lab. After completing this lab, you will be able to:

➤ Sequence network protocols for better performance.

➤ Disable the File and Printer Sharing service.

Requirements

➤ A Windows 2000 server or Windows computer configured for file sharing using both the NetBEUI and TCP/IP protocols.

Estimated completion time: **10 minutes**

ACTIVITY

1. If necessary, start your computer, and log on as an administrator.

2. Follow the steps below to sequence the protocol bindings for better network usage.

    a. Right-click **My Network Places** and click the **Properties** option.

    b. Click the **Advanced** option from the Network and Dial-up Connections menu bar.

    c. Click the **Advanced Settings** option to display a Bindings window similar to the one shown in Figure 8-4.

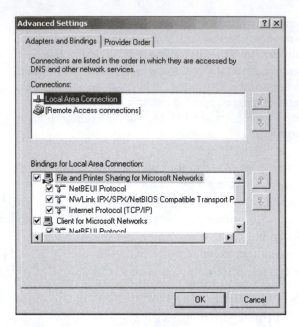

Figure 8-4 Advanced Settings window

    d. On your Lab 8.5 Student Answer Sheet, record the binding order for the Microsoft client.

    e. On your Student Answer Sheet, record the binding sequence for the Novell client.

    f. On your Student Answer Sheet, record the binding sequence for the File and Printer Sharing service.

    g. Because File and Printer Sharing use only the NWLink protocol, you can disable the NetBEUI protocol by removing the check mark from the **NetBEUI Protocol** check box under the File and Printer Sharing service. Next, click the **NWLink** protocol, and use the up-arrow to put it first in the File and Printer Sharing for Microsoft Networks binding list.

    h. Under the Client for Microsoft Networks bindings, verify that the NetBEUI protocol is listed first.

    i. Click **OK** to save your changes, and return to the Network and Dial-up Connections window.

3. Having File and Printer Sharing active on a computer also takes up network bandwidth, and can therefore decrease overall network performance. Therefore, if no files or printers are shared on a Windows 2000 Professional computer, it is best to disable the service.

    a. Double-click the **Local Area Connection** icon, and then click the **Properties** button.

    b. To disable file and printer sharing on this computer, click the **File and Printer Sharing for Microsoft Networks** check box to remove the check mark.

    c. On your Student Answer Sheet, describe an advantage of disabling the protocol, as compared to uninstalling it.

    d. Click **OK** to save your changes, and return to the Local Area Connection Status window.

4. Click **Close**, close the Network and Dial-up Connections window, and log off.

LAB 8.6 RESTORING NETWORK COMPONENTS

Objective

Now that you have completed the labs from Chapters 7 and 8, you should restore your Windows 2000 network components to the original configuration you recorded in Lab 7.1. After completing this lab, you will be able to:

➤ Remove existing network components.

➤ Modify the network components to return a computer to its original configuration.

Requirements

➤ Network component configuration recorded on Lab 7.1 Student Answer Sheet.

➤ Another computer or server to test your restored network configuration.

Estimated completion time: **15 minutes**

ACTIVITY

1. If necessary, start your computer, and log on as an administrator.

2. To return your computer to its original network component configuration, in this step you will remove any existing protocols and services from your Windows 2000 Professional computer.

    a. Right-click **My Network Places** and click **Properties**.

    b. Double-click **Local Area Connection**. Record the requested connection information on your Lab 8.6 Student Answer Sheet.

    c. Click the **Properties** button to display the Local Area Connection Properties window.

d. Click a protocol, and then use the **Uninstall** button to remove it. Record the steps you perform on your Student Answer Sheet. Note that you do not need to restart your computer until all components have been removed.

e. Repeat Steps 2a through 2d to remove all protocols.

f. Click on a service and use the **Uninstall** button to remove it. Record the steps you perform on your Student Answer Sheet.

g. Repeat Step 2f to remove all services.

3. Restart your computer, and log on as an administrator.

4. Right-click **My Network Places** and click the **Properties** button.

5. Double-click **Local Area Connection**, and record the requested connection information on your Student Answer Sheet.

6. Click the **Properties** button to display the Local Area Connection Components window.

7. Use the **Install** button to add the protocols you recorded on the Lab 7.1 Student Answer Sheet.

8. Use the **Install** button to add the clients you recorded on the Lab 7.1 Student Answer Sheet.

9. Use the **Install** button to add the services you recorded on the Lab 7.1 Student Answer Sheet.

10. Restart your computer, and log on as administrator.

11. Test your configuration by accessing a shared folder on another computer attached to your network.

REMOTE ACCESS SERVICES

Microsoft MCSE Exam #70-210 Objectives	
Objective	Lab
Connect to computers by using dial-up networking	
Create a dial-up connection to connect to a remote access server	9.1
Connect to the Internet by using dial-up networking	9.2
Configure and troubleshoot Internet Connection Sharing	9.3
Connect to computers by using a virtual private network (VPN) connection	9.4
Connect to shared resources on a Microsoft network	9.1
Manage and troubleshoot the use and synchronization of offline files	9.5
Manage and troubleshoot Web server resources	9.6

Note

Student Answer Sheets to accompany the labs in this chapter can be downloaded from the Online Companion for this manual at *www.course.com*.

Lab 9.1 Installing and Configuring Remote Access Services

Objective

Computer Technology Services was contacted by Carl Dauer, a local real estate agent who wants to network the computers at the Blue Hills Realty office, as well as provide access to the office network from his home. Currently the Blue Hills Realty office consists of Carl, another real estate agent, and a secretary. Each agent and the secretary have a peer-to-peer network consisting of networked Windows 2000 Professional computers in their offices. Carl recently purchased a notebook computer (also running Windows 2000 Professional) and plans to use the notebook computer to access the office network from his home. The Windows 2000 Professional computer in Carl's office will act as his office computer, as well as the server for shared access to files and printers. You have been asked to set up Remote Access Services (RAS) between the office server and Carl's notebook computer. After completing this lab, you will be able to:

➤ Configure a Windows 2000 computer to accept incoming connections.

➤ Install and configure RAS on a client computer.

➤ Connect two computers using a null modem cable.

➤ Access shared folders using Remote Access Services.

Requirements

➤ Access to another computer running Windows 2000 Professional. If you are working in a classroom environment, you need to team up with another student. Your partner's computer will simulate the remote station, and your computer will simulate the server.

➤ A null modem cable to connect the COM or LPT ports of the Windows 2000 computers to simulate the remote connection.

Estimated completion time: **25 minutes**

Activity

1. To simulate setting up your computer as the Windows 2000 Professional computer in Carl's office, if necessary, start your computer with Windows 2000, and log on as an administrator.

2. Create a user named Carl who can log on to your "server" computer from the remote system.

   a. Open **Control Panel**.

   b. Double-click **Users and Passwords**.

   c. Click the **Add** button, and enter the following user information:

- User Name: **Carl**
- Full name: **Carl Dauer**
- Description: **Carl's remote user account**

   d. Click **Next** and enter a password that you can remember. On your Lab 9.1 Student Answer Sheet, record the password you use.

   e. Click **Next** and click the **Restricted user** option button.

   f. On your Lab 9.1 Student Answer Sheet, describe a reason for restricting a remote user account.

   g. Click **Finish** to create the user account and return to the Users and Passwords window. Verify that the new user account for Carl is included in the Users for this computer box.

   h. Click **OK** to save your changes and return to Control Panel.

   i. Close the Control Panel window.

3. Now you need to configure the Windows 2000 Professional server in Carl's office to accept incoming connections.

   a. Right-click **My Network Places** and click the **Properties** option.

   b. Double-click **Make New Connection**. If the Location Information window appears, enter your area code and click OK twice to continue. Click **Next** to display the Network Connection Type window shown in Figure 9-1.

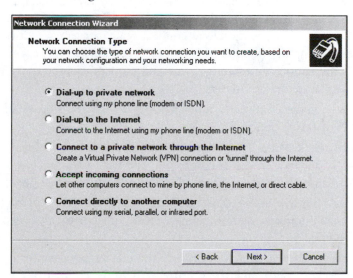

Figure 9-1 Network Connection Wizard

c. Click the **Accept incoming connections** option button, and click **Next** to display the Devices for Incoming Connections window.

d. Record the device options on your Student Answer Sheet.

e. Click either the **Serial** port or **Direct parallel** (LPT1) port, depending on your cable type, and click **Next** to display the Virtual Private Network Connection.

f. At this time, click the **Do not allow virtual private connections** button. (In a later lab, you will change this to enable and test a virtual private connection.)

g. Click **Next** to display the Allowed Users window. This window is used to determine which users can access the computer through Remote Access Services. If necessary, remove the check mark from the Administrator user, and place a check mark in front of Carl's user name to allow only Carl to log on remotely.

h. Click **Next** to display the Networking Components window.

i. On your Student Answer Sheet, record the network components available.

j. To reduce network traffic, remove the check mark from the **NetBEUI** protocol if it exists.

k. Click **Next** to display the connection name text box.

l. Record the default connection name on your Student Answer Sheet, and click **Finish** to return to the Network and Dial-up Connections window.

m. Close the Network and Dial-up Connections window.

4. In this step, you simulate a dial-up connection from a remote computer (Carl's notebook computer) to the server computer (Carl's office computer). You will use a null-modem cable to connect your partner's Windows 2000 Professional computer (the remote computer) to your (server) computer. You configure the remote computer to use a null modem cable to make the connection to your server computer.

a. On the remote computer, right-click **My Network Places** and click the **Properties** option.

b. Double-click **Make New Connection**. If the Location Information window appears, enter your area code and click **OK** twice to continue. Click **Next** to display the Network Connection Type window.

c. On your Student Answer Sheet, record what option you would choose if you were using a modem to connect to the office network over a dial-up phone line.

d. Because in this lab you will simulate the dial-up connection using a null-modem cable, click the **Connect directly to another computer** option, and click **Next** to display the Host or Guest window.

e. On your Student Answer Sheet, briefly describe the difference between Host and Guest modes.

f. Click the **Guest** option button, and click **Next** to display the Select a Device window.

g. On your Student Answer Sheet, list the devices available on your computer.

h. Select the either the **serial** port or **Direct parallel** (LPT1) port, depending on the cable you will use, and click **Next** to display the Connection Availability window.

i. On your Student Answer Sheet, record the connection availability options, along with the default, and click **Next** to accept the default option.

j. In the name for this connection text box, enter the name **Office Connection**, and click **Finish** to display the Connect Office Connection window.

k. Click **Cancel** to exit the Office Connection window and return to the Network and Dial-up Connections window.

l. Close all windows and shut down the system.

5. In this step you test your remote access configuration by using a null modem cable to connect the remote computer to your server computer. (For this step, you need to work with another student, and take turns.)

a. If necessary, shut down both the server and remote computers.

b. Connect a null modem cable between your server computer and your remote computer.

c. Disconnect the remote computer from the network cable.

d. Start both computers.

e. From the remote computer, right-click **My Network Places** and click **Properties**.

f. Double-click **Office Connection** to display the Office Connection window.

g. Enter the User name **Carl** along with the password, and click the **Connect** button.

h. On your Student Answer Sheet, record the steps you took to connect to the server computer.

i. Use **My Network Places** to browse to the server computer and access a shared folder. Record the results on your Student Answer Sheet.

j. Close all windows, and shut down your computers.

k. Connect the remote computer to the network cable.

9

6. If you have sufficient time and are working with a partner, reverse the roles of your computers to make the computer that was the remote become the server computer, and vice versa, and then perform the following process:

   a. If necessary, shut down both the server and remote computers.

   b. Disconnect the new remote computer from the network cable.

   c. Start both computers.

   d. From the new remote computer, right-click **My Network Places**, and click **Properties**.

   e. Double-click **Office Connection** to display the Office Connection window.

   f. Enter the User name **Carl** along with the password, and click the **Connect** button.

   g. On your Student Answer Sheet, record the steps you took to connect to the server computer.

   h. Use **My Network Places** to browse to the server computer and access a shared folder. Record the results on your Student Answer Sheet.

   i. Close all windows and shut down your computer.

   j. Reconnect the remote computer to the network.

LAB 9.2 INSTALLING DIAL-UP ACCESS TO THE INTERNET

Objective

Accessing real estate information and advertising on the Internet is becoming an important part of doing business at the Blue Hills Realty office. As a result, each agent and the secretary currently have modems installed in their computers and use them for dial-up access to the Internet. In addition to configuring the dial-up connection to the office network, Carl also wants you to configure a dial-up connection to the Internet from his new notebook Windows 2000 Professional system. After completing this lab, you will be able to:

➤ Install and configure dial-up access to the Internet.

Requirements

➤ An Internet account with the following parameters. If you do not have access to a dial-up Internet Service Provider (ISP), you still can perform the setup process by supplying the supplemental information in parentheses.

   ■ ISP phone number _____ (your home phone number)

- Username: _____ (cdauer)
- Password: _____ (ab1B22CD)
- Optional e-mail address: _____
  (cdauer@isp.net)
  - Optional mail server name or address: _____
    (mail.isp.net)

➤ A Windows 2000 compatible modem installed in your computer.

➤ If you have already configured the modem, follow the steps below to remove the modem configuration from your computer.

1. If necessary, log on as the administrator.

2. Open **Control Panel**.

3. Double-click the **Phone and Modem** icon.

4. Click the **Modems** tab.

5. Record the existing modem configuration on your Lab 9.2 Student Answer Sheet.

6. If your modem appears, select it and click the **Remove** button.

7. Confirm the removal of the modem configuration and close all windows.

9

Estimated completion time: **20 minutes**

ACTIVITY

1. If necessary, start your computer with Windows 2000, and log on as an administrator.

2. Right-click **My Network Places** and click **Properties**.

3. Double-click the **Make New Connection** icon, and click **Next** to display the Network Connection Type window.

4. Click the **Dial-up to the Internet** option button, and click **Next** to start the Internet Connection Wizard.

5. On your Student Answer Sheet, record the three connection types.

6. Click the **I want to set up my Internet connection manually** option, and click **Next**.

7. Click the **I connect through a phone line and a modem** option button. Record the other option on your Student Answer Sheet.

8. Click **Next** to display the Install New Modem Wizard.

9. Click **Next** to have Windows 2000 auto-detect your modem hardware and install the required software drivers.

10. After your modem has been installed, click **Finish** to display the Internet account connection information window shown in Figure 9-2.

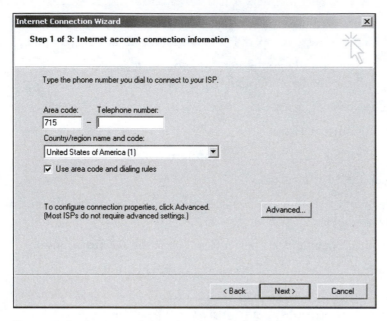

Figure 9-2   Internet Connection Wizard

11. Click the **Advanced** button, and record the default options on your Student Answer Sheet.

12. Click **Cancel** to return to the Internet account connection window.

13. Enter the ISP phone number you specified in the Requirements section, and then click **Next**.

14. Enter the username and password necessary to connect to the ISP, as specified in the Requirements section.

15. Click **Next** and enter **Internet Connection** for the Connection name.

16. Click **Next** to display the Internet Mail Account setup window.

17. If you want to set up an Internet mail account, click **Yes** and follow the steps below.

    a. Click **Next**, and enter the display name you want to use for outgoing mail.

    b. Click **Next**, and enter your e-mail address.

c. Click **Next**, and enter the name or address of your incoming and out-going mail server(s).

d. Click **Next**, and enter the mail Account name and password provided by your ISP.

e. Click to remove the check mark from **To connect to the Internet immediately, select this box and click Finish**.

f. Click **Next**, and then click **Finish** to complete the Internet Connection Wizard.

18. Create a shortcut to your Internet connection on the desktop.

a. Right-click the Internet connection you created in Step 17, and click **Create Shortcut**.

b. Click **Yes** to create the shortcut on the desktop.

c. Close the Network and Dial-up Connections window.

19. Test your Internet connection by performing the following steps. Record the results of the test on your Student Answer Sheet. (*Note*: If you do not have an actual Internet account or ISP, you still can perform this step and verify that the system dials the phone number you specified in the Requirements section.)

a. From the desktop, double-click the **Shortcut to Internet Connection** icon you created.

b. Verify that the user name and password fields are filled in, and click the **Dial** button.

c. Observe the dialing and connection process, and record any messages on your Student Answer Sheet.

LAB 9.3 SHARING AN INTERNET CONNECTION

Objective

The Blue Hills Realty office is increasing its use of the Internet for accessing land prices and advertising recreational properties. The agency has only one Internet account. When one person is using the Internet, the other users need to wait for that person to disconnect before they can dial in. You recently informed Carl that Windows 2000 can help solve this problem by sharing an Internet connection. Carl wants you to configure the other computers in his office so that they share the Internet connection on the Windows 2000 Professional computer in his office. After completing this lab, you will be able to:

➤ Use Windows 2000 to share an Internet connection.

➤ Configure another computer to use the shared Internet connection.

➤ Test the shared connection by accessing the Internet from another computer.

To perform this lab, students need to work in teams consisting of at least two computers—where one computer shares its Internet connection with the other computer(s). When sharing an Internet connection, the computer hosting the Internet connection needs to provide IP addresses to the client computer(s). As a result, to perform this lab, the computers sharing an Internet connection need to be isolated from other lab computers that use a separate hub or network cable. Consult your instructor or lab assistant to determine if it is feasible to do these activities in your lab environment.

Requirements

➤ Completion of Lab 9.2.

➤ Another Windows 2000 Professional computer attached to an isolated network hub or cable.

➤ Determine which computer will share its Internet connection (referred to as the "server" computer) and which computer will be the "client."

➤ In a classroom environment, you need to obtain permission from the instructor or lab assistant to disconnect both your computer and your lab partner's computer from the main network. You then can connect them using a separate hub or crossover cable to simulate the Blue Hills Realty office network. This is necessary for the computer you select to host the shared Internet connection and automatically provide IP addresses to only your client computer.

➤ The hub to which your computers are connected cannot have a DHCP server running, because the Internet-sharing computer must be the only one that can give out IP addresses to other computers.

Estimated completion time: **25 minutes**

ACTIVITY

1. If working in a classroom environment, you and your lab partner should disconnect your computers from the classroom network, and then connect them using a separate hub or crossover cable.

2. Start the shared Internet connection (server) computer with Windows 2000, and log on as an administrator.

3. Share the Internet connection by performing the following procedure on the Internet connection host computer.

   a. Right-click **My Network Places** and click **Properties**.

   b. Right-click the **Internet Connection** icon, and click **Properties** to display the Internet Connection Properties window shown in Figure 9-3.

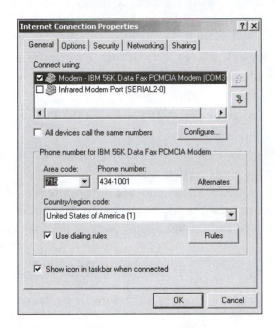

Figure 9-3   Internet Connection Properties window

   c. Click the **Sharing** tab, and click the **Enable Internet Connection Sharing for this connection** check box.

   d. On your Lab 9.3 Student Answer Sheet, describe the option that is enabled by default when you enable Internet connection sharing.

   e. Click the **Settings** button.

   f. Click the **Services** tab. On your Student Answer Sheet, record the services that may be provided to the remote client. Note any services provided by default, and which, if any, you think would benefit the Blue Hills Realty agency.

   g. Click **Cancel** to return to the Internet Connection Properties window.

   h. Click **OK** to save your configuration.

   i. On your Student Answer Sheet, record the requested IP Address information from the message you receive. Also record how you think you would set the IP addresses of the client computers.

    j. Click **Yes** to enable sharing and return to the Network and Dial-up Connections window.

    k. Close all windows and log off.

4. If necessary, start the client computer and log on as an administrator.

5. Before the client computer can share the Internet connection on your server computer, you first need to configure the client computer's TCP/IP protocol so it obtains IP address information automatically.

    a. Right-click **My Network Places** and click the **Properties** option.

    b. Right-click the **Local Area Connection** icon, and click **Properties** to display the Components window.

    c. Click the **Internet Protocol (TCP/IP)** and click the **Properties** button.

    d. Document the current TCP/IP configuration (manual or automatic IP addressing) on your Student Answer Sheet.

    e. If necessary, click the **Obtain an IP address automatically** option button, and click **OK** to return to the Components window. Your client computer now gets its IP address and default gateway from the computer that is sharing its Internet connection. The default gateway for the client will be set to the computer with the Internet connection so IP packets are routed to the Internet.

    f. Click **OK** twice to save your changes and return to the Network and Dial-up Connections window.

6. Click **OK** to close the Network and Dial-up Connections window.

7. Test the shared Internet connection from the client computer.

    a. Find and record the client computer's IP address and default gateway by doing the following:

       ■ Open a Command Prompt window.

       ■ Enter the command **IPCONFIG/All** and record the IP address information on your Student Answer Sheet.

       ■ Enter the command **EXIT** to close the Command Prompt window.

    b. Right-click **Internet Explorer** and click **Properties**.

    c. Click the **Connections** tab, and then click the **LAN Settings** button.

    d. Verify that the **Use a proxy server** option is not checked. Click **OK** twice.

    e. Close all windows.

f. Start **Internet Explorer**. When Internet Explorer attempts to send a packet to the Internet it will be redirected using the gateway IP address to your shared Internet computer. The shared Internet computer then will dial up the ISP and make the connection. Both computers now can share access to the Internet.

8. If you have established a connection with an Internet Service Provider, check your connection status.

   a. On the Internet connection server, point to the Internet connection icon located in the lower-right on the status bar.

   b. On your Student Answer Sheet, record the connection speed, along with bytes sent and received.

   c. Attempt to run Internet Explorer from both computers.

   d. Exit Internet Explorer on both computers.

   e. On your shared Internet computer, double-click the Internet Connection icon, and disconnect from the Internet.

9. After both you and your partner have completed Steps 3–8, return your TCP/IP configuration to the settings you recorded in Step 5.

10. If you are working in a classroom environment, shut down both computers and reattach them to the classroom network.

11. Start both computers and verify that they are operating correctly on the classroom network. Have your instructor or lab assistant confirm system operation, and initial your Student Answer Sheet.

LAB 9.4 CREATING A VIRTUAL PRIVATE NETWORK CONNECTION

Objective

The remote access service you installed for Carl Dauer has proven to be a valuable asset in accessing the real estate office network from home. Recently Carl hired Lucas Fenske as a part-time real estate broker for Blue Hills Realty. Carl thinks being able to access the office network also would assist Lucas' sales efforts. The problem is that Lucas lives in a different region and long-distance phone call costs to access the office network would be prohibitive. Because Lucas has a local Internet service provider, you have suggested using the Point-to-Point Tunneling Protocol (PPTP) to create a Virtual Private Network (VPN) using the Internet to connect to the Blue Hills Realty network. After completing this lab, you will be able to:

➤ Configure Remote Access Services on your computer to accept connections from the Internet.

➤ Configure a client to use Point to Point Tunneling Protocol (PPTP) to establish a Virtual Private Network (VPN) connection to Remote Access Services.

➤ Establish a connection between the computers using PPTP.

Requirements

➤ One other Window 2000 Professional computer attached to the network.

➤ In a classroom environment, you will work with your lab partner to determine which computer will act as the "server" and which computer will be the remote client. The client will be used to make a Virtual Private Network connection to the "server" using your network to simulate the Internet.

Estimated completion time: **20 minutes**

ACTIVITY

1. If necessary, start your server computer with Windows 2000, and log on as an administrator.

2. Lucas Fenske needs a user account so he can access the office network from a remote location. In this step, you create a user account for Lucas on the computer you have identified as the Blue Hills office server. On your Lab 9.4 Student Answer Sheet, record the name of the user account and password you create for Luke. Also record whether the account type should be normal or restricted.

3. Modify the Incoming Connections option on the computer identified as the Blue Hills office server computer so access is allowed from the Internet.

    a. Right-click **My Network Places** and then click **Properties**.

    b. Right-click **Incoming Connections** and click **Properties** to display the Incoming Connections window similar to the one shown in Figure 9-4.

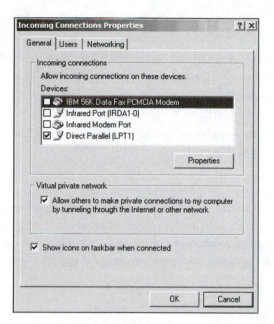

Figure 9-4 Incoming Connections Properties window

c. If necessary, place a check mark in the **Allow others to make private connections to my computer by tunneling through the Internet** check box by clicking it.

d. Click the **Users** tab.

e. Click the check box in front of the user name you created for Lucas Fenske.

f. Click the **Networking** tab, and, if necessary, place a check mark in the **Internet protocol (TCP/IP)** check box by clicking it.

g. Click **OK** to save your changes, and then close the Network and Dial-up connections window.

4. Prior to making a Virtual Private Network connection from the computer designated as the remote client, you need to follow the steps below to determine the IP address of the computer identified as the Blue Hills office server.

a. Open a command prompt window on the Blue Hills office server by clicking **Start**, **Programs**, **Accessories**, **Command Prompt**.

b. Enter the command **IPCONFIG** and press **Enter**.

c. On your Student Answer Sheet, record the IP address of the computer identified as the Blue Hills office server.

d. Enter the **Exit** command and press **Enter** to close the Command Prompt window.

5. Create a Virtual Private Network connection option on the computer identified as the remote client.

    a. If necessary, start your client computer and log on as an administrator.

    b. Right-click **My Network Places** and click the **Properties** option.

    c. Double-click the **Make New Connection** icon, and click **Next** to display the Network Connection Type window.

    d. Click the **Connect to a private network through the Internet** option button, and click **Next**.

    e. If you have an Internet Connection configured on your client computer, the Public Network window shown in Figure 9-5 will appear. Click the **Do not dial the initial connection** option button, and click **Next** to display the Destination Address window. If your computer is accessing a shared Internet connection, this step will be skipped, and the Destination Address window will appear.

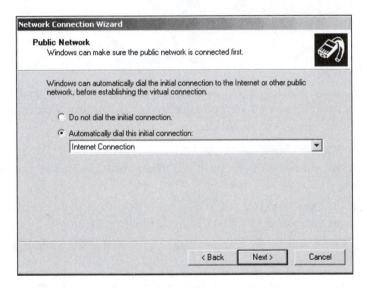

Figure 9-5   Virtual Private Network Connection Wizard

    f. In the Host name or IP address text box, enter the IP address of your server computer, and click **Next**.

    g. In the Connection Availability window, click the **For all users** option button, and click **Next** to display the final connection name window.

    h. Enter **Blue Hills Network** in the Name you want to use for this connection text box, and click **Finish**.

    i. Click **Cancel** to bypass the Connect Blue Hill Network window.

6. In this step, you test your Virtual Network configuration by simulating a connection from the remote client computer to the Blue Hills office server. You will use your local network as if it were the Internet.

   a. If you were accessing the office server from a remote client, you first would need to use your Internet Connection option to establish a connection to the Internet. In this step, you will use your Local Area Network to simulate the Internet connection. Therefore, you can assume that a connection to the Internet has already been established.

   b. If necessary, right-click **My Network Places** and click **Properties**.

   c. Double-click the **Blue Hills Network** connection icon.

   d. Enter Lucas Fenske's user name and password you recorded in Step 2.

   e. Click **Connect** and, on your Student Answer Sheet, record the requested Connection Results window information.

7. Remove the Blue Hills Network connection from the remote client computer.

   a. If necessary, log on to the remote client computer as the administrator.

   b. Right-click **My Network Places** and click **Properties**.

   c. Right-click the **Blue Hills Network** connection, and click **Delete**.

   d. Click **Yes** to confirm the deletion process.

   e. Close the Network and Dial-up Connections window, and log off.

8. Remove the Virtual Private Network connection from the server computer.

   a. If necessary, log on to the server computer as the administrator.

   b. Right-click **My Network Places** and click **Properties**.

   c. Right-click **Incoming Connections** and click **Properties**.

   d. Click to remove the check mark from the **Allow others to make private connections to my computer** check box.

   e. Click **OK** to save your changes.

   f. Close the Network and Dial-up Connections window, and log off.

9. If time permits, repeat the lab by reversing the roles of the computers. Make the old server computer the remote client, and the old remote client computer the new server.

LAB 9.5 USING OFFLINE FILES AND FOLDERS

Objective

Carl spends a lot of time out of the office with clients, working on real estate deals. He wants to use his notebook to access the customer and real estate databases on the office server computer. He also wants to be able to select certain files from the office shared folder so he can work with them while on the road. After discussing these ideas with Carl, you have determined that Windows 2000 Professional offline files and folders can be configured to help him access and update files while away from the office. Some files, such as the real estate database, can be configured to automatically synchronize with his notebook, while other files can be manually selected for offline work. After completing this lab, you will be able to:

➤ Manually create offline files.

➤ Configure a shared folder for automatic offline access.

➤ Synchronize offline files.

Requirements

➤ One other Windows 2000 Professional computer to act as the server. If you are working in a classroom environment, you and your lab partner need to identify which computer will act as the server and which computer will be the client.

Estimated completion time: **25 minutes**

ACTIVITY

1. If necessary, start your server computer with Windows 2000, and log on as an administrator.

2. If necessary, create users named Carl on both the server and client computers, as described in Lab 9.1, Step 2.

3. Create and share a folder named **ForSale**. In the shared ForSale folder, create a file named **SkiHill**. Use Notepad to enter the following description notes:

   Owner: James Gruenhagen

   Location: Near the town of Horseman.

   Description: 500 vertical feet drop, 5 major hills, one chair lift, and two "T" bars. Large chalet with dining room and bar facing the ski hill.

4. Carl is going to visit the SkiHill property to collect additional descriptive data for advertising. He wants to take the existing file, update it, and then synchronize his changes on the server. In this step, you demonstrate how offline files can be used to access information when away from the network.

    a. Log on to the client computer as the user named Carl.

    b. Open the shared ForSale folder as follows:

        ■ Click **Start**, **Run** and enter the following command. Replace *servername* with the name of the server computer. (*Note*: this cannot be your local computer.)

        servername\\ForSale

        ■ Click **OK** to open the shared folder.

    c. Right-click the **SkiHill** file, and then click **Make Available Offline**.

    d. On the Welcome to the Offline Files Wizard window, click **Next**.

    e. On your Lab 9.5 Student Answer Sheet, record the default synchronization option, and then click **Next**.

    f. The SkiHill file is now synchronized with the client computer, and you should notice an offline symbol on the SkiHill file. Describe the offline symbol on your Student Answer Sheet.

    g. Double-click the **SkiHill** file to open it with Notepad.

    h. Close all windows and log off.

5. To simulate Carl going to SkiHill, disable the local network connection of your client computer.

    a. Log on as the network administrator.

    b. Right-click **My Network Places** and click **Properties**.

    c. Right-click **Local Area Connection** and click **Disable**.

    d. Close the Network and Dial-up Connections window, and log off.

6. Perform the following procedure to simulate Carl's ability to access and update the SkiHill file while on the road:

    a. Log on to the client computer as Carl.

    b. Click **Start**, **Run** and enter the following command. Replace *servername* with the name of your server computer:
        servername\\ForSale

    c. Click **OK** to open the shared folder.

    d. Click the computer icon in the lower-right of the status bar to display the Offline Files Status window shown in Figure 9-6.

9

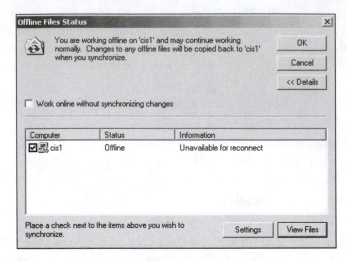

Figure 9-6 Offline Files Status window

e. Click the **View Files** button to view available offline files.

f. Close the Offline Files Folder window.

g. Close the Offline Files Status window.

h. Double-click the **SkiHill** file to open it with Notepad, and add the following line:

   Asking price: 349,000.00

i. Save the file and close Notepad.

j. Restart your computer.

7. Perform the following procedure to simulate Carl returning to the office and synchronizing his files.

a. Enable network communications as follows, to simulate plugging the notebook back into the office network:

 ■ Log on as an administrator. (Ignore the file synchronization message.)

 ■ Right-click **My Network Places** and click **Properties**.

 ■ Click **Enable**.

 ■ Close all windows and log off.

b. Log on as Carl. On your Student Answer Sheet, record the synchronization message.

c. Right-click the computer icon in the lower-right status bar, and click the **Synchronize** option.

d. Access the file from your server computer, and verify that the changes have been synchronized.

8. Working with offline files requires the user to manually select a file and configure offline access from the client computer. Another option is to enable the shared folder for automatic caching. In this step, you work on the server computer to create a shared RealEstate folder, and then enable the RealEstate folder for automatic caching.

   a. Create and share a folder named **RealEstate** on the computer you designated as the server.

   b. Create a text file named **Prices** in the RealEstate folder. Include in the Prices file an entry for the price of the SkiHill property.

   c. Open **Control Panel** and double-click **Administrative Tools**.

   d. Double-click **Computer Management** and, if necessary, expand **System Tools** by clicking the **+** symbol.

   e. If necessary, expand **Shared Folders** by clicking its **+** symbol.

   f. Click **Shares** to display all existing shared folders in the detail pane, as shown in Figure 9-7.

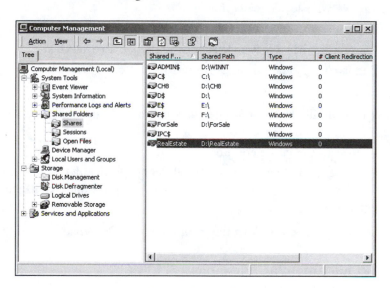

Figure 9-7   Shared folders in Computer Management window

   g. In the detail pane, right-click **RealEstate**, and then click **Properties**.

   h. Under the **General** tab of the RealEstate Properties dialog box, click the **Caching** button.

   i. On your Student Answer Sheet, list the settings available for caching.

   j. On your Student Answer Sheet, describe the Manual cache setting.

   k. In the **Settings** box of the **Caching Settings** window, click **Automatic Caching for Documents**, and then click **OK**.

    l. On your Student Answer Sheet, describe the Automatic cache option.

    m. Click **OK** to close the RealEstate Properties window.

    n. Close Computer Management.

9. Opening and closing a file in a folder set for automatic caching causes the file to be cached in the local computer. In this step, you simulate Carl accessing the Prices file before he leaves the office network.

    a. Log on to your client computer as Carl.

    b. Click **Start**, **Run** and enter the following command. Replace *servername* with the name of your server computer:
    *servername***RealEstate**

    c. Click **OK** to open the shared folder.

    d. Double-click the **Prices** file to open it with Notepad.

    e. Close the file and log off.

10. To simulate removing the client computer from the network, in this step you disable your local area connection.

    a. Log on as an administrator.

    b. Right-click **My Network Places** and click **Properties**.

    c. Right-click **Local Area Connection** and click **Disable**.

    d. Log off.

11. Now that the file has been cached, in this step you simulate Carl accessing the file from a remote location.

    a. Log on to the client computer as Carl.

    b. Click **Start**, **Run** and enter the following command. Replace *servername* with the name of your server computer: *servername***RealEstate**

    c. Click **OK** to open the shared folder.

    d. Double-click the **Prices** file to open it with Notepad, and add the following line:

    Ski hill grooming equipment: $75,000.00

    e. Save and close the Prices file, and log off.

12. To simulate reconnecting your computer to the network, in this step you enable your local area connection.

    a. Log on as an administrator.

    b. Right-click **My Network Places** and click **Properties**.

    c. Right-click **Local Area Connection** and click **Enable**.

    d. Record the synchronization message on your Student Answer Sheet.

    e. Click the Computer icon in the lower-right of the status bar. On your Student Answer Sheet, record the synchronization status.

      f. Close the status window, and record any synchronization action on your Student Answer Sheet.

      g. Close all windows and log off.

      h. Attempt to access the Prices file from the other server computer, and verify whether any changes were synchronized. Record your results on the Student Answer Sheet.

LAB 9.6 CONFIGURING INTERNET INFORMATION SERVICES

Objective

Your local Home Town Library has been assigned a permanent Internet address, and wants to set up and manage their Web site. You have volunteered to help them install and configure Internet Information Services (IIS) on a Windows 2000 Professional system in the office of Kristen Nickel. Kristen has been assigned to develop the library's Web page. Prior to installing the IIS software on the library's Windows 2000 Server, she wants to use the Windows 2000 Professional Internet Information Services on her machine to develop and test the Web page. After completing this lab, you will be able to:

➤ Install Internet Information Services on a Windows 2000 Professional system.

➤ Configure Internet Information Services.

Requirements

➤ Access to a copy of the Windows 2000 Professional CD-ROM.

➤ Optionally, another computer on the network to access your Web server.

Estimated completion time: **30 minutes**

ACTIVITY

1. If necessary, start your computer with Windows 2000, and log on as an administrator.

2. Install Internet Information Services for Windows 2000 Professional.

      a. Insert the Windows 2000 Professional CD-ROM, and click **Exit** to close the Windows 2000 CD window.

      b. Open Control Panel by clicking **Start**, **Settings**, **Control Panel**.

      c. Double-click the **Add/Remove Programs** icon. (If the Add/Remove Programs icon is disabled, follow Step 16 in Lab 6.2 to enable it.)

    d. Click the **Add/Remove Windows Components** icon to start the Windows Components Wizard.

    e. If necessary, click the **Internet Information Services (IIS)** check box, and click **Next** to start the installation. The process to copy files might take several minutes, so this may be a good time for a break.

    f. After all files have been copied, click **Finish** to close the installation wizard and return to the Add/Remove Programs window.

    g. Close the Add/Remove Programs window.

3. After Internet Information Services has been installed, you can modify Web server parameters such as the path to the Web site files, the default Web page name, and access capabilities. For example, assume Kristen wants to use Index.htm for her opening page. In this step, you document the path to the Web site files, and include Index.htm as one of the default Web page names.

    a. Start the Personal Web Manager application as follows:

       ■ Click **Start**, **Settings**, **Control Panel**.

       ■ Double-click **Administrative Tools**.

       ■ Double-click **Personal Web Manager** and read the Tip of the Day.

       ■ Record the tip on your Lab 9.6 Student Answer Sheet.

       ■ Click **Close** to exit the Tip of the Day, and display the Personal Web Manager window shown in Figure 9–8.

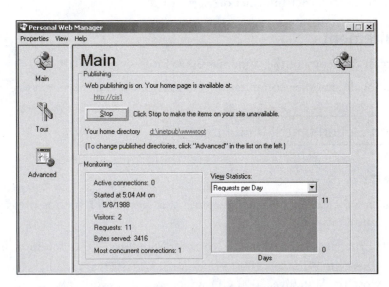

Figure 9-8 Personal Web Manager window

    b. Record the four View Statistics options on your Student Answer Sheet.

    c. On your Student Answer Sheet, document the path to the home directory.

    d. Stop the Web service by clicking the **Stop** button.

    e. Click the **Advanced** button.

    f. To allow Index.htm as a default document name, add **Index.htm** to the end of the Default document(s) text box.

    g. Click the **Main** button, and click **Start** to restart the Web server.

    h. Use the **Properties** option to exit the Personal Web Manager.

4. Now that she understands how the Web server can be configured, Kristen is ready to do some testing. To test basic Web server operation, you place an HTML file in the Library folder, and view the content of the file through Internet Explorer.

    a. Create a text file named **Index.htm** in the Web server home directory you identified in Step 3c on your Student Answer Sheet.

    b. Use Notepad to open the Index.htm text file, and insert the following HTML code:

<html>

<title>

Home Town Library

</title>

<body>

<P><img src="web.gif">

Welcome to the Home Town Library

<img src="web.gif">

</body>

</html>

    c. Save the document and exit Notepad.

    d. Test the Web page from Internet Explorer as follows:

- Start Internet Explorer, and click the **Edit** menu, **Work Offline** option.
- Click **File, Open** and enter **localhost**.
- If you receive the "Web page unavailable while offline" message, click the **Connect** button.
- Your "Welcome to the Home Town Library" page should appear.
- Close Internet Explorer.

5. A neighboring library in the town of Mikana would like the Home Town Library to host a Web page for their library as well. A Web server can host multiple Web sites by adding virtual directories. In this step, you create a folder for Mikana, and then add a virtual Web site to your Web server configuration.

9

    a. Use **My Computer** to browse to the **Inetpub** folder located on your Windows 2000 system drive.

    b. Create a folder named **Mikana** in the Inetpub folder.

    c. Copy the following files from the wwwroot folder you identified in Step 3c into the newly created Mikana folder:

- Index.htm
- Web.gif

    d. Rename the Index.htm file as **Default.htm**.

    e. Use Notepad to edit the Default.htm file, and change "Home Town Library" to **Mikana Public Library** in both the <title> and <body> sections.

    f. Save the Default.htm file, and exit Notepad.

    g. Start the Personal Web Manager, and click the **Advanced** button.

    h. To create a new virtual directory, click the **Add** button, click the **Browse** button, browse to the **Mikana** folder, and click **OK**.

    i. On your Student Answer Sheet, record the possible access permissions for this directory.

    j. On your Student Answer Sheet, record the possible application permissions for this directory.

    k. In the **Alias** text box, enter **Mikana** and click **OK** to save the virtual directory information.

    l. Click the **Main** button, and then click **Stop**.

    m. Click **Start** and then close Personal Web Manager.

6. In this step, you test the new virtual Web directory for the Mikana library.

    a. Clear the Internet Explorer cache as follows:

- Right-click **Internet Explorer** and click **Properties**.
- Click the **Delete Files** button, and click **OK** to confirm the deletion.
- Click **OK** to exit the Internet Properties window.

    b. Start Internet Explorer, and click **Edit**, **Work Offline**.

    c. Click **File**, **Open** and enter the following URL: **localhost/Mikana**.

    d. Click **Connect** to view the Welcome to Mikana Public Library page.

    e. Click **File**, **Open** and, to display your Home Town Library page, enter the following URL: **localhost**.

7. Close Internet Explorer and log off.

CHAPTER TEN

PRINTING

Labs included in this chapter

➤ Lab 10.1 Installing and Sharing Printers

➤ Lab 10.2 Configuring and Securing Shared Printers

➤ Lab 10.3 Managing Print Jobs and Printers

➤ Lab 10.4 Setting Up and Accessing Internet Printers

➤ Lab 10.5 Troubleshooting Network Printing

➤ Lab 10.6 Configuring Fax Services

Microsoft MCSE Exam #70-210 Objectives	
Objective	Lab
Connect to local and network print devices	10.1
Manage printers and print jobs	10.2, 10.3
Control access to printers by using permissions	10.2
Connect to an Internet printer	10.4
Monitor, configure, and troubleshoot I/O devices, such as printers…	10.5
Configure and troubleshoot fax support	10.6

Student Answer Sheets to accompany the labs in this chapter can be downloaded from the Online Companion for this manual at *www.course.com*.

LAB 10.1 INSTALLING AND SHARING PRINTERS

Objective

The Home Town Library is pleased with your work to help them configure Internet Information Services and set up their Web site (Lab 9.6). Now the library wants you to help them set up network printing in their Microlab and office. In addition to the HP LaserJet printer already directly attached to the Microlab network cable, they have recently obtained two color ink-jet printers for use in printing graphical information in the Microlab. Both ink-jet printers are to be attached to LPT ports on one of the Windows 2000 workstations. Rather than have users decide to which color ink-jet printer to send their output, the head librarian wants the Windows 2000 operating system to automatically balance the load between the two color ink-jet printers. Then the users have only two printer choices: laser or color ink-jet. This can be accomplished through the Windows 2000 printer pooling feature, which allows multiple (identical) print devices attached to the print server's LPT ports to share the same printer name and driver. After completing this lab, you will be able to:

➤ Install and share a local printer.

➤ Configure printer pooling to allow one network printer to manage two print devices.

➤ Install a network printer on a Windows 2000 Professional workstation.

Requirements

➤ A Windows 2000 Professional CD-ROM or other source for printer drivers.

➤ Optionally, a printer attached to your Windows 2000 Professional computer.

➤ Optionally, another Windows 2000 Professional computer to use as a client. If you are in a classroom lab environment, you can team up with a partner when installing the networked printer.

Estimated completion time: **20–30 minutes**

ACTIVITY

1. Fill out the Lab 10.1 Printer Planning Worksheet that follows this Activity. Include each printer to be used in your networked printer environment. If you have a physical printer device attached to your computer, use that printer device to simulate one of the color ink-jet printers in the lab scenario.

2. If necessary, start your computer with Windows 2000, and log on as an administrator.

3. In this step, you simulate setting up the Windows 2000 computer that will share the two ink-jet printers. If you have a printer attached to your computer, use that printer and associated printer driver to simulate one of the color ink-jet printers. Follow the steps below to create and share a local printer on the LPT1 port.

   a. Click **Start**, **Settings**, **Printers** to open the Printers window.

   b. Double-click the **Add printer** icon, and click **Next** to start the Add Printer Wizard.

   c. Verify that the **Local printer** option button is selected, and if necessary, click to remove the check mark from **Automatically detect and install my Plug and Play Printer** check box. Click **Next** to display the Select Printer Port window.

   d. List the available printer port options on your Lab 10.1 Student Answer Sheet.

   e. Select **LPT1: Printer Port** and click **Next**.

   f. Select the correct printer manufacturer and model identified on your Lab 10.1 Printer Planning Worksheet for this printer, and click **Next**.

   g. Enter the Printer name you specified on your Lab 10.1 Printer Planning Worksheet for this printer.

   h. Click **No** to the default printer question.

   i. Click **Next** to display the Printer Sharing window.

   j. Click the **Share as** option button, and record the default name of the printer on your Student Answer Sheet.

   k. Enter the printer name you specified on your Lab 10.1 Printer Planning Worksheet, click **Next**, and record the warning message on your Student Answer Sheet.

   l. If you changed the default shared name, click **Yes** to use the new shared name.

   m. In the Location and Comment window, enter the printer location and comment information you specified on your Lab 10.1 Printer Planning Worksheet, and click **Next**.

   n. If you have a print device attached to your LPT1 port, click **Yes** to print a test page. If you do not have a print device attached to your computer, click **No**.

   o. Click **Next** to view the printer summary information. Verify that the printer information matches what you specified on your Lab 10.1 Printer Planning Worksheet.

   p. Click **Finish** to add the printer to the Printers window. If you selected the option to print a test page, after the test page prints click **OK** to continue.

10

4. Configure Printer Pooling to allow the printer attached to the LPT2 port to use the same logical printer as the one you just created.

   a. Right-click the printer you created in Step 3, and click **Properties**.

   b. Click the **Ports** tab to display the window shown in Figure 10-1.

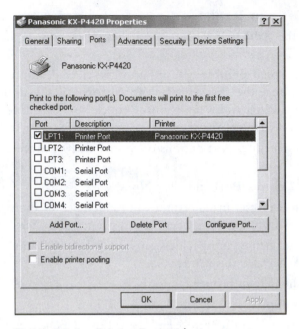

Figure 10-1   Printer Ports tab

   c. Try clicking the port number you specified for the second ink-jet printer, and observe the results.

   d. Click port **LPT1** to reestablish it as the selected printer port.

   e. Click the **Enable printer pooling** check box.

   f. Click the port number you specified for the second ink-jet printer on your Lab 10.1 Printer Planning Worksheet.

   g. On your Student Answer Sheet, record what happens differently when you click this port, as compared to Step 4c.

   h. Click **OK** to save the printer pooling configuration.

   i. On your Student Answer Sheet, briefly describe how enabling printer pooling will make sending output to the ink-jet printers easier for the Microlab users.

5. Install a network printer on the client computer. (*Note*: If you do not have another partner or computer to work with, you can install the network printer on the same computer as your print server.)

a. If necessary, start the client computer, and log on as administrator. (If working with a lab partner, obtain a copy of their Lab 10.1 Printer Planning Worksheet, and simply use your computer as the client to their shared printer.)

b. If necessary, click **Start**, **Settings**, **Printers** to open the Printers window.

c. Double-click **Add printer** and click **Next** to start the Add Printer Wizard.

d. Click the **Network printer** option button, and click **Next** to display the Locate Your Printer window.

e. Enter the shared printer name as shown below, replacing *printserver* with the computer identified as the print server computer, and replacing *printer* with the shared name of the printer, as identified on the Printer Planning Worksheet.

   *printserver**printer*

   (If you do not know the shared name of the network printer, you can click the **Next** button, navigate to the shared printer, click to select it, and click **Next**.)

f. Click the **No** option button to the ...use this printer as the default printer? question, and click **Next** to display the summary window.

g. Verify that the location and comment information specified on the Lab 10.1 Printer Planning Worksheet is correct, and click **Finish** to add the network printer to your Printers window. (*Note*: If you are adding the network printer to the print server computer, no additional printer icon is shown, because the computer recognizes the network printer as being the same printer as the existing printer icon.)

h. On your Student Answer Sheet, describe the difference between the local and network printer icons.

i. Close all windows.

6. Test the network printer.

   a. Start **WordPad**.

   b. Create a sample document describing the difference between the local and network printer icons.

   c. Click the **File**, **Print** option, and then click the network printer icon. Record the Status, Location, and Comments information on your Student Answer Sheet.

   d. Click the **Print** button.

   e. If you have no printer attached to the print server computer, record the error message you receive on your Student Answer Sheet, and click **Cancel**.

10

f. Pause the print server printer by right-clicking the shared printer, and then clicking the **Pause Printing** option.

g. On the client computer, repeat Steps 6c and 6d, and record the results on your Student Answer Sheet.

h. On the print server computer, double-click your shared printer.

i. Click the document and then click the **Document** menu, **Properties** option.

j. Click the **Properties** button, and record the Owner, Pages, Priority, and Submitted information on your Student Answer Sheet.

k. Click **Cancel** to return to the printer window.

l. Right-click the document, and click the **Cancel** option to remove it from the printer window.

m. Close the printer windows and log off.

Lab 10.1 Installing and Sharing Printers
Printer Planning Worksheet

Name: _____   Computer ID: _____

Print Server ID	Printer Name/ Shared Name	Print Driver	Location	Pooled Y or N	Print Device Make/Model	Port

Note: For pooled printers, include Print Device, Port, and Location information for each printer.

10

LAB 10.2 CONFIGURING AND SECURING SHARED PRINTERS

Objective

Windows 2000 allows you to create multiple logical printers that share the same print device. In this lab, you create multiple logical printers to meet the office needs of the Home Town Library. Because their new Lexmark laser printer can operate in either Postscript or standard PCL modes, users should be able to select the appropriate mode as if it were a separate printer.

The laser printer will be attached to Kristen Nickel's Windows 2000 Professional system, and her computer will act as the print server. Although Kristen will be the operator, three other office staffers, including the head librarian, will be accessing the printer. In addition, the head librarian some-times needs to print a rush job, and therefore should be able to submit jobs with a high priority. This can be accomplished by creating a separate logical printer for the Lexmark laser that has a higher priority, and is available only to the head librarian.

The library also wants to be able to print large jobs after hours so they do not conflict with other printing needs. This can be accomplished by creating another logical printer for the Lexmark laser whose jobs print only during a specified time. Because the Microlab and office networks are linked together, it is important to ensure that only users on the office network, not the Microlab users, can send output to the Lexmark laser printer. After completing this lab, you will be able to:

➤ Install and share the office laser print device as multiple logical printers with different print configurations, priorities, and times.

➤ Secure printers for special user access.

➤ Use separator pages when switching a printer between Postscript and PCL modes.

Requirements

➤ A Windows 2000 Professional system which may optionally include an attached printer for testing.

➤ A Windows 2000 CD-ROM or other source for the printer drivers.

Estimated completion time: **20–25 minutes**

ACTIVITY

1. Fill out the Lab 10.2 Printer Planning Worksheet that follows this Activity for each of the following logical printers. If you have another print device that is capable of using both PCL and Postscript languages, you may use it rather than the Lexmark Optra Plus printer identified below. If the print device attached to your computer does not support PCL/Postscript printing, garbled output might result when the PCL or Postscript header page is printed.

   - Lexmark Optra Plus printer using the PCL language, available to all office staff.

   - Lexmark Optra Plus PS printer using the Postscript language, available to all office staff.

   - A high-priority Lexmark Optra Plus printer using PCL language, available only to the head librarian.

   - A Lexmark Optra Plus Postscript printer to be used for printing large jobs during off hours.

2. If necessary, start your computer with Windows 2000, and log on as an administrator.

3. Rather than provide individual users with permissions to use a printer, Microsoft recommends you give the permissions to a group, and then make the users who need to access the printer members of that group. In this step, you create any users or groups you identified on your Lab 10.2 Printer Planning Worksheet (if necessary, review Lab 5.1 on how to create users and groups). Record the user names and passwords, and group names on the Lab 10.2 Student Answer Sheet.

4. Create and share the Lexmark Optra Plus (PCL) printer as a logical printer.

   a. Open the printer window by clicking **Start**, **Settings**, **Printers**.

   b. Double-click **Add Printer** and click **Next** to start the Add Printer Wizard.

   c. Verify that **Local printer** is selected, and that there is no check mark in the **Automatically detect and Install my Plug and Play Printer** check box. Click **Next**.

   d. Click the **LPT1** port, and click **Next**.

   e. Select **Lexmark Optra Plus PS** and click **Next**.

   f. Enter the name you specified for this printer on your Lab 10.2 Printer Planning Worksheet, and click **Next**.

   g. Click the **Share as** option button, enter the shared printer name from the Printer Planning Worksheet, and click **Next**.

10

h. Enter the Location and Comments specified on your Lab 10.2 Printer Planning Worksheet, and click **Next**.

i. Click **No** to prevent printing a test page, and click **Next**.

j. Verify the summary information, and click **Finish** to add the printer to the Printers window. If requested, insert your Windows 2000 Professional CD-ROM.

k. With printers that support both PCL and Postscript languages, separator page files located in the WINNT\SYSTEM32 folder can be used to select the printer language to be used to print a specific job. This saves the operator from having to manually select the language prior to printing the job. Now, to create a separator page that specifies output from a PCL printer, right-click the newly created printer, and click **Properties**.

l. Click the **Advanced** tab to display the window shown in Figure 10-2.

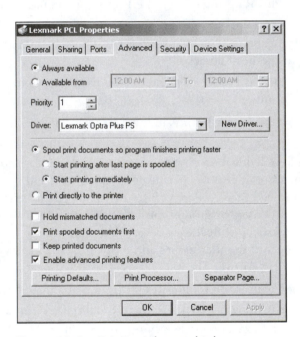

Figure 10-2   Printer Advanced tab

m. Click the **Separator Page** button, and click **Browse**.

n. On your Student Answer Sheet, record the separator page options (files ending with the .sep extension).

o. Double-click the **pcl.sep** file to send the commands to automatically switch the printer into PCL mode.

p. Click **OK** to save the separator page selection.

q. To set security options, click the **Security** tab.

r. Use the **Advanced** button, and, on your Student Answer Sheet, record the rights given to the creator/owner, which documents these rights apply to, and any differences between the rights of Administrators and Power Users.

s. Click **Cancel** to return to the Security tab.

t. Remove **Everyone** as a user of the printer.

u. Add the users and groups that you identified on your Lab 10.2 Printer Planning Worksheet as having rights to use this printer.

v. Click **OK** to save your security changes.

5. Create the Lexmark Optra plus (Postscipt) logical printer.

a. Follow Steps 4b through 4j to create the Lexmark Postscript printer. On the Use Existing Driver window, select the option to **Keep existing driver**.

b. Right-click the newly created printer, and click **Properties**.

c. Click the **Advanced** tab.

d. Click the **Separator Page** button, and click **Browse**.

e. Double-click the **pscript.sep** file to send the commands to automatically switch the printer into Postscript mode.

f. Click **OK** to save the separator page selection.

g. Click the **Security** tab.

h. Remove **Everyone** as a user of the printer.

i. Add the users and groups you identified on your Lab 10.2 Printer Planning Worksheet as having rights to use this printer.

j. Click **OK** to save your security changes.

6. Create the high-priority logical printer for the head librarian.

a. Follow Steps 4b through 4j to create the Lexmark Postscript printer you identified on your Lab 10.2 Printer Planning Worksheet. On the Use Existing Driver window, select the option to **Keep existing driver**.

b. Right-click the newly created printer, and click **Properties**.

c. Click the **Advanced** tab.

d. Change the Priority to **5**.

e. Click the **Separator Page** button, browse to the language specified on your Printer Planning Worksheet, and click **OK**.

f. Click the **Security** tab.

g. Remove **Everyone** as a user of the printer, and add the users and groups you identified on your Printer Planning Worksheet.

h. Click **OK** to save your security changes.

7. Create a NightPrinter logical printer.

a. Follow Steps 4b through 4j to create the NightPrinter printer.

b. Right-click the newly created printer, and click **Properties**.

10

c. Click the **Advanced** tab.

d. Click the **Available from** option button, and enter a duration that starts approximately 10 minutes from now and ends approximately 15 minutes from now. (If you were actually setting up the printer for evening printing, you would specify evening hours.)

e. Click the **Separator Page** button, and select the separator page for the language specified on your Printer Planning Worksheet.

f. Click the **Security** tab.

g. Remove **Everyone** as a user of the printer.

h. Add the users and groups you identified on your Printer Planning Worksheet.

i. Click **OK** to save your security changes.

8. Create network printers on the client computer. If you are working with a lab partner, you need to wait for your partner to reach this step, and then you must swap computers.

a. If necessary, create users on the client computer that match the user-names and passwords on your print server computer.

b. Add the following network printers to your client:

■ Lexmark PCL printer

■ NightPrinter

9. Part of checking out your network printing environment in this lab involves viewing the status of print jobs, and verifying that the night printer does not print until the specified time. To do so, in this step you will pause any printer except the NightPrinter by repeating the following procedure. (*Note:* You will not pause the NightPrinter to verify that the jobs do not start printing until the scheduled time.)

a. If necessary, open the **Printers** window.

b. Right-click all printers except the NightPrinter, and click **Pause**.

10. Test the printing configuration by sending output from the client to each printer.

11. From the print server computer, check the printers and verify print job status.

a. If necessary, wait for your lab partner to reach this step, and then swap back to your print server computer.

b. On the print server computer, open the Printers window by clicking **Start**, **Settings**, **Printers**.

c. Double-click the **Lexmark PCL** printer, and record the job contents on your Student Answer Sheet.

d. Double-click the **NightPrinter**, and record the properties of the print job on your Student Answer Sheet.

e. Wait for the time specified for the NightPrinter, and on your Student Answer Sheet, record the results you observe when the printer time occurs.

f. Close all windows and log off.

Lab 10.2 Configuring and Securing Shared Printers
Printer Planning Worksheet

Name: _____   Computer ID: _____

Print Server ID	Printer Name/ Shared Name	Driver	Port	Location	Language	Priority	Pool Y/ N	Print Device Make/Model	Printer Group	Operators

In the Printer Group column, identify the name of the group to be given access to this printer. Fill in a Users and Group Planning form (see Chapter 5) to define the members of the group.

10

LAB 10.3 MANAGING PRINT JOBS AND PRINTERS

Objective

The head librarian wants you to write some instructions for the users of the Microlab and office printers. The instructions should note how to perform certain printer management tasks such as pausing and restarting the printer, and holding or canceling print jobs. In addition, because the office laser and Microlab laser printer are the same model, in the event the office printer is down, the printer operators should have information on how to transfer output to the Microlab laser printer. After completing this lab, you will be able to document how to:

➤ Pause and restart the printer.

➤ View print jobs and printer statistics.

➤ Cancel and hold print jobs.

➤ Rearrange print-job sequence, and change priorities.

➤ Redirect output from one printer to another.

Requirements

➤ A lab partner with another Windows 2000 Professional computer, to use for redirecting output from one printer to another.

Estimated completion time: **20 minutes**

ACTIVITY

1. If necessary, start your computer with Windows 2000, and log on as an administrator.

2. Use WordPad or another word-processing application, and design a Printer Procedure form to be used to document the following printing procedures:

   ■ Pause and resume printing.

   ■ Check print-job size and status.

   ■ Change print-job priority.

   ■ Cancel a print job.

   ■ Redirect output from one printer to another.

3. When clearing a paper jam or changing paper or ink cartridges, operators should first pause the printer. After the task has been completed, the printer should be restarted. Follow the steps below to use the Windows 2000 Help

information to find the procedure operators should use to pause and resume printing.

    a. Click **Start, Help** to open the Windows 2000 Help window.

    b. Click the **Search** tab. In the Type in the keyword to find: text box, enter **pause**, and click the **List Topics** button.

    c. Double-click the **Pause or resume printing of a document** topic.

    d. Document the process on the Printer Procedure form you created in Step 1.

    e. Test your procedure for pausing and resuming printing to verify that it works as described.

4. Users might want to check the printer status before sending output. Double-click the **View documents waiting to print** topic from the Windows 2000 Help information window. Use the Printer Procedure form you created in Step 1 to document the process for checking printer status. Test your procedure for viewing the status of documents waiting to print, and verify that it works as described.

5. A user whose print job is waiting in the print queue might want to know the size of the preceding jobs. Double-click the **Print queue overview** topic from the Windows 2000 Help information window. Use the Printer Procedure form you created in Step 1 to document the process you use to view information on the current print queue. Test your procedure to verify that it works as written.

6. When you are finished documenting and testing the procedures in Steps 2 through 5, close the Windows 2000 Help window.

7. If someone on the office staff needs to quickly print a job on the Microlab ink-jet printer, but there are several jobs in the print queue, the print operator could get the rush job to print next. The staff member does this by changing the print priority of the rush document to be greater than that of the other documents. In this step, you send two jobs to the printer, and then change the second job's priority. Document the procedure you use on your Printer Procedure form.

    a. If you have a print device attached to your workstation, pause that local printer. If you do not have print device on your workstation, pause the **Lexmark PCL** printer.

    b. Start **WordPad**, and create a document that contains a line that reads **Created first.**

    c. If you have a print device attached to your workstation, print this document to that printer. If you do not have a print device on your workstation, print the document to the Lexmark PCL printer.

    d. Modify the document to read **Created last.**

10

   e. If you have a print device attached to your workstation, print this document to that printer. If you do not have a print device on your workstation, print the document to the Lexmark PCL printer.

   f. Exit WordPad without saving the document.

   g. Open the **Printers** window, and double-click the printer you used.

   h. Double-click the second document, and change its priority to **5**.

   i. Close the printer document list window.

   j. If you have a print device attached to your workstation, restart that printer.

   k. Document the procedure for changing print priority of a document on your Printer Procedure form.

8. Sometimes a user might send the wrong information or document to the printer, and realize it before the output is printed. Use the Windows 2000 Help information to document on your Printer Procedure form how to pause and cancel a specific print job. Test your procedure for pausing and canceling a document to verify that it works as described.

9. The head librarian wants to be able to redirect output from the library's office Lexmark laser to the Microlab Lexmark laser in the event the office laser is down. In this step, you practice this process by redirecting output from your Lexmark PCL printer to your lab partner's Lexmark PCL printer.

   a. On your Student Answer Sheet, record your partner's Lexmark PCL printer name, along with a name of a user and password you can use to attach to their computer.

   b. Create a connection to your lab partner's computer as follows:

   ■ Click **Start**, **Run** and enter *printserver* where *printserver* represents the name of your lab partner's computer.

   ■ If you see an Enter Network Password dialog box, enter the user name and password provided by your partner.

   ■ Close all windows.

   c. Open the Printers window by clicking **Start**, **Settings**, **Printers**.

   d. Pause your **Lexmark PCL** printer.

   e. Right-click your **Lexmark PCL** printer, and click **Properties**.

   f. Click the **Ports** tab, and then click **Add Port**.

   g. Click the **New Port** button, and enter the UNC name of your partner's printer as follows: *printserver**printer* where *printserver* represents the name of your partner's computer, and *printer* represents the name of their Lexmark PCL printer.

   h. Click **OK** to create the connection.

      i. Click **Close** and verify that the new printer connection is selected as the port for your Lexmark PCL laser printer.

      j. Close the Printer Properties window.

      k. Start WordPad, and print a job to your Lexmark PCL printer.

      l. From your partner's print server, verify that the job is placed in their printer.

      m. Document the procedure for redirecting output of a document on your Printer Procedure form.

10. Close all windows and log off.

LAB 10.4 SETTING UP AND ACCESSING INTERNET PRINTERS

Objective

The Elder Services department at the Maple County Courthouse wants their social workers to be able to print client status reports at the office, whether the social workers are at home or on the road. Mary is one of the social workers who spends a lot of time out of the office. Being able to print to the office's laser printer over the Internet would save her a lot of time. You recently installed a Web server on the office manager's Windows 2000 Professional workstation, and now you plan to use the Internet Printing Protocol (IPP) to allow Mary to access the Internet to send output to the office laser printer. After completing this lab, you will be able to:

➤ Install and download printer drivers using the Internet Printing Protocol.

➤ Send output over the Internet to a printer attached to a computer running Windows 2000 Professional Peer Web Services.

Requirements

➤ Installation of Peer Web Services on your Windows 2000 Professional computer, as described in Lab 9.6.

➤ Another Windows 2000 computer with Internet Explorer 4 or later installed. If working in a lab environment, you can work with a partner to access a printer on their Windows 2000 Professional system.

➤ IP address of the print server computer: _____._____._____._____

10

Estimated completion time: **15 minutes**

ACTIVITY

1. If necessary, start your computer with Windows 2000, and log on as an administrator.

2. Create a restricted user named **Mary**. On your Lab 10.4 Student Answer Sheet, record the username and password for Mary.

3. Create and share a Lexmark Optra Plus PS printer named **MapleCoPr**. (If necessary, review Lab 10.1, Step 3, on creating and sharing a local printer.) Verify that Mary has rights to use the printer.

4. Use the procedure you documented in Lab 10.3 to pause the **MapleCoPr** printer.

5. Use your intranet to connect to the shared MapleCoPr from a client computer. If you are working in a classroom lab, coordinate this step with your lab partner by connecting to their shared MapleCoPr printer.

    a. Open the Printer window by clicking **Start**, **Settings**, **Printers**.

    b. Double-click **Add Printers**, and click **Next** to start the Add Printer Wizard.

    c. If necessary, click the **Network printer** option button, and click **Next**.

    d. Click the **Connect to a printer on the Internet or on your intranet** option button.

    e. Enter the URL for the intranet printer as follows: ***http://ip_address/printers/MapleCoPr/.printer*** where *ip_address* represents the IP address of the server containing the shared MapleCoPr. Record the URL you enter on your Student Answer Sheet.

    f. Click **Next** to display the Enter Network Password window.

    g. Enter Mary's username and password from Step 2, and click **OK**.

    h. Complete the printer installation, and on your Student Answer Sheet, record the remaining steps. Click **No** when asked if you want to print a test page.

6. Send output to the MapleCoPr intranet printer.

    a. Start **WordPad**.

    b. Create a document named **InternetPrint** that contains your name along with the following line:

       This is a test of Mary's Internet printing.

    c. Click **File**, **Print**, and click the **MapleCoPr** printer in the Select Printer window.

    d. Click **OK**.

    e. From the print server computer, open the **Printers** window, and double-click the **MapleCoPr** printer. Verify that the InternetPrint document is in the print job window.

    f. Close all windows.

7. Use Internet Explorer to manage Internet printers.

    a. Start **Internet Explorer** and enter the following URL: **http://*ip_address*/printers** where *ip_address* is the IP address of the print server computer.

    b. Enter the administrator name and password, and click **OK** to display an All Printers window similar to the one shown in Figure 10-3.

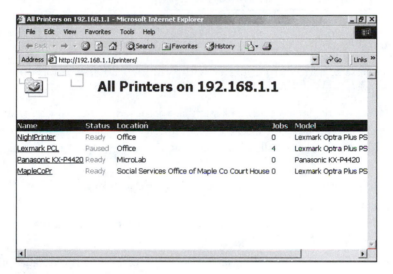

Figure 10-3   Internet All Printers window

    c. Click the **MapleCoPr printer,** and on your Student Answer Sheet, record the Printer and Document actions available.

    d. Close all windows and log off.

LAB 10.5 TROUBLESHOOTING NETWORK PRINTING

Objective

Setting up and managing network printing often involves identifying and fixing problems. There are several techniques that you can use to help you identify and correct common network printing problems. After completing this lab, you will be able to use the following troubleshooting techniques to help resolve network printing problems:

➤ Check for stalled print jobs.

➤ Verify that the printer is online (a device setting).

➤ Terminate and reshare the printer on the print server.

➤ Re-create the network printer on the client.

➤ Reinstall the print driver.

➤ Stop and restart the print spooler.

Estimated completion time: **15 minutes**

ACTIVITY

1. If necessary, start your computer with Windows 2000, and log on as an administrator.

2. Physical print device problems such as a jammed printer, loose cable, or defective print device can cause a document to become stalled in the printer. Perform the following process to simulate creating a stalled document condition.

   a. Identify a shared printer on either your computer or your partner's computer.

   b. If the printer is attached to your print server computer, disconnect the printer cable from the printer.

   c. On the client computer, set the selected printer as the default printer, as follows:

      ■ Open the Printers window.

      ■ Right-click the network printer, and click the **Set as Default Printer** option.

   d. Start **WordPad** from the client computer, create a document, and enter the following text: **This is a test of a stalled document.**

   e. Print the document to the default printer.

   f. On the print server, double-click the selected printer, and cancel all documents:

      ■ Click the **Printer** option from the menu bar.

      ■ Click the **Cancel All Documents** option, and click **Yes** to confirm.

   g. Pause the document being deleted by right-clicking the document, and clicking **Pause**.

h. If you have a print device connected to your print server, disconnect and then reconnect the printer cable, and turn the printer on.

i. From the client computer, print another copy of the document.

j. From the print server computer, view the document list, and on your Lab 10.5 Student Answer Sheet, record your observations.

3. To free the stalled document, perform the following tasks to restart the document.

a. Fix the printer problem (in this case, make sure the cable is reconnected), and then restart the document by right-clicking it and clicking the **Restart** option. Record the results on your Student Answer Sheet.

b. Attempt to delete the stalled document by right-clicking it, and clicking **Cancel**.

c. Resume printing by right-clicking the document, and clicking the **Resume** option.

4. When output from client computers or the local print server does not print, the problem might be that the printer is set for offline printing, as demonstrated by the following procedure.

a. Open the **Printers** window on the print server computer.

b. Right-click the shared printer, and click **Use Printer Offline**.

c. From the client computer, print a document to the shared printer.

d. On the print server computer, click the shared printer, and record the status on your Student Answer Sheet.

e. Double-click the shared printer, and verify that the document is in the print queue.

f. Click the **Printer** option from the menu bar, and click **Use Printer Offline** to remove the check mark. Record the results on your Student Answer Sheet.

5. The print driver on the client computer might become corrupt or damaged. A corrupt network print driver can be fixed by reinstalling the print driver or network printer on the client computer. In this step, you work from the client computer to reinstall the print driver, and then delete and reinstall the network printer.

a. Right-click the network printer, and click **Properties**.

b. Click the **Advanced** tab to display the window shown previously in Figure 10-2.

c. Click the **New Driver** button, and click **Next** to start the New Driver wizard.

d. Select the printer manufacturer and model, and click **Next**.

10

e. Click **Finish,** and if necessary, insert the Windows 2000 Professional CD-ROM and click **OK**.

f. To delete the network printer, right-click the printer, and click the **Delete** option.

g. Click **Yes** to confirm the deletion.

h. You can now reinstall the network printer by referring back to Lab 10.1, and following Step 3.

6. If multiple client computers are having problems printing, the print spooling service on the print server might be malfunctioning. This type of problem often can be fixed by stopping and then restarting the print spooler, as demonstrated by performing the following procedure.

a. Stop the print spooler service:

- Open **Control Panel**.
- Double-click **Administrative Tools**.
- Double-click **Services** to display a window of services existing on your print server computer.
- Scroll down until you find the Print Spooler service.
- Right-click the **Print Spooler** service, and click **Stop**.

b. Print a document to the shared printer from the client, and on your Student Answer Sheet, record the message you receive.

c. Start the Print Spooler service by right-clicking the **Print Spooler** service and clicking **Start**.

d. Print a document from the client, and record your results on your Student Answer Sheet.

7. If restarting the print spooler service does not fix the problem, you might need to delete the shared printer and reinstall it. This process can be time-consuming because the client computers also might need to reinstall the network printers associated with the shared printer. In this step, you delete the shared printer from your print server, and then reinstall it.

a. Click **Start, Settings, Printers** to open the Printers window.

b. Right-click the shared printer to be deleted, and click **Properties**.

c. On your Student Answer Sheet, record the name and driver information about the printer to be deleted.

d. Click **Cancel** to close the Properties window.

e. Right-click the printer, and click **Delete** to delete the shared printer from your print server.

f. Attempt to print from the client. Record the result on your Student Answer Sheet.

g. Install a new printer using the same name and driver.

    h. Attempt to print to the network printer from the client. Record the results on your Student Answer Sheet.

    i. If necessary, delete and reinstall the network printer on the client computer.

    j. Close all windows, and log off both computers.

LAB 10.6 CONFIGURING FAX SERVICES

Objective

The fax capability of Windows 2000 Professional can be very useful for small offices or home users who occasionally need to send and receive faxes. For example, assume you work at home and need to submit an expense report to your manager at Computer Technology Services for some equipment you recently received. Unfortunately, you cannot seem to find the invoice, so you call the vendor who agrees to fax you a copy of the sale information. After completing this lab, you will be able to:

➤ Configure your Windows 2000 Professional computer to receive a fax through your modem.

10

Requirements

➤ This lab requires a fax-enabled modem to be installed on your computer. If student computers do not have fax-enabled modems available, the instructor may choose to demonstrate this lab to the class.

Estimated completion time: **15 minutes**

ACTIVITY

1. If necessary, start your computer with Windows 2000, and log on as an administrator.

2. Create a shared folder named **Faxes** off the root of your Windows 2000 system drive.

3. Open the Control panel by clicking **Start**, **Settings**, **Control Panel**.

4. Double-click the **Fax** icon, and enter your username and fax number in the User Information window.

5. Click the **Advanced Options** tab, and on your Lab 10.6 Student Answer Sheet, record the available option buttons.

6. Click the **Open Fax Service Management Console** button to display the Fax Service Management window.

7. In the Tree pane, click the **Devices** object to display your fax modem in the right-side Device pane.

8. Right-click your fax modem, and click **Properties** to display the Properties window shown in Figure 10-4.

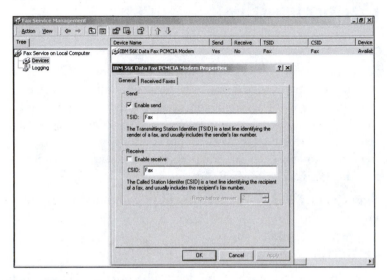

Figure 10-4 Fax Modem Properties window

9. Click the **Enable receive** check box, and set the Rings before answer to **1**.

10. Click the **Received Faxes** tab, and record the options on your Student Answer Sheet.

11. Click the **...** button, and browse to the **Faxes** folder you created in Step 2.

12. Click **OK** to save your settings.

13. Close the Fax Service Management window.

14. Close all windows and log off.

CHAPTER 11

PERFORMANCE TUNING

Labs included in this chapter

➤ Lab 11.1 Working with Task Monitor

➤ Lab 11.2 Establishing a Baseline with Performance Monitor

➤ Lab 11.3 Recognizing Memory Bottlenecks

➤ Lab 11.4 Recognizing Processor Bottlenecks

➤ Lab 11.5 Recognizing Disk Bottlenecks

➤ Lab 11.6 Using Event Viewer

Microsoft MCSE Exam #70-210 Objectives	
Objective	Lab
Optimize and troubleshoot performance of the Windows 2000 Professional desktop	
Optimize and troubleshoot memory performance	11.1, 11.2, 11.3
Optimize and troubleshoot processor performance	11.1, 11.2, 11.4
Optimize and troubleshoot disk performance	11.2, 11.5
Optimize and troubleshoot processor utilization	11.2
Optimize and troubleshoot network performance	11.2
Install, configure, and troubleshoot network adapters	11.6
Implement, configure, manage, and troubleshoot auditing	11.6

 Student Answer Sheets to accompany the labs in this chapter can be downloaded from the Online Companion for this manual at *www.course.com*.

LAB 11.1 WORKING WITH TASK MONITOR

Objective

Dennis Geisler from the Animal Care Center recently called and reported that the Windows 2000 Professional computer they are using to share their folders and printers seems to be running slower. Dennis explained that the problem seems to get worse later in the day, almost as if the machine is getting tired. When you ask if they have changed anything recently, Dennis reports that they added a few new applications, including a client/server system that has a program that loads on the server when it starts. Also, the program he occasionally uses to help diagnose animal health problems seems to slow down the system. Dennis wants you to see if you can do anything to speed up the system. After completing this lab, you will be able to:

➤ Use Task Manager to view currently running applications.

➤ Use Task Manager to see which processes are using the most system resources.

➤ Use Task Manager to terminate a process.

➤ Use Task Manager to observe processor and memory utilization.

Requirements

➤ Access to performance utilities found on the Windows 2000 Professional Resource Kit (you installed the Resource Kit in Lab 2.2).

➤ A copy of the cpustres.exe and leakyapp.exe files from the Windows 2000 Professional Resource Kit. Copy the files from either the kit, or another location specified by your instructor to a folder on your Windows 2000 system drive. Rename them as follows:

■ If necessary, create a folder named **Apps** on your Windows 2000 system drive.

■ Use My Computer or Windows Explorer to open a window to the Resource Pro Kit\Program Files folder.

■ Copy the following files to the Apps folder: **cpustres.exe** and **leakyapp.exe**.

■ Rename cpustres.exe to **diagmon.exe**.

■ Rename leakyapp.exe to **datamgr.exe**.

Estimated completion time: **20 minutes**

ACTIVITY

1. If necessary, start your computer with Windows 2000, and log on as an administrator.

2. To check the processor utilization of the animal diagnosis software that Dennis runs:

   a. Use My Computer or Windows Explorer to open a window to your Apps folder. Simulate starting the diagnostic software by double-clicking the **diagmon.exe** application from the Apps folder.

   b. Start Task Manager by pressing **Ctrl+Alt+Del** and clicking the **Windows Task Manager** button.

   c. Click the **Performance** tab to display a Performance window similar to the one shown in Figure 11-1.

11

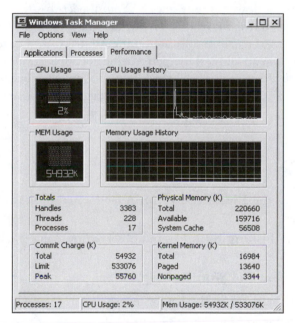

Figure 11-1   Task Manager Performance tab

   d. Record the CPU Usage range on your Lab 11.1 Student Answer Sheet. This CPU Usage range is for one low-activity thread, the Diagmon.exe application.

   e. Change the Diagmon.exe application to a busy thread by clicking **CPU Stress** from the Windows 2000 status bar, and then change Thread 1 activity to **Busy**.

f. Switch to Task Manager by clicking **Windows Task Manager** from the Windows 2000 status bar, and then record the CPU Usage range on your Student Answer Sheet.

g. To simulate using the Diagmon application, continue to activate all threads at **medium** activity until CPU Usage regularly exceeds 80%. On your Student Answer Sheet, record the number of medium active threads it takes to bring your CPU Usage to above 80%.

h. Click the **Processes** tab. Determine which process is using the most CPU time by clicking the **CPU** column heading to sort the process list by CPU time. On your Student Answer Sheet, record the application using the most CPU time.

i. On your Student Answer Sheet, briefly describe ways that Dennis could improve the performance of his computer when he runs the Diagmon.exe software.

j. Close the Diagmon.exe software.

3. Dennis explained that even when he's not running the Diagmon software, the system seems to get slower as time goes by. You suspect that the client/server database software might be overloading the system. To test the effect of the client/server database software on the Animal Care Center computer, you want to run and test the performance of applications before and after starting the client/server database. Use the following process to test the computer's performance before the client/server database is loaded.

a. Start the following applications from the Start, Programs, Accessories menu:

- WordPad
- Paint

b. From Paint, open the **Blue Lace 16.bmp** file located in the WINNT folder.

c. Open the **Gone Fishing.bmp** file, and observe how long it takes to load the file.

d. Minimize the **Paint** and **WordPad** applications.

4. Start the simulated client/server database software.

a. Use My Computer to browse to the **Apps** folder.

b. From the Apps folder, double-click **datamgr.exe** to simulate Dennis running the database server software.

c. To simulate a faulty program that continues to use up system memory, in the My Leaky App window, click the **Start Leaking** button.

5. Check the system performance with datamgr.exe running.

   a. Activate **Paint** and load the **Blue Lace 16.bmp** graphic file. On your Student Answer Sheet, record any observations regarding the current speed of loading the file, as compared to Step 4.

6. To find out what is slowing down the system, start Task Manager by pressing the **Ctrl+Alt+Del** key sequence, and clicking the **Windows Task Manager** button. Then do the following:

   a. Click the **Applications** tab, and record the applications and their status on your Student Answer Sheet.

   b. Click the **Performance** tab, and record the CPU Usage range on your Student Answer Sheet. Is this usage range causing the performance problem? Note your response on your Student Answer Sheet.

   c. Click the **Processes** tab, and record the names of the column headings on your Student Answer Sheet.

   d. On your Student Answer Sheet, record the application that is using the most memory.

   e. Add Handle Count columns to the Processes display:

      ■ Click the **Select Columns** option from the View menu.

      ■ Click the **Handle Count** check box.

      ■ Click **OK** to add the selected columns to the Processes tab.

   f. On your Student Answer Sheet, record the process that has the most Handles open.

7. Determine the number of page faults required to open the **Gone Fishing.bmp** file using the Paint application.

   a. Close the Paint application.

   b. Add Page Faults and Virtual Memory Size columns to the Processes display:

      ■ If necessary, click the **Processes** tab.

      ■ Click the **Select Columns** option from the View menu.

      ■ Click the **Page Faults** check box.

      ■ Click the **Virtual Memory Size** check box.

      ■ Click **OK** to add the selected columns to the Processes tab.

   c. Start the **Paint** application.

   d. On your Student Answer Sheet, record the number of page faults for the **mspaint.exe** process.

   e. Open the **Gone Fishing.bmp** graphic.

   f. Switch to the **Windows Task Manager** window.

11

      g. On your Student Answer Sheet, calculate the number of page faults required by MSPAINT to load the Gone Fishing.bmp graphic by subtracting the Initial number of page faults from the number of page faults after loading Gone Fishing.

      h. Close Paint.

  8. Exit the datamgr.exe application, and observe how page faults are affected.

      a. Click the **Processes** tab.

      b. Click the **datamgr.exe** process.

      c. Click the **End Process** button.

      d. Click **Yes** to terminate the application.

      e. Start the **Paint** application, switch to the **Task Manager** window, and on your Student Answer Sheet, record the number of Initial page faults.

      f. Open the **Gone Fishing.bmp** graphic.

      g. Switch to **Task Manager**, and on your Student Answer Sheet, record the number of page faults for MSPAINT.

      h. On your Student Answer Sheet, calculate the number of page faults required by MSPAINT to load the Gone Fishing graphic.

  9. Start **datamgr.exe** and click the **Start Leaking** button. Look at the Virtual Memory size (VM Size) column, and on your Student Answer Sheet, record what application is using the most virtual memory. Also record what you observe happening.

  10. Close all windows and log off. On your Student Answer Sheet, make a recommendation to Dennis regarding what you believe should be done to fix the client/server database performance problem.

LAB 11.2 ESTABLISHING A BASELINE WITH PERFORMANCE MONITOR

Objective

Dave Mansfield is the Information Systems Manager for the Maple County Courthouse. Maple County recently implemented a Web server, and Dave is concerned about its effect on the performance of computer systems at the courthouse. Dave and his staff are quite busy implementing new systems, and need your help to set up a network monitoring system and to establish performance baselines. After completing this lab, you will be able to:

➤ Use Performance Monitor to view current system performance.

➤ Configure counter logs in Performance Monitor to record system performance.

➤ Capture system activity.

➤ Use counter logs to create a performance baseline.

➤ Configure alerts to notify the administrator when performance counters exceed predefined values.

Requirements

➤ Peer Web Services installed on your Windows 2000 Professional system (Peer Web Services were installed in Lab 9.6).

➤ Optionally, another Windows 2000 computer to create network activity.

➤ In the Apps folder, use Notepad to create a file named **Work.bat** that contains the following commands, pressing **Enter** at the end of each line:

MD \Labtemp

Start PING ip_address −n 20

For %%a in (1 2 3 4 5 6 7 8 9 0 a b c d e f) do call Tran.bat RD \Labtemp

where *ip_address* is the IP address of another computer on your network. If no other computers are available, use your computer's IP address.

➤ In the Apps folder, create a file named **Y.txt** that contains the following:

Y

➤ In the Apps folder, create a file named **Trans.bat** that contains the following commands:

COPY \WINNT \Labtemp

DEL \Labtemp <Y.txt

Estimated completion time: **30 minutes**

ACTIVITY

1. If necessary, start your computer with Windows 2000, and log on as an administrator.

2. Start **Performance Monitor**.

   a. Open **Control Panel**.

   b. Double-click **Administrative Tools**.

   c. Double-click **Performance** to open a Performance Monitor window similar to the one shown in Figure 11-2.

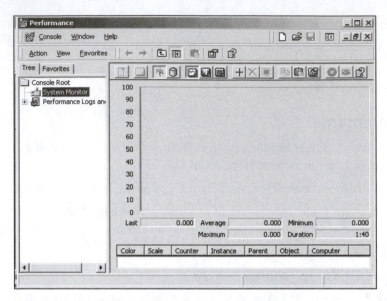

Figure 11-2 Performance Monitor Chart window

3. Performance Monitor can be used to view current system activity, or to view activity from a log of past activity. In this step, you identify the options available to monitor, and view system activity with Performance Monitor.

   a. Counters are used to view the activities of system objects. To add a counter to the graph, click the plus sign (**+**) toolbar icon in the right-side view pane to display the Add Counters window, as shown in Figure 11-3.

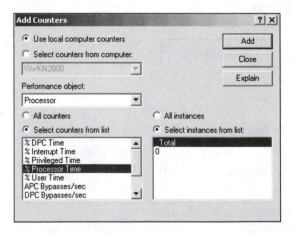

Figure 11-3 Add Counters window

b. Counters can be added for activities on your computer or on other computers on the network. To add counters for activities on your computer, click the **Use local computer counters** option button.

c. Before selecting the counters, you must identify the performance object you wish to monitor. By default, the **Processor** object is selected first. Each occurrence of the same object is referred to as an instance. Using the Instances options, you can select to include all instances of the object, a specific object instance, or a Total of the object instances. Verify that the **Total** option is selected.

d. To include all counters for the Processor object, click the **All counters** option button, and click **Add**.

e. To view a specific counter, such as the number of pages per second, click the scroll button to the right of the Performance object window, scroll up and click the **Memory** object.

f. To view just Pages/second activity, click the **Select counters from list** option button, and, if necessary, use the scroll bar to scroll down until you see the **Pages/sec** counter.

g. Click the **Explain** button to display an explanation of the selected counters.

h. Click the **Pages/sec** counter, and click the **Add** button to add Pages/sec to the counter list.

i. Use the Explain window, and on your Lab 11.2 Student Answer Sheet, describe how Pages/sec is calculated.

j. Click the **Close** button to return to the Performance Monitor chart window.

k. Starting with the left side of the chart window, place your insertion point on each toolbar button, and record its description on your Student Answer Sheet.

l. When there are many counters visible, it is difficult to monitor one of the values. The Highlight button allows you to focus on a specific counter. For example, to highlight just the Percent of Processor utilization counter, click the **% Processor Time** counter in the counter window, and then click the **Highlight** button. Move the mouse around, and observe the effect of placing the mouse on processor utilization.

m. Click the **View Histogram** button to view bars representing the relative system usage of each selected counter.

n. Move your mouse around, and on your Student Answer Sheet, record the two counters that show the highest activity levels on the histogram.

o. Click the **View Report** button, and move the mouse around. On your Student Answer Sheet, record the counter with the highest value.

11

p. Click the **View Chart** button to return to Chart view.

q. To clear all counters, click the **New Counter Set** button.

4. In addition to viewing performance statistics, you also can use Performance Monitor to create a log file to help you fill out the Baseline Data Worksheet. When creating a baseline, an advantage of a log file is that it allows you to start and stop logging on a predefined schedule. In this step, you use Performance Monitor to add the objects and counters on the Lab 11.2 Baseline Data Worksheet at the end of this activity to a log file.

a. In the left-side pane, click the **Performance Logs and Alerts** option.

b. In the right-side results pane, right-click **Counter Logs**, and click the **New Log Settings** option.

c. Enter **baseline** for your log filename and click **OK** to display the **baseline** window shown in Figure 11-4.

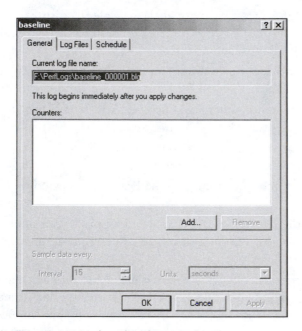

Figure 11-4 baseline log window

d. To add counters to the window, click the **Add** button. Use the Add Counters window described in Step 3 to add the objects and counters listed in the Counters column on your Baseline Data Worksheet.

e. After all counters have been added, click **Close** to return to the Baseline properties window.

f. Click the **Log Files** tab, and record the path to your log file and log filename on the Student Answer Sheet.

g. Click the **Schedule** tab, and record the default start time on your Student Answer Sheet.

h. Click **Manually** in the Start log window, and then click **OK** to save the baseline log configuration and return to the Performance Logs and Alerts window.

5. Now that you have configured the baseline log counters, the next step in creating a baseline is to log normal usage of the system. In this step, you will manually start the logging process, and then generate system activity using the batch file created in the Requirements section of this lab.

a. To manually start the logging process, double-click **Counter Logs** in the right-side results pane to display the existing log files.

b. Right-click your **baseline** log file, and click **Start**.

c. Minimize **Performance Monitor**.

d. Start **Paint** and load the **Gone Fishing.bmp** file.

e. Run the **Work.bat** file created in the Requirements section:

- Click **Start, Run**.

- Click the **Browse** button, and navigate to your Apps folder.

- Double-click the **Work.bat** file.

- Click **OK** to start the program.

f. While the Work.bat file is running, start **WordPad** and create and save a document file.

g. Run the **Work.bat** file a second time.

h. Wait a few minutes for system activity to settle down.

i. Maximize **Performance Monitor**.

j. Right-click your **baseline** log, and click the **Stop** option.

6. After typical system activity has been logged, you next need to view the Baseline performance log, and then record baseline data on your Baseline Data Worksheet. The baseline worksheet can then be used to determine alert values.

a. In the left-side tree pane, click **System Monitor**.

b. To view logged data, click the **View Log File Data** button, and if necessary, navigate to the **D:\PerfLogs** folder, then double-click your **baseline** file.

c. Click the **Add** or **+** button to display the Add Counters window.

d. Click the **Use local computer counters** option button.

e. Click the scroll button to the right of the Performance Object text box. Notice that because you are viewing the contents of the log file, only the objects and counters you logged are included in object and counter windows.

11

f. For any performance object listed, click the **All counters** button, and then click **Add**.

g. After all counters are added to the chart, click the **Close** button.

h. From the chart window, click each counter, and record the maximum and minimum values on your Baseline Data Worksheet.

i. Click the **View Report** button, and record the average value listed for each counter on your Baseline Data Worksheet.

j. On your Baseline Data Worksheet, use the average and maximum values to define alert values near the maximums.

7. Now that you have determined alert values, in this step you configure Performance Monitor to use these alert values when monitoring the system.

a. In the left-side tree pane, right-click **Alerts**, and click the **New Alerts Settings** option.

b. Enter the name **BaseAlerts** and click **OK** to display the BaseAlerts properties window.

c. Click the **Add** button, and add each object's counter for which you identified an alert.

d. After all alert counters have been added, click the **Close** button to return to the BaseAlerts properties window.

e. On the **General** tab, select each counter and enter the Alert limit as specified on your Baseline Data Worksheet.

f. When all limit values have been set, click the **Action** tab, and on your Student Answer Sheet, record the possible actions, along with the default.

g. Click the **Schedule** tab, and click the **Manually** start scan option.

h. Click **OK** to save the alert settings.

i. Exit Performance Monitor, and close all windows.

j. If you are finished working, log off. In the next lab, you will trigger and evaluate the alerts by inducing additional system activity.

LAB 11.2 ESTABLISHING A BASELINE WITH PERFORMANCE MONITOR

Baseline Data Worksheet

Computer ID: _____   **Date:** _____

Counter	Minimum	Maximum	Average	Alert Value
Memory				
Available KBytes				
Pages/Second				
% Committed Bytes in Use				
Processor				
% Processor Time				
Interrupts/sec				
% Privileged Time				
Network Interface				
Current Bandwidth				
Bytes Received/sec				
Bytes Sent/sec				
Packets Received Errors				
Packets/sec				
Output Queue Length				
Physical Disk				
Avg Disk Queue Length				
% Disk time				
Avg Disk Bytes/Read				
Avg Disk Bytes/Write				
Avg Disk Bytes/Transfer				
System				
File Data Operations/sec				
Thread				
% Processor Time				
Process				
Page Faults/sec				
Thread count				

11

LAB 11.3 RECOGNIZING MEMORY BOTTLENECKS

Objective

Dave Mansfield from the Maple County Courthouse recently called regarding an alert message from Performance Monitor. In addition, some of the users have been complaining about the slow response times when accessing the server. Your job is to determine what is causing the alert message, and identify the system performance bottleneck. After completing this lab, you will be able to:

➤ Trigger and view alert messages.

➤ Use Event Viewer to view and filter alert messages.

➤ Use Performance Monitor to track and identify bottlenecks.

Requirements

➤ Completion of Labs 11.1 and 11.2.

Estimated completion time: **15 minutes**

ACTIVITY,

1. If necessary, start your computer with Windows 2000 and log on as an administrator.

2. Start **Performance Monitor**, and start the BaseAlerts log.

   a. Open **Control Panel**.

   b. Double-click **Administrative Tools**.

   c. Double-click **Performance** to open a Performance Monitor window.

   d. In the left-side tree window, expand **Performance Logs and Alerts**, and then click the **Alerts** object.

   e. In the right-side results window, right-click the newly created **BaseAlerts** log, and click **Start**.

   f. Performance Monitor now will begin monitoring system activity.

3. Perform the following procedure to simulate activity at the courthouse.

   a. Start the **datamgr.exe** application and click the **Start Leaking** button.

   b. Run the **Work.bat** file.

   c. Start **Paint**, and load the **Gone Fishing.bmp** file.

   d. Allow the system to run for a few minutes.

4. Exit the datamgr.exe application.

5. You have just arrived at the courthouse to check the performance of Dave's Windows 2000 system. In this step, you use Event Viewer to look for any alert messages placed in the application event log.

   a. Open **Control Panel**.

   b. Double-click **Administrative Tools**.

   c. Double-click **Event Viewer**.

   d. In the left-side tree pane, click **Application Log**.

   e. Double-click the first **Information message** to display the Event Properties window.

   f. Use the down arrow to scan the event log until you come to an alert message.

   g. Record the date, event ID, type, category, and source information on your Lab 11.3 Student Answer Sheet.

   h. Click **Cancel** to return to the Event Viewer window.

6. You can sort the Event Log window on any of the columns simply by clicking a column heading. For example, click the **Source** column heading to sort by the application that originated the message. On your Student Answer Sheet, record up to five sources of application messages.

7. When you view a log that has events from many sources, it is often beneficial to reduce the messages you see to include messages only from a specified source, event ID, or time. In this step, you filter the application log to view messages only from Performance Monitor.

   a. To filter application messages to view messages only from Performance Monitor, click the **Filter** option on the **View** menu.

   b. In the Event source text box, scroll to locate, and then click the **SysmonLog** event.

   c. Click **OK** to include only Performance Monitor messages.

   d. Click the Event Column to sort the list by event. Scan the Performance Monitor messages, and record each different event ID on your Student Answer Sheet.

   e. Use the filter option of Event Viewer (**View**, **Filter**) to count the number of messages for each event ID recorded in Step 7d. Record the number on your Student Answer Sheet.

8. Prior to clearing the log and continuing to troubleshoot the problem, it is often a good idea to archive the log for future use or auditing. In this step, you archive the Application log, and then view the archived log file.

   a. Minimize **Event Viewer**.

   b. Create a folder named **Logs** off the root of the Windows 2000 system disk.

11

c. Maximize **Event Viewer**.

d. Be sure that the **Application log** is selected in the left-side tree pane.

e. Click the **Action** menu, **Save Log File As** option.

f. In the **Save in:** text box, browse to the **Logs** folder.

g. Enter **Alerts** in the File name text box.

h. Verify that the file type is **Event Log (*.evt)**, and click **Save**.

i. Clear events from the application log by clicking the **Action** menu, **Clear all Events** option.

j. Click **No** to the save Application Log message.

k. Perform the steps shown below to view the archived application log file:

- Click the **Action** menu, **Open Log File** option.
- In the Log Type text box, scroll to select the **Application** log.
- Navigate to your **Logs** folder, and double-click the **Alerts.evt** log file.

9. On your Student Answer Sheet, describe the performance bottleneck.

10. You need to save the file in a text format so it can be viewed or edited by other programs. In this step, you save the log in text format, and then view it from Notepad.

a. Click the **Action** menu, **Save Log File As** option.

b. If necessary, use the scroll button to the right of the Save in text box to browse to the **Logs** folder.

c. Enter the name **Alerts** in the File name text box.

d. Use the scroll button to the right of the Save as type text box to select the **Text (Tab delimited) (*.txt)** type, and then click the **Save** button.

e. Minimize **Event Viewer**.

f. Use **My Computer** or **Windows Explorer** to navigate to the Logs folder.

g. Double-click the **Alerts.txt** file to open it with Notepad.

h. On your Student Answer Sheet, identify an advantage and disadvantage of viewing the log from an application such as Notepad.

i. Exit Notepad, and close all windows.

LAB 11.4 RECOGNIZING PROCESSOR BOTTLENECKS

Objective

Maple County Courthouse is still having performance problems when running certain applications such as the Drawman.exe graphics design program. Your job is to help determine what is causing the performance bottleneck when running this program. After completing this lab, you will be able to:

➤ Trigger and view alert messages.

➤ Use Event Viewer to view and archive messages.

➤ Use Performance Monitor to track and identify processor bottlenecks.

Requirements

➤ Completion of Lab 11.3.

➤ To simulate a graphics design program, use My Computer or Windows Explorer to navigate to your Apps folder, and rename diagmon.exe to **drawman.exe**.

Estimated completion time: **10–15 minutes**

11

ACTIVITY

1. If necessary, start your computer with Windows 2000, and log on as an administrator.

2. Start **Performance Monitor**, and start the **BaseAlerts** log.

   a. Open **Control Panel**.

   b. Double-click **Administrative Tools**.

   c. Double-click **Performance** to open a Performance Monitor window.

   d. In the left-side tree window, expand **Performance Logs and Alerts**, and then click the **Alerts** object.

   e. In the right-side results pane, right-click the **BaseAlerts** log, and click **Start**. Performance Monitor now begins monitoring system activity.

3. Perform the following procedure to simulate activity at the courthouse.

   a. Use **My Computer** or **Windows Explorer** to navigate to your Apps folder. Start the **drawman.exe** application by double-clicking **Start**.

   b. Set Thread 1 activity level to **Busy**.

   c. Activate Thread 2 and Thread 3 at **Medium** activity levels.

    d. Run the **Work.bat** file.

    c. Allow the system to run for a few minutes.

4. Exit the Drawman.exe application by clicking the **Close** button in the CPU Stress window.

5. Use Event Viewer to look for any alert messages placed in the application event log.

    a. Open **Control Panel**.

    b. Double-click **Administrative Tools**.

    c. Double-click **Event Viewer**.

    d. In the left-side tree pane, click **Application Log**.

    e. Filter the application log to view messages only from Performance Monitor. Click **View**, **Filter**, and scroll to and click **SysmonLog** in the Event source text box.

    f. Scan the Performance Monitor messages.

    g. On your Lab 11.4 Student Answer Sheet, identify any counters exceeding the alert value.

    h. Archive the log by clicking the **Action** menu, **Save Log File As** option, with the name **Processor** in the File name text box. If necessary, browse to the Logs folder you created in the Save in: text box in Lab 11.3, Step 8.

    i. Clear the log (**Action**, **Clear all Events**), and click **No** if you are asked to save a log file. Exit Event Viewer.

6. If necessary, start **Performance Monitor**, and do the the following.

    a. Click the **Add (+)** button, and add the counters you identified in Step 5.

    b. Minimize **Performance Monitor**.

7. Start the **drawman.exe** program, and set the activity of Thread 1 to **Busy**.

8. Use Performance Monitor to monitor the counter(s) you identified in Step 5.

    a. Run the **Work.bat** file, and then maximize **Performance Monitor**.

    b. Observe the Performance Monitor chart, and when the chart is full, click the **Freeze Display** button.

    c. Start **Event Viewer**, and check for any Performance Monitor application messages.

    d. Use Event Viewer along with the Performance Monitor chart, and, on your Student Answer Sheet, record the values of any counters that have exceeded their Alert settings.

    e. Archive the Application log, using the name **Processor_x** (replace *x* with the step number).

f. Clear the Application log, and exit Event Viewer.

g. In the Performance Monitor window, click the **Freeze Display** (red **X**) button to reactivate performance scanning.

9. In the **drawman** window, set Thread 2 to **medium** activity, and then repeat Step 8, recording counters exceeding alert values on your Student Answer Sheet.

10. In the **drawman** window, set Thread 3 to **medium** activity and then repeat Step 8, recording counters exceeding alert values on your Student Answer Sheet.

11. Exit Performance Monitor, and close all windows.

12. Analyze the usage data you collected in Steps 7 through 10, and, on your Student Answer Sheet, identify the thread activity level that caused each counter you identified in Step 5 to exceed its alert value.

LAB 11.5 RECOGNIZING DISK BOTTLENECKS

Objective

The disk system can be the cause of performance problems. Disk performance problems usually can be identified when disk-related counters, such as queue length, % Disk Time, or Disk Bytes/Transfer, increase above the baseline. After completing this lab, you will be able to:

➤ Use the *diskperf* command, along with Performance Monitor, to collect logical disk information.

➤ Use Performance Monitor to track and identify disk bottlenecks.

Requirements

➤ Completion of Lab 11.4.

Estimated completion time: **10–15 minutes**

ACTIVITY

1. If necessary, start your computer with Windows 2000, and log on as an administrator.

2. Start **Performance Monitor**, and attempt to add Logical Disk counters.

a. Open **Control Panel**.

b. Double-click **Administrative Tools**.

c. Double-click **Performance** to open a Performance Monitor window.

d. If necessary, click the **New Counter Set** button to clear any existing counters.

e. If necessary, click the **View Current Activity** button.

f. Click the **Add** button, and attempt to add PhysicalDisk counters. Record the results on your Lab 11.5 Student Answer Sheet.

3. Run the *diskperf* command.

a. Open a Command Prompt window by clicking **Start**, **Programs**, **Accessories**, **Command Prompt**.

b. Enter the command **diskperf –y**, and press **Enter**.

c. Record the message you receive on your Student Answer Sheet.

d. Type **Exit**, and press **Enter** to exit the Command Prompt window.

4. Restart your system by clicking **Start, Shutdown, Restart**.

5. Start **Performance Monitor**, and again attempt to add Logical Disk counters.

a. Open **Control Panel**.

b. Double-click **Administrative Tools**.

c. Double-click **Performance** to open a Performance Monitor window.

d. If necessary, click the **New Counter Set** button to clear any existing counters.

e. If necessary, click the **View Current Activity** button.

f. Click the **Add** button, and attempt to add the following PhysicalDisk counters. Record the results on your Student Answer Sheet:

- % Disk Time
- Current Disk Queue Length
- Disk Bytes/sec

6. Click **Close** to return to the Performance Monitor chart window.

7. Minimize **Performance Monitor**.

8. Create disk activity by running the following applications.

a. Start **datamgr.exe**, and click the **Start Leaking** button.

b. Run the **Work.bat** file.

9. Maximize **Performance Monitor**.

10. After the graph page fills, click the **Freeze Display** button.

11. On your Student Answer Sheet, record each counter's acceptable value range, and its observed range.

12. Exit Performance Monitor.

13. Exit datamgr.exe.

14. Monitoring logical disk performance takes away from system performance. As a result, when you finish monitoring logical disk activity, you should use the *diskperf* command to disable logical disk monitoring.

   a. Open a Command Prompt window.

   b. Enter the following command, **diskperf –NV,** and press **Enter**.

   c. Record the message you receive on your Student Answer Sheet.

15. Close all windows and log off.

LAB 11.6 USING EVENT VIEWER

Objective

Sebastian Melendres from the Melendres and Associates law firm telephoned to inform you that he can no longer access the network from his Windows 2000 Professional system. You have been assigned the task of troubleshooting and correcting the problem. After completing this lab, you will be able to:

➤ Use Event Viewer to view system and security messages.

➤ Use Event Viewer to view other computer event logs.

11

Requirements

➤ An additional Windows 2000 Professional computer to use to view a remote computer's event log.

Estimated completion time: **15 minutes**

ACTIVITY

1. If necessary, start your computer with Windows 2000, and log on as an administrator.

2. Perform the following procedure to simulate a network cable problem that Mr. Melendres is having with his computer.

   a. Unplug the network cable from your computer.

   b. Wait a few minutes and then plug the cable back in.

   c. Repeat steps a and b two more times.

3. Use Event Viewer to view current System messages.

   a. Start **Event Viewer** by clicking **Start, Programs, Administrative Tools, Event Viewer**.

   b. Click the **System Log** option.

   c. On your Lab 11.6 Student Answer Sheet, record message information regarding the cable connection.

4. Mr. Melendres is suspicious that someone is attempting to log on to the office network. He wants to be able to check the Security log files on the systems in his office. In this step, you prepare to demonstrate how to monitor security by creating some security audit messages on your computer.

   a. Open **Control Panel**, and double-click **Administrative Tools**.

   b. Double-click **Local Security Policy** to view the Local Security Settings window.

   c. Expand the **Local Policies** object, and click **Audit Policy** to display a window similar to the one shown in Figure 11-5.

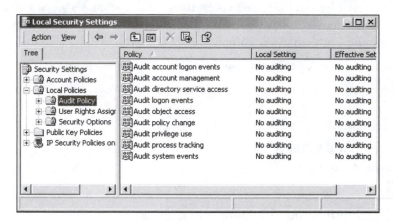

Figure 11-5   Local Audit Policy window

   d. Double-click **Audit logon events**, and click **Failure** to begin recording failed log on attempts.

   e. Click **OK** to save the audit setting.

   f. Exit the Local Security Settings window, and log out.

   g. Attempt to log on as Administrator using an incorrect password.

   h. Attempt to log on again, using an invalid username and password.

   i. Attempt to log on a third time, using a valid username and an incorrect password.

j. Log on as Administrator (with the correct password), and start **Event Viewer**.

k. Click **Security Log**, and, on your Student Answer Sheet, record the time, date, and username of each invalid access attempt.

5. In this step, you show Mr. Melendres how to check the Security log on another computer.

a. If your partner's computer has a different password for the Administrator user, do the following to make a connection to their computer:

 - Click **Start**, **Run**, and enter **\\computername**, replacing *computername* with the name of your partner's computer. (If you do not know your partner's computer name, right-click **My Computer**, click **Properties**, and then click the **Network Identification** tab.)

 - Enter the administrator's username and password in the Enter Network Password window, and click **OK**.

 - Close all windows except Event Viewer.

b. In the left-side tree pane, right-click the **Event Viewer (Local)** object, and then click the **Connect to another computer** option.

c. Enter the name of your partner's computer, or use the **Browse** button to find it.

d. Click **OK** to change to your partner's Event Viewer log.

e. Click **Security Log**, and, on your Student Answer Sheet, record the time, date, and username of each invalid access attempt.

6. Close all windows, and log off.

11

WINDOWS 2000 APPLICATION SUPPORT

Labs included in this chapter

➤ Lab 12.1 Working with DOS Applications

➤ Lab 12.2 Working with 16-bit Windows Applications

➤ Lab 12.3 Working with Win32 Applications

Microsoft MCSE Exam #70-210 Objectives	
Objective	Lab
Optimize and troubleshoot performance of the Windows 2000 Professional desktop	
Optimize and troubleshoot application performance	12.1, 12.2, 12.3

Student Answer Sheets to accompany the labs in this chapter can be downloaded from the Online Companion for this manual at *www.course.com*.

LAB 12.1 WORKING WITH DOS APPLICATIONS

Objective

The Animal Care Center is considering purchasing a new Windows 2000 Professional-based system from your company. This new computer will replace one of their older Windows 3.1 computers. One of the requirements for the new system is that it must be able to continue using some older DOS and Window 3.1 applications, until the applications can be replaced with Win32-based applications. After completing this lab, you will be able to:

➤ Configure AUTOEXEC.NT and CONFIG.NT files for a DOS application.

➤ Customize execution parameters for DOS applications.

➤ Use Task Manager to view virtual DOS machines (VDMs), and change base priorities.

Requirements

➤ Optionally, another computer that can be used to test network connections.

Estimated completion time: **15 minutes**

ACTIVITY

1. If necessary, start your computer with Windows 2000, and log on as an administrator.

2. DOS applications often require certain driver and configuration settings to be made to the system through the CONFIG.SYS and AUTOEXEC.BAT files when the computer starts. Windows 2000 Professional provides for this need by allowing each virtual DOS machine to process commands from the CONFIG.NT and AUTOEXEC.NT files located in the WINNT\SYSTEM32 folder. To demonstrate the use of the AUTOEXEC.NT file, in this step you create a shortcut for the DOS Edit application, modify the AUTOEXEC.NT file, and observe how modifying the file affects starting the Edit application.

   a. Create a shortcut to the Edit application named DOSApp1 (to use as if it were one of the Animal Care Center's DOS applications), as follows:

   ■ Use My Computer or Windows Explorer to open the **WINNT\system32** folder.

   ■ Right-click the **edit.com** application, and click the **Create Shortcut** option.

- Drag and drop the **Shortcut to MS-DOS Editor** to your desktop.
- Close the **system32** window.
- Rename the Shortcut to MS-DOS Editor to **DOSApp1**.

b. Double-click **DOSApp1** shortcut to load the DOS editor.

c. Exit the MS-DOS Editor.

d. Use My Computer to open the **WINNT\system32** folder.

e. Right-click **AUTOEXEC.NT**, and then click **Open With**.

f. Double-click **Notepad**, and record all commands except REM on your Lab 12.1 Student Answer Sheet.

g. Insert the word **REM** in front of the @echo off command at the beginning of the AUTOEXEC.NT file.

h. Exit Notepad, and save your changes.

i. Double-click the **DOSApp1** shortcut, and note any changes in the load process on your Student Answer Sheet.

j. Exit the DOS editor.

3. If a DOS application requires unique startup instructions, you can specify separate AUTOEXEC.NT and CONFIG.NT files for that DOS application by using the execution parameters.

a. Create another shortcut to the Edit application named DOSApp2 (to simulate another DOS application), as follows:

- Use My Computer or Windows Explorer to open the **WINNT\system32** folder.
- Right-click the **edit.com** application, and click the **Create Shortcut** option.
- Drag and drop the **Shortcut to MS-DOS Editor** to your desktop.
- Close the **System32** window.
- Rename the Shortcut to MS-DOS Editor to **DOSApp2**.

b. Double-click the **DOSApp2** shortcut to load the DOS editor. On your Student Answer Sheet, record whether or not you see the statements from the AUTOEXEC.NT file when starting DOSApp2.

c. Right-click the **DOSApp2** shortcut icon, and click the **Properties** button to display the Shortcut Properties window.

d. Click the **Program** tab to display the application execution properties shown in Figure 12-1.

12

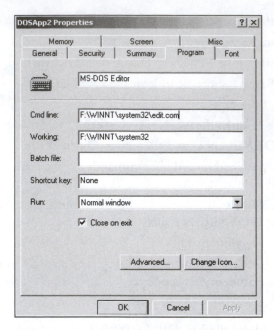

Figure 12-1 MS-DOS application Properties window

e. Click the **Advanced** button, and record the existing Autoexec and Config filenames on your Student Answer Sheet.

f. Change the Autoexec filename to **AUTO2.NT**.

g. Click **OK** to save your changes.

h. Click **OK** to close the Shortcut Properties window.

i. Use My Computer or Windows Explorer to open the **WINNT\system32** folder.

j. Double-click the **AUTOEXEC.NT** file to open it with Notepad.

k. Remove the **REM** from in front of the @echo off command.

l. Save the file as **AUTO2.NT:**.

- Click the File menu, **Save as** option.
- In the Save as type text box, select **All Files**.
- In the File name text box, enter **AUTO2.NT**.
- Click the **Save** button.

m. Exit Notepad.

n. Double-click **DOSApp2** shortcut to load the DOS editor. On your Student Answer Sheet, record whether or not you see the statements from the AUTOEXEC.NT file.

    o. Try using the DOSApp1 shortcut, and record your observations on your Student Answer Sheet.

    p. Exit both DOS applications, and close all windows.

4. In addition to the CONFIG.NT and AUTOEXEC.NT files, Windows 2000 allows other DOS application execution parameters to be configured through application properties. In this step, you identify several DOS application configuration parameters.

    a. Right-click **DOSApp1**, and click **Properties**.

    b. Click the **Security** tab, and on your Student Answer Sheet, record who is able to run this shortcut, along with their permissions to this file.

    c. Click the **Program** tab, and on your Student Answer Sheet, record the Cmd line and Working path.

    d. Change the icon to a picture of a computer:

       ■ click the **Change Icon** button.

       ■ Click the computer icon to select it.

       ■ Click **OK** to return to the Program tab.

    e. Remove the check mark from the **Close on exit** check box.

    f. Click the **Font** tab, and record the default fault size on your Student Answer Sheet.

    g. Click the **Memory** tab, and reduce the Conventional memory setting to **400**. On your Student Answer Sheet, record the default DPMI memory setting.

    h. Click the **Screen** tab, and change the Usage to **Full-screen**. On your Student Answer Sheet, record the default Performance settings.

    i. Click the **Misc** tab, and record the default settings on your Student Answer Sheet.

       ■ If necessary, disable the screen saver.

       ■ If necessary, enable mouse exclusive mode.

    j. Click **OK** to save the program parameters.

    k. Start **DOSApp1** from the shortcut, and on your Student Answer Sheet, describe the different appearance of the window, and what caused this change.

    l. Exit DOSApp1, and describe what happens and why, on your Student Answer Sheet.

    m. Close all windows.

12

5. By default, each DOS application runs in its own virtual DOS machine (VDM), and all VDMs have equal processing priority. In this step, you load multiple DOS applications, and then use Task Manager to modify the base priority of the DOS applications.

   a. Start **DOSApp1**.

   b. Use the **Alt+Esc** key sequence to rotate to the Windows 2000 desktop, and start **DOSApp2**.

   c. Start **Task Manager** by using the **Ctrl+Alt+Esc** key sequence to display the Windows Security window, and then clicking **Task Manager**.

   d. Click the **Processes** tab.

   e. DOS applications run in VDMs. On your Student Answer Sheet, record the CPU Time, Memory Usage, and Handles for each VDM application.

   f. Right-click the second VDM (representing DOSApp2), and record the process options on your Student Answer Sheet.

   g. Click **Set Priority**, and record the priority options on your Student Answer Sheet.

   h. Click **High** priority, and summarize the warning message on your Student Answer Sheet.

   i. Click **Yes** to the change priority class message.

   j. On your Student Answer Sheet, record any changes to the VDM parameters you documented in Step 5e.

   k. Right-click the first DOSApp1 VDM (representing DosApp 1), and click **End Process**. Click **Yes** to continue.

   l. Close **Task Manager**.

   m. Close **DOSApp2**, and log off.

LAB 12.2 WORKING WITH 16-BIT WINDOWS APPLICATIONS

Objective

In addition to the DOS applications, the original Windows 3.1 computer at the Animal Care Center has two Windows 3.x applications that will need to run on the new Windows 2000 Professional system. After completing this lab, you will be able to:

➤ Determine the system requirements needed to run multiple Win16 applications in the same VDM.

➤ Determine the system requirements needed to run multiple Win16 applications in separate VDMs.

➤ Use Task Manager to terminate Win16 applications, and free up system resources.

Estimated completion time: **15 minutes**

ACTIVITY

1. If necessary, start your computer with Windows 2000, and log on as an administrator.

2. Record system resources in use.

   a. Start **Task Manager**.

   b. Click the **Performance** tab, and record the requested initial system usage statistics on your Lab 12.2 Student Answer Sheet.

3. Copy a Windows 16-bit application to the desktop as follows:

   a. Use My Computer or Windows Explorer to open a window to your **WINNT** folder.

   b. Right-click **winhelp.exe**, and click **Copy**.

   c. Right-click your desktop, and click **Paste**.

   d. Rename winhelp.exe to **Win16App1.exe**, to simulate an Animal Care Center Windows 3.1 application.

4. Repeat Step 3 to create another 16-bit application named **Win16App2.exe**.

5. Start **WIN16App1.exe**, and record virtual DOS machine information.

   a. Double-click the **Win16App1.exe** application.

   b. Start **Task Manager**.

   c. Click the **Processes** tab, and on your Student Answer Sheet, record all applications running in the virtual DOS machine.

   d. Minimize **Task Manager**.

6. Start **WIN16App2**, and record virtual DOS machine information and performance statistics.

   a. Double-click the **Win16App2** application.

   b. Activate **Task Manager**.

   c. Click the **Processes** tab, and on your Student Answer Sheet, record all applications running in the virtual DOS machine.

12

d. Click the **Performance** tab, and record the requested statistics on your Student Answer Sheet.

e. Minimize **Task Manager**.

7. Close the 16-bit Windows applications, and record the results.

a. Close **Win16App1** and **Win16App2**.

b. Switch to **Task Manager**, and on your Student Answer Sheet, record the requested statistics for the two virtual DOS machines (ntvdm).

c. Click the **Performance** tab, and record the requested statistics on your Student Answer Sheet.

d. Click the **Processes** tab, then use Task Manager to close the virtual DOS machine as follows:

- Right-click the **ntvdm.exe** application, and click **End Process**.

- Click **Yes** to terminate the process.

e. Minimize **Task Manager**.

8. Configure the Win16App2 application to use a separate memory space.

a. Right-click **Win16App2**, and click **Create Shortcut**.

b. Right-click the **Shortcut to Win16App2.exe**, and click **Properties** to display a Shortcut window similar to the one shown in Figure 12-2.

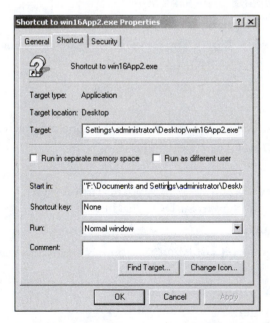

Figure 12-2 Windows 16-bit Shortcut Properties window

c. Click the **Run in separate memory space** option, and click **OK**.

9. Start **WIN16App1**.

10. Start **WIN16App2**, and record Task Manager processes and usage statistics.

    a. Double-click the **Shortcut to Win16App2.exe** application.

    b. Activate **Task Manager**.

    c. On your Student Answer Sheet, record all applications running in each virtual DOS machine.

    d. Click the **Performance** tab, and record the requested statistics on your Student Answer Sheet.

    e. Compare usage statistics to those gathered in Step 6. Record any observations on your Student Answer Sheet.

    f. Minimize **Task Manager**.

11. Exit the WinApp1.exe application, and record the Task Manager processes.

    a. Exit WinApp1.exe, and switch to **Task Manager**.

    b. On your Student Answer Sheet, record all applications running in each virtual DOS machine.

    c. Minimize **Task Manager**.

12. Exit the WinApp2.exe application, and record Task Manager processes.

    a. Exit WinApp2.exe and switch to **Task Manager**.

    b. On your Student Answer Sheet, record all applications running in each virtual DOS machine.

    c. Minimize **Task Manager**.

13. Use Task Manager to close all virtual DOS machines.

    a. Right-click the **ntvdm.exe** application, and click **End Process**.

    b. Click **Yes** to terminate the process.

    c. If necessary, repeat steps a and b to remove any remaining VDMs.

14. Exit all applications, and log off.

12

LAB 12.3 WORKING WITH WIN32 APPLICATIONS

Objective

One of the major considerations when the Animal Care Center purchased their Windows 2000 Professional-based computers was that they be able use a new veterinary software package. The veterinary software package requires that a path be set to the Public folder on the server when a user logs on. One way to establish a path is to use the AUTOEXEC.BAT file to configure Windows 2000 environment variables. When Windows 2000 starts, it will check for an

AUTOEXEC.BAT file in the system drive, and then scan the AUTOEXEC file for any environment variables or path settings. After completing this lab, you will be able to:

➤ Use AUTOEXEC.BAT to configure path and environmental variables for Win32 applications.

➤ Verify path and environmental variable settings.

➤ Use Task Manager to view the resources used by Win32 applications.

Requirements

➤ An additional Windows 2000 computer to be used as a server. In a classroom environment, you should work with lab partner using their computer as the "server." The server computer needs to have a shared folder named Public.

➤ Performance utilities found on the Windows 2000 Professional Resource Kit. (These utilities were installed to complete Lab 11.1. See Lab 11.1 requirements.)

Estimated completion time: **10 minutes**

ACTIVITY

1. If necessary, start your computer with Windows 2000, and log on as an administrator.

2. Modify the AUTOEXEC.BAT file to provide a path to the Public folder on the computer you have identified as the server.

   a. Use My Computer or Windows Explorer to open a window to the root of your system drive. (Your system drive is the drive that is marked as active, normally the C: drive.)

   b. Right-click the **AUTOEXEC.BAT** file and click **Edit**.

   c. Insert the following commands at the end of the AUTOEXEC.BAT file:

      - **SET VetDrive=P**
      - **SET VetPath=**server_name**\Public** (where server_name is the name of your partner's computer)
      - **SET VetUser=administrator**
      - **PATH=P**

   d. Save **Autoexec.bat**, and exit Notepad.

   e. To implement the new commands you've added to your Autoexec.bat file, you need to restart your computer, by clicking **Start, Shutdown, Restart**.

3. To verify that the environment variables and path settings have been made, you can use either the Command Prompt or the Registry Editor. In this step, you use the Command Prompt to verify the settings. (In Chapter 13 you will learn how to use a Registry Editor to view or modify Registry values.)

    a. Log on to your computer as the administrator.

    b. Open a Command Prompt window.

    c. To view environment variables, type the command **SET**, and press **Enter**.

    d. Record the variable settings on your Lab 12.3 Student Answer Sheet.

4. Dennis is running two Win32 applications on his computer. One of the applications is interactive and needs to run faster than the other application that runs in the background. In this step, you simulate running two applications, and then use Task Manager to view resource usage after changing application priorities.

    a. Right-click the **Drawman** application you renamed in Lab 11.4, and click the **Copy** option.

    b. Right-click the desktop, and click **Paste** to create a copy of the Drawman.exe application.

    c. Rename the copy of Drawman.exe to **Background.exe**.

    d. Start the **Drawman** application you created in Lab 11.1.

    e. Activate three threads at **medium** activity level.

    f. Start the **Background** application.

    g. Start **Task Manager**, and click the **Processes** tab.

    h. Click the View menu, **Select Columns** option.

    i. If necessary, click the **Thread Count** check box.

    j. Click **OK** to return to the Processes window.

    k. On your Student Answer Sheet, record the values from the CPU and Threads columns.

    l. Set the priority of Drawman to Realtime, as follows:

      ■ Right-click the **Drawman** application, and click **Set Priority**.

      ■ Click the **Realtime** priority option. Click **Yes** on the warning window that appears.

    m. Set the priority of the Background application to **Below Normal**:

      ■ Right-click the **Background** application, and click **Set Priority**.

      ■ Click the **Below Normal** priority option. Click **Yes** on the warning window that appears.

12

n. From the Task Manager Processes window, record on your Student Answer Sheet any changes to the CPU Usage for the Drawman and Background applications.

o. From Task Manager, exit the Drawman and Background applications by right-clicking the application, and clicking the **End Process** option.

p. Exit Task Manager.

q. Close all windows, and log off.

WORKING WITH THE WINDOWS 2000 REGISTRY

Labs included in this chapter

➤ Lab 13.1 Backing Up the Registry

➤ Lab 13.2 Exploring the Registry

➤ Lab 13.3 Changing Registry Data Through Control Panel

➤ Lab 13.4 Working with HKEY_LOCAL_MACHINE

➤ Lab 13.5 Backing Up and Restoring Registry Keys

➤ Lab 13.6 Working with User Data

➤ Lab 13.7 Restoring the Registry

Microsoft MCSE Exam #70-210 Objectives	
Objective	Lab
Recover systems and user data	13.1, 13.4, 13.5, 13.7
Optimize and troubleshoot performance of the Windows 2000 Professional desktop	13.2, 13.3, 13.6
Optimize and troubleshoot application performance	13.4

Student Answer Sheets to accompany the labs in this chapter can be downloaded from the Online Companion for this manual at *www.course.com*.

LAB 13.1 BACKING UP THE REGISTRY

Objective

The Windows 2000 Registry plays a critical role in the operation of your computer by storing hardware and software configuration information. The Registry is a complex information structure that is maintained by the Windows 2000 operating system, and is usually modified using Control Panel or through an application's installation process. Occasionally it is necessary for a system administrator to directly access and modify the Registry to correct a problem or modify a setting that is not accessible via Control Panel. To become more familiar with the Registry and how to work with it, the labs in this chapter require you to access and make changes to Registry values. Because modifying information in the Registry can affect your computer's operation and performance, it is important to make a backup of the Registry data prior to making any changes. Although the Windows 2000 Backup program is covered in detail in Chapter 15, in this lab you will use the Backup program to make a backup of your computer's Registry. After completing this lab, you will be able to:

➤ Use the Windows 2000 Backup program to make a backup of the Registry.

Requirements

➤ Approximately 300 MB of free space on your hard disk to store the system backup information.

Estimated completion time: **10–15 minutes**

ACTIVITY

1. If necessary, start your computer with Windows 2000, and log on as an administrator.

2. Use My Computer or Windows Explorer to create a folder named **RegBack** on your Windows 2000 operating system drive.

3. Start the **Backup** utility by clicking **Start**, **Programs**, **Accessories**, **System Tools**, **Backup**.

4. Click the **Backup Wizard** button, and click **Next** to display the What to Back Up window.

5. Click the **Only backup the System State data** option button, and click **Next**.

6. In the Backup media or file name text box, click the **Browse** button, and navigate to the **RegBack** folder you created in Step 2.

7. Type **Registry.bkf** in the File name text box, and click **Open**.

8. Click **Next** to select the RegBack\Registry.bkf file.

9. Click **Finish** to start the Registry backup process.

10. Record the requested Backup Progress information on your Lab 13.1 Student Answer Sheet.

11. Click **Report**, and check for any error messages. Record the requested report information on your Student Answer Sheet.

12. Exit Notepad, and click **Close** to return to the Welcome to Backup window.

13. Exit the Backup utility.

LAB 13.2 EXPLORING THE REGISTRY

Objective

You are representing your company, Computer Technology Services, on the Superior Technical College CIS program advisory council. At the last council meeting, you volunteered to give a talk to the council about the Windows 2000 Registry. Your presentation will consist of two parts. In the first part you will show how Registry data is organized, and then in the second part you will demonstrate how Registry values can be modified using the Control Panel and Registry Editor tools. In this lab, you will prepare for the first part of the presentation by reviewing the Registry key structure using the Regedit and Regedt32 programs. After completing this lab, you will be able to:

➤ Use the Regedit program to find and view Registry key information.

➤ Use Control Panel to modify Registry settings.

➤ Identify the relationship between certain Registry keys.

➤ View Registry size limitations.

> Estimated completion time: **15 minutes**

ACTIVITY

1. If necessary, start your computer with Windows 2000, and log on as an administrator.

13

2. When the system is in use, the Registry resides in the paged pool portion of memory, allowing it to be swapped out to disk when not in use. To prevent the Registry from consuming too much of the page pool, thus causing excessive paging activity, Windows 2000 imposes a maximum size for the Registry. The ceiling initially should be set to ¼ (25%) of the page pool, and can be viewed or changed using the Virtual Memory dialog box. In this step, you use the Virtual Memory dialog box to view, and, if necessary, modify the maximum Registry size.

   a. Open **Control Panel** and double-click the **System** icon.

   b. Click the **Advanced** tab, and then click the **Performance Options** button.

   c. Click the **Change** button to display the Virtual Memory dialog box.

   d. On your Lab 13.2 Student Answer Sheet, record the currently allocated total paging file size for all drives, the Current Registry size, and the Maximum Registry size.

   e. Divide the Maximum Registry size by the currently allocated page size, and, on your Student Answer Sheet, record the results as the Percent of page file used by the Registry.

   f. For best performance, Microsoft recommends that the Maximum Registry size be set to approximately ¼ (25%) of the allocated page pool size. Divide your currently allocated page size by 4 to calculate what your computer's Maximum Registry size should be.

   g. If necessary, change the Maximum Registry size to ¼ (25%) of the total page pool memory. Record the new Registry size on your Student Answer Sheet.

   h. Click **OK** twice to return to the System Properties window.

   i. Click **OK** to return to Control Panel.

   j. Close the Control Panel window.

3. The Registry contains hardware and software configuration information stored in sections called keys that are arranged in a tree-type structure. In this step, you use the Regedit program to identify the major keys and subkeys that make up the Registry tree.

   a. To run the Regedit program, click **Start**, **Run**, and type **regedit**. Click **OK**, or press **Enter** to display the Registry Editor window.

   b. Record the five major keys on your Student Answer Sheet.

   c. Expand the **HKEY_LOCAL_MACHINE** key by clicking its plus (+) symbol.

   d. On your Student Answer Sheet, record the five subkeys of HKEY_LOCAL_MACHINE.

   e. Exit Regedit.

4. Create shortcuts for Regedit and Regedt32.

    a. Use My Computer or Windows Explorer to open the **WINNT** folder.

    b. Right-click the **regedit.exe** program, and click **Copy**.

    c. Right-click your desktop, and click the **Paste Shortcut** option.

    d. Repeat the above process to copy a shortcut of **Regedt32.exe** from the System32 folder to the desktop.

5. The HKEY_LOCAL_MACHINE\HARDWARE subkey is automatically loaded with hardware information when Windows 2000 starts. If there are problems with certain devices, or if you are wondering what devices, such as serial ports, were detected on a computer, you can view the contents of the HARDWARE subkey to determine the system configuration. In this step, you use the HARDWARE subkey to document device settings on your Windows 2000 system.

    a. Start **Regedit** by double-clicking your desktop shortcut.

    b. Expand the **HARDWARE\DESCRIPTION\System** subkey.

    c. Expand the **CentralProcessor** key, and observe the number of processors in your computer (each processor will have a key associated with it).

    d. On your Student Answer Sheet, record the value of the **Identifier** and **Vendor Identifier** for each processor.

    e. Expand the keys until you find the **SerialController** subkey.

    f. On your Student Answer Sheet, record the path to the SerialController key.

    g. Use the SerialController subkey, and, on your Student Answer Sheet, record the port used for each serial controller.

    h. Minimize all HARDWARE subkeys, and exit Regedit.

6. Some Registry keys such as HKEY_LOCAL_MACHINE\HARDWARE are built on the fly when Windows 2000 boots. However, certain device and security information needs to be stored and then loaded from the WINNT\Config folder each time Windows 2000 starts. In this step, you identify the key information that is stored, and then loaded, each time Windows 2000 boots.

    a. Use My Computer or Windows Explorer to open the **WINNT\ system32\config** folder.

    b. On your Student Answer Sheet, record each subkey of HKEY_LOCAL_MACHINE represented in the Config folder.

    c. Double-click each log file that is associated with a Registry key, and record the message you receive on your Student Answer Sheet.

    d. Close all windows.

13

7. The HKEY_LOCAL_MACHINE\SYSTEM subkey contains control set keys that store information, such as device loading sequence, service startup credentials, and startup parameters needed to start Windows 2000. In this step, you use Regedt32 to identify the control set subkeys on your system, and then determine which control set is the current control set, and which control set contains the Last Known Good configuration start settings.

   a. Start **Regedt32** by double-clicking the desktop shortcut.

   b. Maximize the **HKEY_LOCAL_MACHINE** window.

   c. Expand the **SYSTEM** key by double-clicking it.

   d. On your Student Answer Sheet, record the name of each control set key.

   e. Click the **Select** key to display values similar to the ones shown in Figure 13-1.

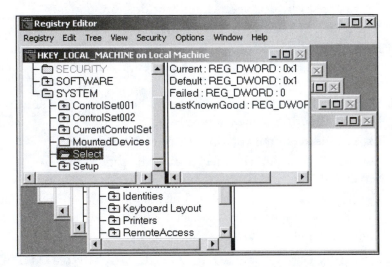

Figure 13-1   Select key values in Regedt32

   f. On your Student Answer Sheet, identify the three parts of a value entry.

   g. The number in the value field of each entry identifies the control set number associated with that configuration. For example, in Figure 13-1 the 0x1 in the Current value entry identifies ControlSet001 as the current control set. On your Student Answer Sheet, identify the control sets to be used for Current, Failed, and Last Known Good configurations.

   h. Exit the Registry Editor.

LAB 13.3 CHANGING REGISTRY DATA THROUGH CONTROL PANEL

Objective

The second part of your presentation is to demonstrate how Registry values can be changed using both the Control Panel and Registry Editor tools. During your presentation, you want to make the following points:

➤ Although you can use the Registry Editor tools, Regedit or Regedt32, to change Registry values, this should be done only as a last resort, and only after backing up the Registry as described in Lab 13.1.

➤ In some keys, changing Registry values might be next to impossible, because the values are stored in binary format or are protected by security settings.

➤ Another possible problem when changing Registry values is that certain keys are copies of other subkeys. If you change a copy, it simply will be overwritten when the system restarts.

➤ Whenever possible, Registry values should be changed using Control Panel tools.

In this lab, you will prepare for the second part of your presentation by practicing using Control Panel along with Regedit and Regedt32 to make changes to Registry values. After completing this lab, you will be able to:

➤ Demonstrate the relationship between the HKEY_CLASSES_ROOT and HKEY_LOCAL _MACHINE keys.

➤ Use Control Panel to add an extension to the HKEY_CLASSES_ROOT key.

➤ Use Control Panel to modify system and user environmental variables.

➤ Use Regedit to find and view environment variables in HKEY_USERS and HKEY_LOCAL_MACHINE keys.

➤ Determine the relationship between HKEY_USERS and CURRENT_USER keys.

13

Estimated completion time: **15 minutes**

ACTIVITY

1. If necessary, start your computer with Windows 2000, and log on as an administrator.

2. The HKEY_CLASSES_ROOT key contains application associations based on file extension data. The contents of this key are copied from another

Registry key, and can be changed by modifying the File Types settings of the Folder Options dialog box. In this step, you modify the contents of the HKEY_CLASSES_ROOT key by using the Folder Options dialog box, and determine which other key contains file extensions.

a. Open **Control Panel** and double-click **Folder Options**.

b. Click the **File Types** tab to display existing file extensions and associated file types.

c. Click the **New** button, and then click **Advanced.**

d. Enter **.let** for the File Extension, and then select **Text Document** for the Associated File Type, as shown in Figure 13-2.

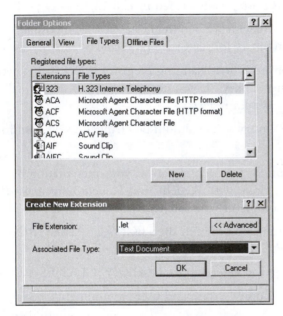

Figure 13-2   Folder Options window

e. Click **OK** to save the entry.

f. Click **Close** to close the Folder Options window.

g. Start the **Regedit** application from the **Start**, **Run** window.

h. In the left Registry Editor pane, highlight **My Computer** by clicking it.

i. Click, **Edit**, **Find** and enter **.let** in the Find what text box. In the Look at dialog box, click to remove checks from the **Values** and **Data** check boxes.

j. Click the **Match whole string only** text box and then click the **Find Next** button.

k. On your Student Answer Sheet, record the key containing the .let file extension.

l. Press the **F3** key to continue searching the entire Registry.

m. On your Student Answeer Shet, record any other keys containing the .let extension.

n. Right-click the last **.let** extension you found and click **Delete**. Click **Yes** to confirm the deletion of the .let extension.

o. Click **View**, **Refresh** to update the Registry Editor data.

p. Repeat steps i through m and record the results of your search on your Student Answer Sheet.

q. Exit the Registry Editor and close all windows.

r. Open **Control Panel** and double-click **Folder Options**. Click the **File Types** tab and use the scroll button to verify that the .let extension has been removed.

3. In this step, you view the results of using Regedit to add another file extension to the HKEY_CLASSES_ROOT key.

a. Start **Regedit** by double-clicking your desktop shortcut.

b. Right-click **HKEY_CLASSES_ROOT**, and click **New**, and then click **Key**.

c. Enter **.prg** for the key name, and press **Enter**.

d. In the right-side results pane, double-click the **Default** entry, and then enter **txtfile** in the Value data text box.

e. Click **OK** to save your key value.

f. Collapse the **HKEY_CLASSES_ROOT** key.

g. Expand the **HKEY_LOCAL_MACHINE** subkey you identified in Step 2.

h. Scan the subkey value entries to determine if the .prg extension has been added to the master key. Record the results on your Student Answer Sheet.

4. Registry keys also are used to contain path and environment variable settings. In this step, you use Control Panel to set user and system environment variables.

a. Open **Control Panel**, and double-click the **System** icon.

b. Click the **Advanced** tab, and then click the **Environment Variables** button to display a window similar to the one shown in Figure 13-3.

c. Under the User variables window, click the **New** button and add the following environment variable for the Administrator user:

- Variable Name: **FirstName**

- Variable Value: [**Your first name**]

d. Click **OK** to return to the Environment Variables window. Notice that your first name has been added to the User variables for Administrator window.

13

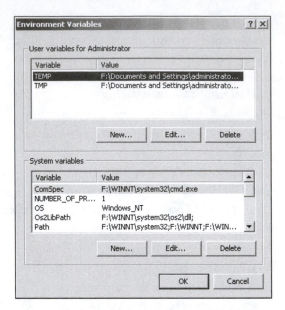

Figure 13-3 Environment Variables window

    e. Click the **New** button under the System variables window, and enter the following environment variable used by all users:

- Variable Name: **Organization**
- Variable Value: **Superior Technical College**

    f. Click **OK** to return to the Environment Variables window.

    g. Click **OK** to close the Environment Variables window.

    h. Click **OK** to close the System Properties window.

    i. Close Control Panel.

5. In this step, you use Registry Editor to find and record the keys used to store user environment variables.

    a. If necessary, strart or activate the **RegEdit.exe** Registry editor.

    b. Click **My Computer** in the Registry window.

    c. From the **Edit** menu, click the **Find** option, and enter **[your first name]** in the Find what text box.

    d. Click the **Find Next** button, and, on your Student Answer Sheet, record the key where your name is found.

    e. Click the **Edit** menu, **Find Next** option and record the next key where your name is found.

    f. Check to see if your first name is found in any other keys. Record your results on your Student Answer Sheet.

    g. Minimize all keys by clicking the **minus (−)** signs.

6. In this step, you use Registry editor to find and record what key(s) are used to store system environment variables.

   a. If necessary, start or activate the **RegEdit.exe** Registry editor.

   b. Click **My Computer** in the Registry window.

   c. From the Edit menu, click the **Find** option, and enter **Superior Technology College** in the Find what text box.

   d. Click the **Find Next** button. On your Student Answer Sheet, record the key where Superior Technical College is found.

   e. Check to see if Superior Technical College is found in any other keys. Record your results on your Student Answer Sheet.

7. Exit Registry Editor and log off.

LAB 13.4 WORKING WITH HKEY_LOCAL_MACHINE

Objective

At the Animal Care Center, Dennis recently installed some trial software on his computer and then removed it. He now receives a message that Vetman.dll is not found. He wants you to find out what caused this message, and to remove it. After completing this lab, you will be able to:

➤ Back up a Registry key.

➤ Add Registry key values.

➤ Find and remove Registry key values.

➤ Restore a Registry key.

Requirements

To simulate the changes made by Dennis's trial application, you should work with a lab partner. Your lab partner will then make changes to your Registry, which you will need to find and remove.

Estimated completion time: **10 minutes**

ACTIVITY

1. If necessary, start your computer with Windows 2000, and log on as an administrator.

2. In this step, you modify the Registry of your partner's computer in order to simulate the modifications made by Dennis's trial software installation.

   a. If necessary, start **Regedit** by double-clicking the desktop shortcut.

    b. Expand the **HKEY_LOCAL_MACHINE\SOFTWARE** subkey.

    c. Right-click the **SOFTWARE** subkey, click **New**, and then click **Key**.

    d. Enter **VetMan** for the key name.

    e. Right-click **VetMan,** click **New**, and then click **String Value**.

    f. For the string value name, enter **Path**.

    g. Double-click **Path**, and in the value text box, type **c:\program files\vetman\vetman.dll**.

    h. Right-click another Software subkey such as ODBC, Program Groups, or Secure.

    i. Click **New**, then click **String Value** and repeat Steps 2f and 2g to make another entry for VetMan.

    j. On your Lab 13.4 Student Answer Sheet, record the modified subkey and the value entry.

    k. Repeat Steps 2h through 2j to place a Binary value in another subkey.

    l. Minimize all keys, and exit Registry editor.

3. When an error message indicates that a DLL or other application from an uninstalled application can't be found, often the message might be a result of an entry or entries that were not removed from the Registry. In this case, one way to completely remove all traces of the application is to use Regedit to find all references to the application in the Registry, and then remove them. Prior to doing this, however, be sure you have a backup of the Registry subkey on which you are working in case you accidentally damage other values. In this step, you use the Regedt32 program on your computer to find and remove the subkey values your lab partner placed in your Registry.

    a. Back up the Registry subkey on which you are working.

    b. Start **Regedt32** by double-clicking your desktop shortcut.

    c. Click the **SOFTWARE** subkey under HKEY_LOCAL_MACHINE to highlight it.

    d. From the View menu, click the **Find Key** option.

    e. In the Find what text box, enter **Vetman**.

    f. If necessary, remove the check mark from the Match whole word only check box by clicking it.

    g. Click the **Find Next** button, and record the results on your Student Answer Sheet.

    h. Click **Cancel** after the search is completed.

    i. Highlight the **VetMan** key, click the **Edit** menu, and then click **Delete**.

    j. Click **Yes** to confirm the key deletion.

    k. Press **F3** to continue searching for any other Vetman keys. Record the results of the search on your Student Answer Sheet.

    l. Exit Registry Editor.

4. In Step 3 you observed that Regedt32 searches only for key names, and not for values. An advantage of using Regedit is that it can find values as well as key names. In this step, you use Regedit to find and remove any other Vet entries made by your lab partner.

    a. Start **Regedit** by double-clicking your desktop shortcut.

    b. Right-click the **SOFTWARE** subkey, and click the **Find** option.

    c. Enter **Vetman** in the Find what text box.

    d. If necessary, remove the check mark from the **Match whole strings only** check box by clicking it.

    e. Click the **Find Next** button.

    f. If found, record the Vetman subkeys and value entries on your Student Answer Sheet. Then remove those subkeys and values.

    g. Press **F3** to continue searching for other Vetman keys until no more value entries are found.

    h. Compare your results to your partner's, and on your Student Answer Sheet, record any values that your partner found but you did not.

    i. Minimize the **SOFTWARE** subkey.

    j. Exit Regedit.

5. Close all windows, and log off.

LAB 13.5 BACKING UP AND RESTORING REGISTRY KEYS

Objective

Mr. Melendres has a new software package named LawManager that he wants you to install on his computer. The software is a 60-day evaluation version that comes with an uninstall program to remove it when the trial period is over. After your experience at the Animal Care Center, you have decided not to trust the uninstall program to clean up its Registry settings. You have decided to create a backup of the Registry prior to installing the software. After completing this lab, you will be able to:

➤ Use Regedit to export and import subkey data.

➤ Use Regedt32 to back up and restore subkeys.

➤ Identify limitations of restoring subkeys with Regedit and Regedt32.

Requirements

➤ Completion of Lab 13.4.

Estimated completion time: **15 minutes**

13

ACTIVITY

1. If necessary, start your computer with Windows 2000, and log on as an administrator.

2. Prior to installing new software or editing the Registry, it is a good procedure to back up the entire Registry, as you did in Lab 13.1. You also should make a copy of the particular keys you are working on. Although you can copy individual Registry keys using either Regedit or Regedt32, you might prefer to use Regedit, because Regedt32 prevents you from restoring system keys that are in use by the operating system. In this step, you use both the Regedit and Regedt32 applications to save the SOFTWARE subkey, prior to installing the evaluation software for Mr. Melendres.

   a. Use My Computer or Windows Explorer to create a folder named **Keybackup** on your Windows 2000 system disk.

   b. Close all windows.

   c. Start **Regedit** by double-clicking your desktop shortcut.

   d. Highlight the **HKEY_LOCAL_MACHINE\SOFTWARE** subkey.

   e. Click **Export Registry File** from the Registry menu.

   f. Verify that the **Selected Branch** option button is selected, and that the Software subkey appears in the Selected Branch text box.

   g. If necessary, browse to your **Keybackup** folder.

   h. Enter the name **Software** in the File name text box, and click **Save**.

   i. Minimize all keys, and exit the Registry Editor.

   j. Start **Regedt32** by double-clicking your desktop shortcut.

   k. In the HKEY_LOCAL_MACHINE window, click the **SOFTWARE** subkey to highlight it.

   l. Click the Registry menu, **Save Key** option.

   m. If necessary, browse to your **Keybackup** folder, enter the name **SoftwareKey** in the File name text box, and click **Save**.

   n. After the save is completed, exit Regedt32.

3. In this step, you simulate the changes made to the Software subkey from the installation of the LawManager software package.

   a. If necessary, start **Regedit** by double-clicking the desktop shortcut.

   b. Right-click the **SOFTWARE** key, and create a new subkey named **LawMan**.

   c. Within the Secure subkey, add a string value named **LawUsers**, with a value of **c:\program files\LawMan\Users.dat**.

   d. Minimize and expand the **SOFTWARE** subkey to verify the LawMan values.

   e. Delete the **ODBC** software subkey.

4. In this step, you use the Import Registry option to restore the SOFTWARE key.

   a. Highlight the **HKEY_LOCAL_MACHINE\SOFTWARE** subkey, and click the Registry menu, **Import Registry File** option.

   b. Double-click the **Software.reg** file you created in Step 2 to start the restore process.

   c. Record the message you receive on your Lab 13.5 Student Answer Sheet. Click **OK** to continue.

   d. The Regedit import process works by merging key data from the import file into the Registry, and therefore restores missing values, but does not remove existing values. Use Regedit to expand and view your restored Software key. On your Student Answer Sheet, record whether importing the Registry removed the LawMan key values and restored the ODBC subkey.

   e. On your Student Answer Sheet, briefly describe two methods you could use to return the Software key to its condition prior to installing the LawManager software.

5. Exit Regedit.

6. As stated earlier, when using Regedt32, you cannot restore a key if any of its subkeys are in use by the system. In this step, you attempt to restore the Software subkey you saved in Step 2.

   a. Start **Regedt32** by double-clicking your desktop shortcut.

   b. Access the **HKEY_LOCAL_MACHINE** window and click the **SOFTWARE** subkey.

   c. With the SOFTWARE subkey highlighted, click the Registry menu, **Restore** option.

   d. Double-click the **SoftwareKey** file, and click **Yes** to continue.

   e. Record any error messages you receive on your Student Answer Sheet.

7. Subkeys that are not in use can be easily saved and restored using Regedt32. In this step, you save the current user's Printers key using Regedt32:

   a. Access the **HKEY_CURRENT_USER** key window.

   b. Click the **Printers** subkey.

   c. From the Registry menu, click **Save Key**. If necessary, browse to your KeyBackup folder, enter the name **Printers** in the File name text box, and click **Save**.

8. To practice restoring a key with Regedt32, in this step, you delete the Printers subkey, and then restore it.

   a. Delete the **Printers** subkey (so that you can restore it in the next step):

      ▪ Click the **Printers** subkey to highlight it.

      ▪ Click the **Edit** menu, **Delete** option, and click **Yes** to confirm.

13

      b. Restore the Printers subkey as follows:

- Click the Registry menu, **Restore** option.

- Double-click the **Printers** Registry entry, and click **Yes** to continue.

- Verify that the Printers subkey has been restored to the HKEY_CURRENT_USER window.

      c. Record the results of restoring the Printers subkey on your Student Answer Sheet.

   9. Exit Regedt32 and log off.

LAB 13.6 WORKING WITH USER DATA

Objective

The Melendres and Associates law firm recently called to report that Mr. Melendres' server computer received a warning message asking for an increase in the maximum size of the Registry. After talking to Mr. Melendres, you discovered that in the last several months the firm has been hiring and releasing a lot of temporary employees. Each time they replaced a temporary employee, the firm deleted the old user account and created a new user. As a result of creating and deleting so many users, you suspect that the HKEY_USERS key might be excessively large. You decide to check the size of the HKEY_USERS key, and to delete any users that no longer exist. After completing this lab, you will be able to:

➤ Use Regedt32 to view the HKEY_USERS key.

➤ Determine the relationship between the HKEY_USERS and CURRENT_USER keys.

➤ Remove users that no longer exist from the HKEY_USERS key.

➤ Use Regedt32 to change Registry key permissions, and back up the SAM and Security subkeys.

Estimated completion time: **15–20 minutes**

ACTIVITY

1. If necessary, start your computer with Windows 2000, and log on as an administrator.

2. Create two new restricted user accounts named **User1** and **User2**. (Refer to Chapter 5 on creating user accounts, if necessary.)

3. Log on as **User1**, and then log off to create a user profile for User1. (User profile information is created when the system starts, by reading all the

NTUSER.DAT files from the user's folders located in the Documents and Settings folder.)

4. Log on as **User2**, and then log off to create a user profile for User2.

5. Log on as Administrator.

6. In this step, you view the user profile information that has been created by logging on and off as User1 and User2.

   a. Open **Control Panel**, and double-click the **System** icon.

   b. Click the **User Profiles** tab to view all users that have logged on.

   c. Record the user profile names on your Lab 13.6 Student Answer Sheet.

   d. Click **Cancel**, and close Control Panel.

   e. Use My Computer or Windows Explorer to open the **Documents and Settings** folder located on the Windows 2000 operating system drive.

   f. Verify that all user profiles have corresponding folders in the Documents and Settings folder.

   g. On your Student Answer Sheet, record any folders that do not have usernames in the User Profiles window.

   h. Close all windows.

7. Delete the User1 and User2 accounts.

   a. Click **Start**, **Settings**, **Control Panel**, and then double-click **Users and Passwords**.

   b. Click **User1**, click the **Remove** button, and respond by clicking **Yes** to confirm the removal. Repeat this process to remove the User2 account.

   c. Click **OK** to exit the Users and Passwords application.

   d. Close Control Panel.

8. Check for profile information from the deleted user accounts.

   a. Open **Control Panel** and double-click the **System** icon.

   b. Click the **User Profiles** tab to view all users that have logged on.

   c. Record the user profile names on your Student Answer Sheet.

   d. Click **Cancel,** and close Control Panel.

   e. Use **My Computer** or **Windows Explorer** to open the **Documents and Settings** folder.

   f. Verify that all user profiles have corresponding folders in the Documents and Settings folder.

   g. On your Student Answer Sheet, record any folders that do not have usernames in the User Profiles window.

   h. Close all windows.

9. Remove any Unknown accounts from the User Profiles window.

   a. Click an **Account Unknown**.

13

b. Click the **Delete** button, and click **Yes** to confirm the removal of the profile information. Repeat this procedure for each unknown account.

c. Use My Computer or Windows Explorer to open the **Documents and Settings** folder.

d. On your Student Answer Sheet, record any folders that do not have user profile information.

10. The SAM subkey contains user account and security information. However, by default, this subkey, along with the Security subkey, is protected by restricting the Administrator's permissions. As a result, before accessing these subkeys, you need to modify your Administrator permissions. Regedt32 needs to be used for this purpose because Regedit does not allow permission changes. To gain experience with changing permissions, in this step you use Regedt32 to change permissions and back up the SAM subkey.

a. Start **Regedt32** by double-clicking your desktop shortcut.

b. Access the **HKEY_LOCAL_MACHINE** key window.

c. Expand the **SAM** key. Notice that the SAM and SECURITY subkeys are grayed out, and you cannot open them to view any key values.

d. Click the grayed out **SAM** subkey, click the **Registry** menu, and click the **Save Key**.

e. Enter the name **SAMKey** in the File name text box and click **Save**. Record the message you receive on your Student Answer Sheet.

f. To change permissions, with the SAM subkey highlighted, click the Security menu, **Permissions** option.

g. Click the **Advanced** button to display the Permissions window shown in Figure 13-4.

h. Click to place a check mark in the **Reset permissions on all child objects and enable propagation of inheritable permissions** check box.

i. With the **Administrators** group highlighted, click **View/Edit**, and record the rights for the Administrator on your Student Answer Sheet.

j. Click to place check marks in the Allow boxes of all permisisons.

k. Click **OK** twice to save the changes, and return to the Permissions window.

l. Check **Yes** to accept the removal of explicitly defined permissions on all child objects, and then Click **OK** to return to Regedt32.

m. With the **SAM** key highlighted, click **Registry**, **Save Key**.

n. If necessary, browse to the Key Backup folder, enter **SAMKey** in the File name text box, and click **Save**.

11. Close all windows, and log off.

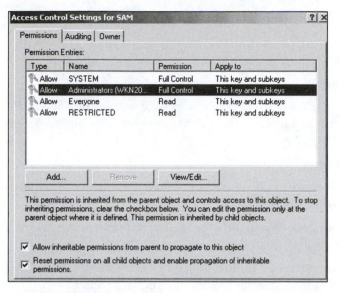

Figure 13-4   Access Control Settings window, Permissions tab

Lab 13.7 Restoring the Registry

Objective

In Lab 13.5 you learned that it can be difficult to use Regedit or Regedt32 to restore Registry keys. Importing a key with Regedit does not remove existing entries, and Regedt32 requires that the key values not be in use by other processes. In this lab, you will use the Windows 2000 Backup utility to simulate restoring the Melendres and Associates computer's Registry to its state prior to installing the LawManager application. After completing this lab, you will be able to:

➤ Use the Windows 2000 Backup program to restore a Registry backup.

Requirements

➤ Your Registry backup from Lab 13.1.

➤ Completion of Lab 13.5.

Estimated completion time: **10 minutes**

ACTIVITY

1. If necessary, start your computer with Windows 2000, and log on as an administrator.

2. Start **Regedt32** by double-clicking its desktop icon.

3. Verify that the LawMan subkey you created within the SOFTWARE key in Lab 13.5 is still there. If the LawMan subkey does not exist, repeat Step 3 of Lab 13.5.

4. Exit the Regedt32 utility.

5. Start the **Backup** utility by clicking **Start**, **Programs**, **Accessories**, **System Tools**, **Backup**.

6. Click the **Restore Wizard** button, and click **Next** to display the What to Restore catalog window.

7. Click the **Import File** button, and, if necessary, use the **Browse** button to select the **Registry.bkf** file from your RegBack folder.

8. Click **OK** to import the Registry backup.

9. Expand the **File** folder in the What to Restore pane.

10. Expand the **Media created** folder to display your System State backup.

11. Click the check box in front of the **System State** folder, and click **Next**.

12. Click **Finish** to display the Backup File Name dialog box.

13. Verify that the Registry.bkf file is selected, and then click **OK** to start the restore process.

14. After the restore process is completed, click the **Report** button, and record the results on your Student Answer Sheet. Compare the results to those you recorded after the backup in Lab 13.1. Note any differences on your Student Answer Sheet.

15. Exit Notepad, and click **Close**.

16. Click **Yes** to restart your computer.

17. Log on as the Administrator.

18. Start **Regedt32** by double-clicking its icon.

19. Expand the **Software** key, and check for the LawMan key.

20. Record the results of your findings on your Student Answer Sheet.

21. Exit Regedt32, and log off.

BOOTING WINDOWS 2000

Labs included in this chapter

➤ Lab 14.1 Working with Startup Options

➤ Lab 14.2 Working with the Boot.ini File

➤ Lab 14.3 Creating a Windows 2000 Boot Disk

Microsoft MCSE Exam #70-210 Objectives	
Objective	**Lab**
Recover systems and user data	14.1, 14.2, 14.3
Troubleshoot system restoration by using Safe Mode	14.1

Student Answer Sheets to accompany the labs in this chapter can be downloaded from the Online Companion for this manual at *www.course.com*.

Lab 14.1 Working with Startup Options

Objective

Kristen, head librarian at the Home Town Library, recently called to report that one of the Window 2000 computers in the Micro-lab periodically "hangs" when it is first started in the morning. When asked if any new software or hardware had been installed on the system, Kristen reported that a Computer Based Training package had been installed but was working fine on the other systems. Occasionally, incorrect configuration settings, driver incompatibility, or hardware problems can disable normal Windows 2000 operations, or prevent the system from starting. To make troubleshooting these problems easier, Windows 2000 provides a number of boot options that can be selected by pressing the F8 key when the boot menu appears. Your job in this lab is to learn how you can use the Windows 2000 boot options to help you troubleshoot and isolate problems of this sort. After completing this lab, you will be able to:

➤ Boot Windows 2000 to Safe Mode using command prompt and network options.

➤ Enable boot logging and interpret the resulting boot log.

➤ Use Last Known Good Configuration to restart a computer.

➤ Identify device-loading Registry parameters.

 In this Lab and the other Labs in this chapter, unless otherwise instructed, select the Microsoft Windows 2000 Professional operating system and press Enter when starting or restarting your computers.

Estimated completion time: **20 minutes**

 ## Activity

1. You just started the Home Town Library Windows 2000 computer in question, and it "hung" during the boot process just after the Microsoft Windows 2000 Professional banner appeared. On your Lab 14.1 Student Answer Sheet, record the last step of the boot process that would have completed successfully.

2. In order to troubleshoot a computer that is "hanging" during the boot process, you need to determine at which step in the loading process the system is halting. One way to do this is to use the startup options to boot the computer, starting with "Safe Mode with Command Prompt" and working up to a Normal boot. In the next few steps, you boot the computer in each of the "Safe" modes, and record the results on your Student Answer Sheet.

a. Start your computer and press the **F8** key when you see the boot selection menu. Record the "Safe" boot options on your Student Answer Sheet.

b. Highlight the **Safe Mode with Command Prompt** option and press **Enter**. Log in as an administrator. On your Student Answer Sheet, describe the steps that occur after you press the Enter key on the command prompt option. When the command prompt appears, record the version and build number on your Student Answer Sheet.

c. One use of the command prompt booting option might be to copy or update system files that have been corrupted or deleted. For example, type the command **Dir ntoskrnl.exe/s** and press **Enter** to search for the Windows 2000 operating system kernel. On your Student Answer Sheet, record the path to the kernel, along with the creation date.

d. Use Task Manager to check system processes and resource usage as follows:

- Use the **Ctrl+Alt+Del** key combination, and click **Task Manager**.
- On your Student Answer Sheet, record the number of Processes running along with CPU Usage and the Physical Memory present. Is the physical memory shown less than the actual memory? Explain this on the Student Answer Sheet.

e. Type **Exit** and press **Enter**. After verifying that the system is operating correctly in the Command Prompt mode, the next step in the troubleshooting process is to use the Safe Mode to boot the system without network support. In this step, you boot the computer to Safe Mode and observe system operation:

f. Restart your computer by pressing **Ctrl+Alt+Del** and clicking the **Shutdown** button. When you see the boot selection menu, press the **F8** key, highlight the **Safe Mode** option (without networking), and press **Enter**.

- Log on using your administrator username and password.
- On your Student Answer Sheet, record the possible causes and suggested action provided in the Desktop Safe Mode message. Click **OK** to continue.
- One source to check for possible system problems is the Event Viewer System log. To do this, open **Control Panel**, open **Administrative Tools**, and start **Event Viewer**. View your error message, and on your Student Answer Sheet, record any devices that failed to load.
- Close **Event Viewer**.

g. After the Windows 2000 kernel loads, it uses the Registry to determine the sequence in which to initialize drivers that were loaded during the boot process. If drivers experience errors as they initialize, the kernel

14

determines what action to take, based on the Error Control Registry entry for that driver. In this step, you use a Registry editor to check the load sequence and error control entries for the disk system on your computer:

- Start **Regedit** from the **Start**, **Run** dialog box.
- Expand the HKEY_LOCAL_MACHINE key to show the \SYSTEM\ControlSet001\Services subkey.
- On your Student Answer Sheet, use the following information, and record the Error Control and Start levels for each of the **Abiosdsk** and **atapi** services.

    Level 0: Ignore.

    Error Level 1: Normal (Message is shown, but boot process continues.)

    Error Level 2: Severe (If Last Known Good Configuration—LKGC—is not in use, restart with LKGC. If LKGC in use, display message and continue.)

    Error Level 3: Critical (If LKGC is not in use, restart with LKGC. If LKGC in use, boot process fails.)

h. Use Regedit to search for any service having a Critical or Severe error level:

- Click **Edit**, **Find** and enter **ErrorControl** in the Find what text box.
- Click to remove the check mark from the **Keys** and **Data** check boxes, leaving only **Values** checked.
- Click **Match whole string only** check box.
- Click the **Find Next** button.
- Press the **F3** key to search for any ErrorControl values greater than 1. Record that service on your Student Answer Sheet.

i. After searching all Services, exit the Registry Editor.

3. Use **My Network Places** to attempt to browse to other computers on your network. Record any message you receive on your Student Answer Sheet.

4. Close all windows.

5. If everything checks out after booting in Safe Mode, the problem could be in the network drivers. In this step, you boot the computer with the Safe Mode with Networking option, and attempt to access computers on the network.

a. Restart your computer.

b. Press **F8** when you see the boot selection menu, and select the **Safe Mode with Networking** option.

c. Log on as administrator.

   d. Use **My Computer** to browse to the network.

   e. On your Student Answer Sheet, record the name of at least one other computer in your workgroup.

6. Because the Safe modes do not load all drivers and services, some problems may only occur in normal boot mode. When this happens, you can use the boot log file to log drivers that load, and if the system hangs, reboot in Safe Mode, then read the logged messages to help determine what driver might have caused the problem. In this step, you practice creating and reading a boot log.

   a. Restart your computer.

   b. Press **F8** when you see the boot selection menu and select the **Enable Boot Logging** option. The system continues to load Windows 2000. Do not log on at this time.

   c. To simulate a system crash, turn off the computer when you see the logon window.

   d. Restart the computer in Safe Mode and log on as the administrator.
   - Press **F8** when you see the Windows 2000 boot selection menu.
   - Verify that **Safe Mode** is selected, and press **Enter**.
   - Log on as the administrator and click **OK** to respond to the Windows is running in Safe Mode message.

   e. Use **My Computer** or **Windows Explorer** to browse to the **WINNT** folder.

   f. Double-click the **ntbtlog.txt** file to open it with Notepad.

   g. On your Student Answer Sheet, record the information requested.

   h. Close Notepad.

   i. Restart your computer in Normal boot mode.
   - Click **Start**, **Shutdown**, select **Restart**, and then click **OK**.
   - Select the Microsoft Windows 2000 Professional operating system from the boot menu, and press **Enter**.
   - Log on as the administrator.

7. Making changes to the system configuration can sometimes cause more problems than it solves. When this happens, you often can correct the problem by booting from the Last Known Good Configuration (LNGC). When you realize that a configuration is bad, it is important not to log on after restarting the system, or the LNGC will be overwritten with the current configuration data. In this step, you simulate using LNGC to correct a screen configuration problem that you create.

   a. Right-click any empty space on the desktop, and click **Properties** to display the Display Properties window.

14

b. Click the **Settings** tab and record the screen resolution on your Student Answer Sheet.

c. Change your screen resolution and click **Apply**. Record the revised screen resolution on your Student Answer Sheet.

d. Click **OK** to test your new settings.

e. Click **Yes** to keep the settings.

f. Click **OK** to close the Display Properties window.

g. Restart the computer.

h. Press the **F8** key when the boot menu appears, and select the Last Known Good Configuration option.

i. Log on as the administrator.

j. Right-click any empty space on the desktop, and click **Properties**.

k. Click the **Setup** tab, and record the restored screen resolution on your Student Answer Sheet. Make sure the restored resolution is the same as the resolution you recorded in Step 6d.

l. Close all windows and log off.

LAB 14.2 WORKING WITH THE BOOT.INI FILE

Objective

Superior Technical College has a computer lab in which the student computers need to be able to boot to multiple operating systems. In addition, because the instructor's station is used for demonstrations, the college wants to make it easy for presenters to boot the computer to various startup modes without having to use the F8 function key. The Boot.ini file identifies the location of the Windows 2000 operating system as well as various startup parameters. Knowing how to modify the Boot.ini file is important when troubleshooting or configuring Windows 2000. After completing this lab, you will be able to:

➤ Identify the proper installation sequence for multiple operating systems.

➤ Use Control Panel to modify the default Boot.ini file parameters.

➤ Use Notepad to modify the Boot.ini file.

➤ Add boot options to the Boot.ini file.

Estimated completion time: **15–20 minutes**

ACTIVITY

1. Superior Technical College has contracted with your company to install the computer systems in the new Web Page Development lab. In addition to Web classes, this lab will be used for teaching DOS and Windows 95. As a result, you need to install all three operating systems on the computers. On your Lab 14.2 Student Answer Sheet, describe the installation sequence you would employ to allow all three operating systems to boot through the Windows 2000 boot selection menu.

2. If necessary, start your computer with Windows 2000, and log on as an administrator.

3. By default, the boot selection menu provides only a short time for the operator to make a selection before booting from the default operating system. Often this does not give users enough time to make a selection. To help prevent booting to the wrong operating system, Superior Technical College wants the computers in the Web lab to wait at least 5 minutes before starting with the default operating system. In this step, you use Control Panel to change the default boot options.

   a. Open **Control Panel** and double-click the **System** icon.

   b. Click the **Advanced** tab and then click the **Startup and Recovery** button to display a Startup and Recovery window similar to the one shown in Figure 14-1.

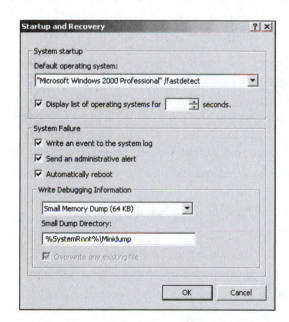

Figure 14-1   Configuring system startup options

14

c. On your Student Answer Sheet, record the default operating system, along with the number of seconds given to display the list of operating systems.

d. Click the down arrow button to the right of the operating system window, and on your Student Answer Sheet, record the possible operating system choices.

e. Change the wait time seconds so the system has to wait for 5 minutes before starting the default operating system. Record the number of seconds you enter on your Student Answer Sheet.

f. Click **OK** twice to save your changes.

g. Close Control Panel.

h. Restart your system and verify that the new wait time is in effect.

4. Because teachers often get interrupted while booting the presentation computer, they want the presentation computer to wait indefinitely for them to make an operating system selection. This can be done by placing a negative number (–1) in the time field. In this step, you attempt to use Control Panel to set the number of seconds to –1.

a. If necessary log on as an administrator.

b. Open **Control Panel** and double-click the **System** icon, and click the **Advanced** tab.

c. Click the **Startup and Recovery** button and attempt to change the wait time to a negative number. Record the results on your Student Answer Sheet.

d. Click **Cancel** until you exit the System window.

e. Close Control Panel.

5. As you can see from Steps 2 and 3, only very limited changes can be made to the boot selection menu from Control Panel. To customize the boot selection menu, you need to edit the boot.ini file using a text editor such as Notepad. In this step, you use Notepad to edit the boot.ini file in order to change the default operating system and set an unlimited wait time.

a. Use My Computer or Windows Explorer to open a window for the C: (system) drive.

b. Click **Tools**, **Folder Options** and click the **View** tab.

c. Verify the following options:

  ■ Show hidden files and folders is selected.

  ■ Hide file extensions for known file types is *not* checked.

  ■ Hide protected operating system files (Recommended) is *not* checked.

d. Click **OK** to return to the LocalDisk (C:) window.

e. Navigate to the root of drive C:, right-click the **boot.ini** file, and click **Properties**.

f. If necessary, remove the check mark in the **Read-only** attribute check box, and click **OK**.

g. Right-click the **boot.ini** file, and click the **Open With** option.

h. Double-click **Notepad** to display the contents of the boot.ini file.

i. Record the operating system lines on your Student Answer Sheet.

j. Modify the timeout line to read: **timeout=-1**

k. Save the boot.ini file, and exit Notepad.

l. Open Control Panel, double-click the **System** icon, and click the **Advanced** tab.

m. Click the **Startup and Recovery** button. Record the error message on your Answer Sheet. Click **OK** to close the message.

n. Click **OK** twice to close the System icon.

o. Close Control Panel.

p. Use Notepad to open the **boot.ini** file. Record the wait time on your Student Answer Sheet.

q. Using the diagram on your Student Answer Sheet, identify the location of your Windows 2000 boot partition.

r. If necessary, change the wait time to **-1** and then save the file and exit Notepad.

s. Close all windows and restart your computer.

t. On your Student Answer Sheet, record the result of booting with the wait time set to -1.

6. Superior Technical College wants to add the following options to the boot selection menu:

- Full Hardware Detect (remove /FASTDETECT and add the /NOGUIBOOT option)

- Command prompt only (use the /SAFEBOOT:MINIMAL (ALTERNATESHELL) option)

- Safe Mode with networking (use the /SAFEBOOT:NETWORK option)

In this step, you use Notepad to add the necessary entries and options to the boot.ini file.

a. Use Notepad to open the **boot.ini** file as described in Step 5.

b. Using the existing multi()disk()partition() information, add a line to your boot.ini file for each of the above options, to make your boot.ini file

14

similar to the one shown in Figure 14-2. (Your information may differ, depending on your disk configuration.) Record the lines you add on your Student Answer Sheet.

```
[boot loader]
timeout=30
default=multi(0)disk(0)rdisk(1)partition(2)\WINNT
[operating systems]
multi(0)disk(0)rdisk(1)partition(2)\WINNT="Microsoft Windows 2000" /fastdetect
multi(0)disk(0)rdisk(1)partition(2)\WINNT="Full Detect" /NOGUIBOOT /SAFEBOOT:MINIMAL
multi(0)disk(0)rdisk(1)partition(2)\WINNT="Command Prompt" /SAFEBOOT:MINIMAL
(ALTERNATESHELL)
multi(0)disk(0)rdisk(1)partition(2)\WINNT="Safe/Network" /SAFEBOOT:NETWORK
```

Figure 14-2   Boot.ini file options

   c. Save the boot.ini file, and exit Notepad.

7. In this step, you test each of your boot options.

   a. Close all windows and restart your system.

   b. Test each boot option and, if necessary, make corrections to your boot.ini file.

   c. If necessary, record any corrections on your Student Answer Sheet, or attach an updated printout of the boot.ini file.

8. Close all windows and log off.

LAB 14.3 CREATING A WINDOWS 2000 BOOT DISK

Objective

Being able to boot from a floppy disk can be important to recovering from corrupted system files or when working with a Windows 2000 server that has mirrored disk drives. When using mirrored disk drives, if the primary drive fails, the boot floppy can be used to boot the computer from the backup or mirrored drive. For example, the Melendres and Associates law firm recently upgraded to Windows 2000 Server mirrored disk drives. In this lab, you will learn how to create a Windows 2000 boot disk that can be used to boot a Windows 2000 Server or Professional system in the event the primary boot drive or boot sector is damaged. After completing this lab, you will be able to:

➤ Format a Windows 2000 disk.

➤ Copy system files to a disk.

➤ Modify the boot.ini file to change the boot partition number.

➤ Identify error messages that occur when attempting to boot from a partition that does not contain the Windows 2000 operating system.

➤ Boot your computer from a disk and recover the NTLDR program.

Requirements

➤ A blank disk.

Estimated completion time: **15 minutes**

ACTIVITY

1. If necessary, start your computer with Windows 2000, and log on as an administrator.

2. Format a disk as follows:

    a. Insert a disk in the A drive, and double-click **My Computer**.

    b. Right-click the **(A:)** drive and click the **Format** option.

    c. Enter **W2KBOOT** in the Volume label text box.

    d. Verify that the Quick Format check box is unchecked. Click **Start** and then **OK** to the warning message to perform a full format. (*Note:* Windows 2000 does not have a System format option. In the next step, you make a system disk by copying the necessary system files to the formatted disk.)

    e. After the format is complete, click **Close** to exit the Format window.

3. Copy files from the C: (system) drive to your newly formatted disk.

    a. Use **My Computer** to open a window to the C: (system) drive.

    b. Copy the following files to your disk:

    ▪ ntldr

    ▪ ntdetect.com

    ▪ boot.ini

    c. Close all windows.

    d. Write **Windows 2000 Boot Disk** on the disk label.

4. If you were working with a mirrored drive on a server, the next step would be to modify the boot.ini file on the disk so you can add an option that would load the kernel and other operating system files from the WINNT folder of the mirrored drive. In this step, you simulate this process by adding such an option to the boot.ini file on your disk.

    a. Use My Computer or Windows Explorer to open a window for the (A:) drive.

    b. Right-click the **boot.ini** file, and click the **Open with** option.

14

   c. Double-click **Notepad** to view the boot.ini file.

   d. Add the following line at the end of the [operating system] lines:

   ■ **multi(0)disk(1)rdisk(0)partition(#)\WINNT="Windows 2000 Mirror Boot"**

If you are using SCSI drives without BIOS support, you need to change the disk numbering to read: SCSI(0)disk(0)rdisk(1)

   e. Save the boot.ini file, and exit Notepad.

5. Test your boot disk by restarting your computer with the disk in the drive and selecting the **Normal** boot option. Record the results on your Lab 14.3 Student Answer Sheet.

6. Test your boot disk again by restarting your computer with the disk in the drive and selecting the **Mirrored drive** boot option. Record the error message you receive on your Student Answer Sheet.

7. Remove the disk from drive A:. Restart the computer and log on as the administrator.

8. In this step, you simulate a problem with your hard drive boot partition by changing the partition number in the Boot.ini file of the C: (system) drive. Then you fix the problem by restarting the computer with the Safe Mode option of the boot disk.

   a. Use My Computer or Windows Explorer to open a window to the C: (system) drive.

   b. Right-click the **boot.ini** file, and click the **Open with** option.

   c. Double-click **Notepad** to open the **Boot.ini** file.

   d. On your Student Answer Sheet, record the Advanced RISC Computing (ARC) path-name for the Windows 2000 normal boot option.

   e. Change the Partition number in the Windows 2000 normal boot option.

   f. Save the **boot.ini** file and exit.

   g. Restart your computer using the modified Windows 2000 normal boot option.

   h. Record the error message you receive on your Student Answer Sheet.

   i. Insert the Windows 2000 Boot disk in the drive, and restart your computer.

   j. After Windows 2000 has booted, log on as the administrator.

k. Repeat steps 8a through 8f to change the partition number back to the original correct number you recorded on your Student Answer Sheet for Step 7d.

l. Remove the Windows 2000 Boot disk from the drive and restart your computer.

9. In this step, you rename the NTLDR file to simulate a corrupted loader, and then fix the problem by booting in Safe Mode from your Windows 2000 boot disk.

   a. Use My Computer or Windows Explorer to open a window to the C: (system) drive.

   b. Rename **ntldr** to **ntldr.bak**. Click Yes to the warning message.

   c. Close all windows.

   d. Remove your Windows 2000 Boot disk from the drive.

   e. Restart your computer, and record the error message on your Student Answer Sheet.

   f. Insert your Windows 2000 Boot disk, and restart the computer using the Command Prompt mode.

   g. In the Command prompt window, enter the following commands from the root of your boot drive. (In the following commands "drive:\>" represents the command prompt path, and "drive:" is your boot drive. You need to enter only the commands shown in bold.)

   drive:\>**ATTRIB A:\NTLDR –H –S** (Remove Hidden and System Attributes)

   drive:\>**COPY A:\NTLDR C:\NTLDR**

   drive:\>**ATTRIB C:\NTLDR +H +S** (Set Hidden and System Attributes)

   h. Remove the Windows 2000 Boot disk from the drive, and restart your computer.

   i. Record the result on your Student Answer Sheet.

   j. Close all windows and log off.

14

DISASTER RECOVERY AND PROTECTION

Labs included in this chapter

➤ Lab 15.1 Establishing a Data Protection and Recovery System

➤ Lab 15.2 Scheduling and Testing Normal User Backups

➤ Lab 15.3 Scheduling and Testing Daily Differential Backups

➤ Lab 15.4 Protecting the Windows 2000 Professional System

➤ Lab 15.5 Recovering from System Problems

➤ Lab 15.6 Installing Applications with Windows Installer

Microsoft MCSE Exam #70-210 Objectives	
Objective	Lab
Recover systems and user data	15.1
Recover systems and user data by using Windows Backup	15.2, 15.4, 15.5
Install applications by using Windows Installer packages	15.3, 15.6

Student Answer Sheets to accompany the labs in this chapter can be downloaded from the Online Companion for this manual at *www.course.com*.

Lab 15.1 Establishing a Data Protection and Recovery System

Objective

As the Melendres and Associates law firm's use of the network has expanded, Mr. Melendres has become more concerned about establishing a system to help protect against data loss and restore system operation if a problem or disaster occurs. After meeting with Mr. Melendres, you have agreed to plan and implement a data protection plan that includes four levels. The first level is to provide protection against power surges and outages through the installation of a quality UPS (uninterruptible power supply) on the server computer. The second level is to synchronize critical case data with the server. Synchronizing the data on the server allows users to maintain a copy of the data on their local computers. In the event that the server is down, users can continue to access case information on their local machines. The third level is to establish a daily backup of the user data on the server. This backup can be used to recover user data in the event of operator error or system disaster. The fourth level is to provide a method to quickly repair problems on the server without having to perform a lengthy reinstall or restore process. In this lab, you will work on the first two levels by configuring a UPS and synchronizing user data. In Labs 15.2 and 15.3, you will continue to set up the data protection plan by implementing levels three and four. In Lab 15.4 you will work with the Recovery Console and create and use an Emergency Repair Disk (ERD). After completing this lab, you will be able to:

➤ Identify the four levels of a data protection plan.

➤ Establish a configuration for an uninterruptible power supply (UPS).

➤ Implement and test folder redirection.

Requirements

➤ Another Windows 2000 computer to act as a server for folder synchronization.

Estimated completion time: **20 minutes**

Activity

1. If necessary, start your computer with Windows 2000, and log on as an administrator.

2. On your Lab 15.1 Student Answer Sheet, describe the four levels of your data protection plan for the Melendres and Associates law firm.

3. Mr. Melendres is considering purchasing either an American Power Conversion Back-UPS Pro 1000 (Serial) for about $400, or an American Power Conversion Smart-UPS 700 (Serial) for about $450. In this step, you look up the UPS models in the Windows 2000 Hardware Compatiblity List (HCL) text file, and then on your Student Answer Sheet, record the UPS you would recommend, and why.

   a. Insert the Windows 2000 Professional CD into your CD drive.

   b. Use My Computer or Windows Explorer to open a window to the **SUPPORT** folder.

   c. Double-click **HCL.TXT** to open it with Notepad.

   d. Use the HCL to determine which UPS would be best to buy, and record the information on your Student Answer Sheet.

   e. Close all windows.

4. You have just finished installing the UPS and connecting its control cable to the serial port of the server computer. In this step, you use the UPS icon from Control Panel to customize the UPS settings.

   a. Open **Control Panel** and double-click **Power Options**.

   b. Click the **UPS** tab and click the **Select** button.

   c. Use the Select manufacturer scroll button to select the UPS manufacturer.

   d. In the Select model window, click the model you selected in Step 3.

   e. Verify that your computer's available COM port is selected. Record the Manufacturer, Model, and COM port on your Student Answer Sheet.

   f. Click the **Finish** button to return to the UPS tab.

   g. Click the **Configure** button to display the UPS Configuration window shown in Figure 15-1.

   h. Record the default settings on your Student Answer Sheet.

   i. The amount of time that the UPS can operate a computer depends on the battery capacity of the UPS and the current draw of the computer. Assume that the UPS you are installing for Mr. Melendres specifies that it can provide power for up to 7 minutes given the power demands of his computer. To provide a 2-minute margin of safety, change the Minutes on battery before critical alarm setting to **5**.

15

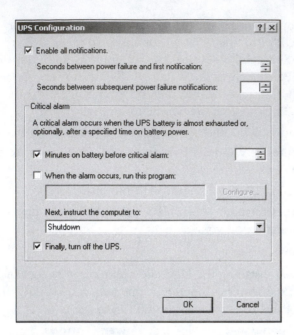

Figure 15-1 UPS Configuration window

    j. Click **OK** to save your configuration, and return to the UPS tab.

    k. Click **OK** to exit Power Options.

    l. Close Control Panel.

5. Currently, the legal assistants copy each client's case information to the My Documents folder on their local computers. The problem with this system is that the case information is not being backed up regularly, and other legal assistants or attorneys cannot access the case files until they are finished and placed back in the shared Cases folder. If the legal assistants work only on case information stored on the server, this could cause a problem if the server or network were down. Folder redirection solves both these problems by allowing data stored on the server to be automatically synchronized with the client in the event the server is down. In this step, you simulate this level of the data protection system by seeing how to set up folder redirection.

To actually implement folder redirection, you need to be able to log on to a Windows 2000 Server domain from your Windows 2000 Professional station.

    a. Start **Windows Explorer** and click the **Tools** menu, **Synchronize** option.

b. From the Items to Synchronize window, click the **Setup** button to display the Synchronization Settings window.

c. From the **Logon/Logoff** tab, record the information in the network connection and Synchronize panes on your Student Answer Sheet.

d. Use the scroll button to the right of the "When I am using this network connection" text box, and use your Student Answer Sheet to record synchronization items for any other network connections.

If the Windows 2000 Professional computer is a member of a Windows 2000 Server domain, at this point you could select to synchronize folders from your local computer to a network share.

e. Click **OK** and then click **Close** to return to Windows Explorer.

f. Close the Windows Explorer window.

LAB 15.2 SCHEDULING AND TESTING NORMAL USER BACKUPS

Objective

After the server contains the User data and is protected from power problems, the next level in the data protection plan is to provide a daily backup of the organization's data. There are three major daily backup options: Full (also called Normal), Incremental, and Differential. In a Full or Normal backup, the selected files are backed up every day even if no changes were made. With an Incremental backup, only the files that changed that day are copied to the daily backup. A Differential backup copies all files that have changed since the last Full backup.

After you discuss these backup options with Mr. Melendres, he decides to use a daily Differential backup with Full backup to be made on Mondays. In this lab, you will set up and test the Monday Full backup. (In Lab 15.3 you will set up and test the daily Differential backups.) After completing this lab, you will be able to:

➤ Create a Backup Operator user account.

➤ Schedule a Monday Full (Normal) backup of selected files.

➤ Perform and verify the Full (Normal) backup.

15

Estimated completion time: **20 minutes**

ACTIVITY

1. If necessary, start your computer with Windows 2000, and log on as an administrator.

2. Rather than use the Administrator account to back up the system, Mr. Melendres wants you to create a user account that has only the privilege to back up and restore system and user data. In this step, you create a user named BackOp that has backup and restore privileges.

   a. Open **Control Panel** and double-click the **Users and Passwords** application.

   b. Click the **Add** button to display the Add New User window.

   c. Enter the following user information:

      - User name: **BackOp**

      - Full name: **Backup Operators**

      - Description: **Account used to back up user data**

   d. Click **Next**.

   e. Enter a password that you can remember, or use **password**, in both Password and Confirm password text boxes.

   f. Click **Next** to select the level of access for this user.

   g. Click the **Other** option button, and use the scroll button to select the **Backup Operators** group.

   h. Click **Finish** to create the BackOp user account.

   i. Click **OK** to save the changes and return to Control Panel.

   j. Close Control Panel.

3. To use the Backup utility on your computer, in this step, you create a folder named **Backups**.

   a. Use My Computer or Windows Explorer to open a window to the drive containing the Windows 2000 operating system files.

   b. Create a new folder named **Backups**.

   c. Minimize **My Computer** or **Windows Explorer**.

4. As described earlier, Mr. Melendres wants to perform a Full (Normal) backup every Monday at 11:55 pm. To simulate the Monday backup, in this step you schedule a Full (Normal) backup of the Documents and Settings folder to occur in 5 minutes.

   a. Start the Backup utility by clicking **Start**, **Programs**, **Accessories**, **System Tools** and double-clicking **Backup**.

b. Click the **Backup Wizard** button from the Welcome tab, and click **Next** to start the Backup wizard.

c. On your Lab 15.2 Student Answer Sheet, record the three backup item buttons.

d. Click the appropriate option to back up only user data, and click **Next** to display the Items to Back Up window.

e. Select the Documents and Settings folder as follows:

- In the right-side tree pane, click the + box to expand **My Computer** and the drive containing the Windows 2000 operating system.

- Click the check box to the right of the **Documents and Settings** folder.

- Click the **Documents and Settings** folder, and notice that all subfolders are checked.

- Remove the check marks from **All Users** and **Default User** to remove these folders from the backup process.

f. Click **Next** to display the Where to Store the Backup window.

g. Use the **Browse** button to navigate to your **Backups** folder.

h. In the File name field, enter **MondayNormal.bkf** and click the **Open** button.

i. Click **Next** to display the Completing the Backup Wizard window:

- To select the type and schedule for the backup, click the **Advanced** button.

- Click the scroll button to the right of the Select the type of backup text box, and record the possible backup types on your Student Answer Sheet.

- Verify that the **Normal** backup type is selected, and click **Next** to display the backup options.

j. Identify the Normal backup options on your Student Answer Sheet.

k. Click the **Verify data after backup** option check box, and click **Next** to display the Media Options window.

l. Click the **Replace the data on the media with this backup** option button, and click **Next** to display the Backup label window:

- For the Backup and Media labels, enter **Monday Normal backup test**.

- Click **Next** to display the When to Back Up window.

m. Click the **Later** button and enter the name and password of the backup user you established in Step 2. Click **OK** to display the Schedule tab.

15

n. Click the **Set Schedule** button, and then click the scroll button to the right of the **Schedule Task** text box. Record the schedule options on your Student Answer Sheet.

o. Click the **Weekly** option to display the schedule window shown in Figure 15-2.

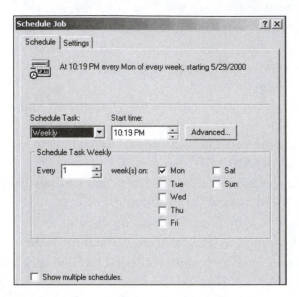

Figure 15-2   Weekly Schedule window

p. Set the start time to start the backup 5 minutes from the current time shown in the lower-right of your status bar.

q. To test the backup today, click the check box next to the current day of the week.

r. Click **OK** to return to the When to Back Up window.

s. Type **Monday Normal backup test** in the Job name text box and click **Next**.

t. Click **Finish** to save your Monday scheduled backup, and return to the Welcome tab window.

u. Click the **Schedule Jobs** tab to display a calendar of scheduled jobs.

v. Click a scheduled job to display the **Monday Normal backup test** job properties. Click **Cancel** to return to the Schedule Jobs calendar.

w. Exit the Backup utility.

5. Test the Monday Normal backup by performing the following procedure.

a. Start **WordPad**.

b. Create a new document that contains the statement **This is Monday's case information.**

c. Save the document as **Case007** in your My Documents folder.

d. Use the **File**, **Save as** option to save the document a second time with the name **Case008**.

e. Wait for your Normal backup to execute.

f. Close all windows and log off.

LAB 15.3 SCHEDULING AND TESTING DAILY DIFFERENTAL BACKUPS

Objective

Once you have verified that the scheduled Monday Normal backup is working, your next step is to configure the Differential backups to occur each remaining day of the week at 11:55 pm. To simulate the daily Differential backups, in this lab you will configure the Tuesday through Friday backups to occur every several minutes. After scheduling the backups, you will enter new data and then test the backups by restoring files. After completing this lab, you will be able to:

➤ Create scheduled Differential backups.

➤ Test the backup system by entering data between scheduled backups.

➤ Restore files using the Differential backup.

Estimated completion time: **25–30 minutes**

ACTIVITY

1. If necessary, start your computer with Windows 2000, and log on as an administrator.

2. If necessary, start the Backup utility (click **Start**, **Programs**, **Accessories**, **System Tools**, and then double-click **Backup**).

3. Create a Differential backup to simulate Tuesday's backup as follows:

a. Start the **Backup Wizard**.

b. Select the option to **Back up selected files** and click **Next**.

c. Repeat Step 4e from Lab 15.2 to select the **Documents and Settings** folder from your Windows 2000 operating system drive, and click **Next**.

d. On the Where to Store the Backup window, click **Browse** and enter **Daily** in the File name text box.

15

e. Click **Open** and then click **Next** to place the Differential daily backup in the Backups folder.

f. Click the **Advanced** button, select the **Differential** option, and click **Next**.

g. Click the **Verify data after backup** option, and click **Next**.

h. Click the **Replace the data on the media with this backup** option, and click **Next**.

i. Enter **Tuesday** in the Backup label text box.

j. Enter **Daily Differential Test** in the Media label, and click **Next**.

k. Click the **Later** option button and enter the name and password of the BackOp user.

l. Click **OK** and then click the **Set Schedule** button.

m. In the Schedule Task text box, click the **Weekly** option and set the start time ten minutes from the current time shown on the right side of the status bar.

n. On your Lab 15.3 Student Answer Sheet, record start times of each Tuesday through Friday differential backup, based on the current time.

o. Click **OK** to save the settings, and return to the When to Back Up window.

p. Enter **Tuesday Differential Backup Test** in the Job name text box, and click **Next**.

q. Click **Finish** to return to the Backup utility.

4. Repeat Step 3 to create a Differential backup to simulate Wednesday's backup.

a. Click the **Append this backup to the media** option, and click **Next**.

b. Enter **Wednesday** in the Backup label text box.

c. Enter **Daily Differential Test** in the Media label.

d. Enter **Wednesday Differential Backup Test** in the Job name text box.

e. Schedule the backup to start at the time you recorded on your Student Answer Sheet.

5. Repeat Step 3 to create a Differential backup to simulate Thursday's backup.

a. Click the **Append this backup to the media** option, and click **Next**.

b. Enter **Thursday** in the Backup label text box.

c. Enter **Daily Differential Test** in the Media label.

d. Enter **Thursday Differential Backup Test** in the Job name text box.

e. chedule the backup to start at the time you recorded on your Student Answer Sheet.

6. You now need to time the next step carefully to make changes between the scheduled backups. In this step, you simulate weekly activity and backups by changing files in your My Documents folder between each scheduled backup.

a. Prior to the Tuesday differential backup, start **WordPad** and open the **Case007** file:

- Add a **This is Tuesday's case information** statement to the end of the file.
- Save the file and exit WordPad.

b. Wait for your Tuesday Differential backup to occur.

c. Prior to the Wednesday Differential backup, start **WordPad** and open the **Case008** file:

- Add a **This is Wednesday's case information** statement to the end of the file.
- Save the file and exit WordPad.

d. Wait for the Wednesday Differential backup to occur.

e. Prior to the Thursday Differential backup, start **WordPad** and then do the following:

- Create and save a new document named **Case009**.
- Exit WordPad.

f. Wait for the Thursday Differential backup to occur.

7. No backup is completed until you can verify that the data can be successfully restored. One of the disadvantages of the Differential backup is that when data is lost, you need to restore both the Full backup and the latest Differential backup. To allow the operator to select folders and files to restore, the Backup utility uses a catalog on the storage device. The backup catalog contains name, location, and other information about each file and folder on the backup media. Before you can restore information you need to import file and folder information from the storage device into the backup catalog. In this step, you make the backup data available by importing catalog entries with the Restore Wizard.

a. Start the **Backup** utility.

b. Click the **Restore Wizard** button, and then click **Next** to display the What to Restore window.

15

c. Import catalog entries for the Monday Normal backup as follows:

- Click the **Import File** button.
- Click the **Browse** button and browse to your **Backups** folder.
- Double-click the **MondayNormal** backup file, and click **OK** to create a catalog entry.

d. Import a catalog entry for the Daily backup as follows:

- Click the **Import File** button.
- Click the **Browse** button, and double-click the **Daily** backup file.
- Click **OK** to create the catalog entry.

e. Expand the **File** folder in the left-side tree window.

f. Expand the Monday Normal backup and all its subfolders as follows:

- In the Backup File Name window, click the **Browse** button, and then click the **MondayNormal** backup file.
- Click **Open** and then click **OK** to expand the Monday Normal backup.

g. Expand the Daily Differential Backup and all its subfolders as follows:

- In the Backup File Name window, click the **Browse** button, and then click the **Daily** backup file.
- Click **Open** and then click **OK** to expand the Differential backup.
- Repeat this process until all subfolders are expanded, as shown in Figure 15-3.

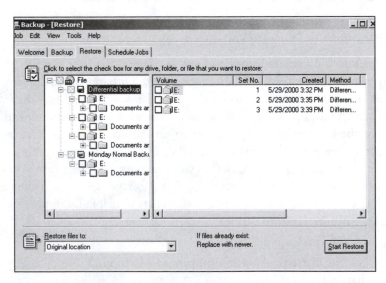

Figure 15-3 Restore catalog window

h. Click **Cancel** to exit the Restore Wizard.

8. In this step, you simulate a Friday morning disaster that deletes all the case files from the My Documents folder of the server computer.

   a. Double-click the **My Documents** desktop icon to open the **My Documents** folder. Delete all the files starting with **Case**.

9. In this step, you test the first phase in the differential restore process by restoring the Monday Normal backup, and then checking the status of the restored files.

   a. If necessary, start the **Backup** utility, and click the **Welcome** tab.

   b. Click the **Restore Wizard** button, and click **Next** to display the What to Restore window.

   c. Expand the **MondayNormal backup** and click the check box to the left of the drive letter to restore it and all its subfolders.

   d. Click **Next** to display a restore summary window.

   e. Click **Finish** to display the Enter Backup File Name dialog box.

   f. Use the **Browse** button to select the **MondayNormal** backup file, and then click **Open**.

   g. Click **OK** and monitor the progress of the Restore program. When the restore is completed, record the requested Restore Progress information on your Student Answer Sheet.

   h. Click the **Report** button and scan for any errors.

   i. Click **Close** to return to the Welcome tab.

   j. Double-click **My Documents** and check to see if all files have been properly restored. Record your findings on the Student Answer Sheet.

10. In this step, you test the second phase in the differential restore process by restoring the Thursday Daily backup, and then checking the file status.

    a. If necessary, start the **Backup** utility and click the **Welcome** tab.

    b. Click the **Restore Wizard** button and click **Next** to display the What to Restore window.

    c. In the left-side What to Restore pane, click the **Daily Differential backup** to display all three backups in the right-side results window.

    d. Click the check box to the left of the **Thursday** backup, and click **Next**.

    e. Click **Finish** to display the Enter Backup File Name window.

    f. Use the **Browse** button to select the **Daily** backup file, and click **Open**.

    g. Click **OK** to start the restore process.

    h. Record the Restore Progress information on your Student Answer Sheet.

    i. Double-click **My Documents** and check to see if all files have been properly restored. Record your findings on your Student Answer Sheet.

11. Exit the Backup utility and log off.

15

LAB 15.4 PROTECTING THE WINDOWS 2000 PROFESSIONAL SYSTEM

Objective

Mr. Melendres wants to know what options are available if the Windows 2000 operating system should become disabled and not boot. Windows 2000 could be reinstalled and the user data restored from the backup, but reinstalling Windows 2000 would take quite a bit of time, especially if you need to re-create the users, assign folder permissions, and reinstall printers and application software. For this reason, the fourth level of data protection involves ways that you can recover or repair the Windows 2000 operating system without having to reinstall it. If the Windows 2000 operating system is damaged and needs to be reinstalled, you still can save a lot of time by being able to use the Backup utility to restore users, printers, and Registry data. After completing this lab, you will be able to:

➤ Use the Backup utility to back up and restore system state data.

➤ Use the Backup utility to create an Emergency Repair Disk (ERD).

➤ Install the Recovery Console.

Requirements

➤ The Windows 2000 Professional CD-ROM to install the Recovery Console in Lab 15.4.

➤ A floppy disk that can be formatted for an Emergency Repair Disk (ERD).

Estimated completion time: **15 minutes**

ACTIVITY

1. If necessary, start your computer with Windows 2000, and log on as an administrator.

2. Backing up system state data provides a way to recover the Registry, system boot files, and user accounts. Although you probably don't need a daily backup of system state data, it's a good idea to back up the system state data before installing applications, and after creating new users or modifying user account policies. In this step, you back up system state data, and then in Step 3 you practice restoring user accounts and Registry settings.

    a. If necessary, start the **Backup** utility.

    b. Click the **Backup Wizard** button and click **Next** to display the What to Back Up window.

    c. Click the **Only backup the System State data** option button, and click **Next**.

    d. Use the **Browse** button to navigate to your **Backups** folder, and enter **System.bkf** in the File name text box.

    e. Click **Open** and then click **Next** to select the **System.bkf** file.

    f. Click **Finish** to start the System State backup process.

    g. Record the requested Backup Progress information on your Lab 15.4 Student Answer Sheet.

    h. Exit the Backup utility.

3. If user accounts become damaged or deleted, you can use the system state backup to restore them. In this step, you use the system state backup you made in Step 2 to restore a deleted user account.

    a. Open **Control Panel** and double-click **Users and Passwords**.

    b. Click the **BackOp** user you created in Lab 15.1, and click the **Remove** button.

    c. Click **Yes** to confirm the action.

    d. Click **OK** to return to Control Panel.

    e. Close Control Panel.

    f. Start the **Backup** utility.

    g. Click the **Restore Wizard** button, and click **Next** to display the What to Restore window.

    h. Click the **Import File** button, and click **OK** to import the System.bkf file into the catalog.

    i. Expand the **System State** backup, and click the check box to the right of the **System State** backup entry. On your Student Answer Sheet, record the three system state items to be restored.

    j. Click **Next** to display the summary window.

    k. Click **Finish** and then click **OK** to select the **System.bkf** file and start the restore process.

    l. Record the requested Restore Progress information on your Student Answer Sheet.

    m. Exit the Backup utility.

    n. Open **Control Panel** and use the **Users and Passwords** utility to verify that the BackOp user was restored.

4. Restoring system state information allows you to recover from problems as long as you are able to boot Windows 2000. The Recovery Console allows you to troubleshoot and fix certain problems that might prevent

15

Windows 2000 from fully booting. In this step, you install the Recovery Console so you can select it when booting to Safe Mode, as described in Chapter 14.

   a. Insert your Windows 2000 CD into your computer's CD-ROM drive.

   b. Click **Start**, **Run**.

   c. Use the **Browse** button to navigate to the **I386** folder of your CD.

   d. Double-click the **WINNT32.EXE** application to insert the Winnt32.exe command in the Open text box.

   e. Press the **Spacebar** and then type **/cmdcons** at the end of the command entry.

   f. Click **OK** and then click **Yes** to install Recovery Console. When installation is completed, a Microsoft Windows 2000 Professional Setup message will appear.

   g. On your Student Answer Sheet, record the method given to start the Recovery Console.

   h. Click **OK** to close the completion message window.

5. If all else fails, and you are unable to boot the computer to a Safe Mode, a last-ditch effort prior to reinstalling Windows 2000 and restoring the backups is to attempt to fix the problem by booting with the Emergency Repair Disk (ERD). In this step, you use the Backup utility to create an ERD, and then you test it in Lab 15.4.

   a. Format a new floppy disk:

     ■ Insert the disk to be formatted in drive A:.

     ■ Double-click **My Computer**.

     ■ Right-click the **A:** drive and click **Format**.

     ■ Enter **ERD** in the Volume label text box.

     ■ If necessary, click to remove any check mark from the **Quick Format** check box.

     ■ Click the **Start** button to format the disk.

     ■ After the disk is formatted, click **Close** and exit My Computer.

   b. Start the **Backup** utility.

   c. Click the **Emergency Repair Disk** button.

   d. Verify that the newly formatted disk is inserted in the drive.

   e. Click the **Also backup the registry** check box to include the ability to recover Registry data.

   f. Click **OK** to start the ERD creation process.

   g. When you see the message that the process is successfully completed, label and remove the ERD.

   h. Click **OK** to exit the completion message.

   i. Exit the Backup utility.

LAB 15.5 RECOVERING FROM SYSTEM PROBLEMS

Objective

Recovering from system problems can range from restoring the Registry after uninstalling an application to fixing a system that does not boot. This lab contains problem scenarios from the Melendres and Associates law firm that will give you practice working with the recovery tools you created in Lab 15.4. After completing this lab, you will be able to:

➤ Use the Backup utility to restore Registry settings.

➤ Use several Recovery Console commands to help restore or troubleshoot the operating system.

➤ Use the Emergency Repair Disk to recover from a damaged operating system.

Requirements

➤ Completion of Lab 15.4.

➤ A set of installation startup disks for Windows 2000. (See Chapter 2 to create a set of startup disks.)

Estimated completion time: **15 minutes**

ACTIVITY

1. If necessary, start your computer with Windows 2000, and log on as an administrator.

2. As described in Chapter 14, most applications modify the Registry when they are installed. Having a system state backup prior to installing an application allows you to restore Registry settings if you need to uninstall an application. For example, in this step, you simulate uninstalling an application for the Melendres and Associates law firm by modifying the Registry and then restoring it from the system state backup you made in Lab 15.4.

    a. Modify the Registry by performing the following steps:

    ■ Start **Regedit** by double-clicking the desktop shortcut you created in Lab 13.1.

    ■ Expand the **HKEY_LOCAL_MACHINE\SOFTWARE** subkey.

    ■ Right-click the **SOFTWARE** subkey and click the **New** menu, **Key** option.

    ■ Enter **LawSuite** for the key name.

    ■ Right-click **PetDiag** and click the **New** menu, **String value** option.

15

- For the string value name, enter **Path**.
- Double-click **Path** and in the value text box, type **c:\program files\lawman\lawman.dll**, and click **OK**.
- Right-click another SOFTWARE subkey such as ODBC, Program Groups, or Secure.
- Click **New**, **String value** to make another entry for LawSuite.
- Minimize all keys and exit the Registry editor.

   b. Restore your System State backup by following the same procedure you performed in Step 3 of Lab 15.4.

   c. Use Regedit to record the results of the restore on your Lab 15.5 Student Answer Sheet.

3. On Monday morning one of the legal assistants at the Melendres and Associates law firm calls to inform you that the Windows 2000 computer at their office is not booting. In this step, you use several commands from the Recovery Console to attempt to get the system operating.

   a. Follow the process you recorded on your Lab 15.4 Student Answer sheet for Step 4g to restart the computer in Recovery Console mode.

   b. Enter the number of the Windows 2000 installation you want to log onto. Record the number on your Student Answer Sheet.

   c. Enter the password for the administrator account, and press **Enter**.

   d. Enter the command **listsvc** and press **Enter** to list all services.

   e. You suspect that the Browser service is causing the system to fail, and decide to disable it. To disable the Browser service, enter the command **disable Browser** and press **Enter**. Record the original and new start values on your Student Answer Sheet.

   f. To reenable the Browser service, enter the command: **enable Browser** and press **Enter**. Record the message you receive on your Student Answer Sheet.

   g. Enter the command: **enable Browser Service_Auto_Start** and press **Enter**. Record the message you receive on your Student Answer Sheet.

   h. Enter the command **diskpart**. Record the information you receive on your Student Answer Sheet.

   i. Now you suspect that the problem may be a damaged boot sector. To repair a damaged boot sector, enter the command **fixboot** and press **Enter**. Record the messages you receive on your Student Answer Sheet.

   j. Sometimes booting with a virus-infected disk can corrupt the master boot record. If this happens, Windows 2000 might not boot or might crash during operation. To repair the master boot record, enter the command **fixmbr** and press **Enter**. On your Student Answer Sheet, record the message you receive. Enter **N** to skip the repair process.

The master boot record also can be repaired by booting with a DOS disk and using the command C:\>FDISK /mbr.

    k. Type **exit** and press **Enter** to end the Recovery Console mode. The system now will automatically restart.

4. Despite all your efforts, the system still will not start, and you suspect problems with some of the operating system files or configuration. In this step, you practice using the Emergency Repair Disk (ERD) to attempt to bring the system back to life.

    a. Insert the Windows 2000 installation disk 1 into the floppy drive, and restart your computer.

    b. Insert the remaining startup disks 2 through 4 as requested.

    c. When the installation options screen appears, type the letter **r** to choose the option to repair the Windows 2000 installation.

    d. Record the two repair options on your Student Answer Sheet.

    e. Select the option to use the ERD.

    f. Select **Manual repair** and record the manual repair options on your Student Answer Sheet.

    g. Press **Enter** to continue the repair process.

    h. On your Student Answer Sheet, record the ERD repair options and associated keys.

    i. Insert your ERD into the floppy drive, and press the key to use your ERD.

    j. Perform the ERD process, and then restart your computer.

    k. Record any additional steps on your Student Answer Sheet.

15

LAB 15.6 INSTALLING APPLICATIONS WITH WINDOWS INSTALLER

Objective

You were recently contacted by Kellie Thiele, the network administrator for Universal Aerospace, about installing Microsoft Office 2000 on their newly purchased Windows 2000 computers. Kellie is used to working with the Novell Z.E.N.works product, which provides options for installing and managing applications over the network. She is concerned whether Windows 2000 has the ability to restore applications in the event a user inadvertently removes essential application or system files, or if the system crashes. You have reassured her that the new Windows Installer Service included with Windows 2000 allows applications, along with software and operating system upgrades, to be seamlessly reinstalled or repaired. After completing this lab, you will be able to:

➤ Use Windows Installer Service to install an application package.

Requirements

➤ A software package, such as Office 2000, to install on Windows 2000 Professional.

Estimated completion time: **15–20 minutes**

ACTIVITY

1. If necessary, start your computer with Windows 2000, and log on as an administrator.

2. Insert your chosen application CD into the CD-ROM drive.

3. Open **Control Panel** and double-click **Add/Remove Programs**. Record the option buttons on your Lab 15.6 Student Answer Sheet.

4. Click the **Add New Programs** button. Record the New Program options on your Student Answer Sheet.

5. Click the **CD or Floppy** button, and click **Next** to start the Install Program wizard.

6. Use the **Browse** button to browse to your CD, and select the **Setup** program.

7. Click **Finish** to start the installation process.

8. On your Student Answer Sheet, record the selections you make in the installation process.

9. Exit the installation process.

10. Close the Add/Remove Programs window.

11. Close Control Panel, and test your application by opening it.

TROUBLESHOOTING WINDOWS 2000

Labs included in this chapter

➤ Lab 16.1 Creating a Computer Information File (CIF)

➤ Lab 16.2 Troubleshooting Network Problems

➤ Lab 16.3 Applying Service Packs

Microsoft MCSE Exam #70-210 Objectives	
Objective	Lab
Install, configure, and troubleshoot network adapters	16.1
Configure and troubleshoot the TCP/IP protocol	16.1, 16.2
Implement, manage, and troubleshoot disk devices	16.1
Configure and troubleshoot desktop settings	16.1
Troubleshoot failed installations	16.2
Monitor, configure, and troubleshoot volumes	16.2
Manage and troubleshoot access to shared folders	16.2
Manage printers and print jobs	16.2
Deploy service packs	16.3

LAB 16.1 CREATING A COMPUTER INFORMATION FILE

Objective

In the last year the consulting company you work for, Computer Technology Services, has added several new accounts and hired additional network support specialists and technicians. To better address customer problems and needs, Computer Technology Services wants a computer information file (CIF) created for computers at each customer site. This will allow faster problem resolution and make it easier for new support staff to understand any changes that have been made to the systems. Because of your experience in the field, your manager has asked you to work with the design team and help create forms for the CTS technical support staff to gather information for the computer information files, as well as to document procedures. To do this lab your instructor may assign you to a student design team. The team should set some design standards and then delegate form designs to various team members. You may wish to use forms found in earlier chapters of this lab manual as samples for your design. At the completion of the project, you might be asked make a presentation of your forms to your classmates in order to simulate a forms training session to the CTS technical support staff. You will work with other students in your design team to design and create the following:

➤ A form to be used to record system and network information

➤ A form to be used to document backup procedures and schedules

➤ A form to be used to document shared folders and permissions

➤ A form to be used to document problems and solutions

➤ A form to be used to document system changes

➤ A heading page that identifies the printouts and documents to be collected in the CIF

After completing this lab, you will be able to:

➤ Use the Computer Management tools to document system information.

➤ Collect necessary printouts and documents for your CIF.

Estimated completion time: **30 minutes**

ACTIVITY

1. Work with the other students in your group and use WordPad or your choice of word-processing software to design and create a Computer and Network Information form that includes spaces for the following. (other information can be added at the discretion of your instructor):

   - OS name, version, and manufacturer
   - System manufacturer, model, type, and name
   - Processor type and speed
   - BIOS version
   - Location of Windows directory (include drive letter, disk number, and partition number)
   - Total physical and virtual memory
   - Page file space
   - Any empty ports and expansion capability, such as empty memory slots and disk bays
   - Network adapter and driver software
   - Protocols in use
   - TCP/IP address, subnet mask, and gateway
   - Network services and clients loaded

2. Use WordPad or your choice of word-processing software to create a Server Backup form that can be used to document backup procedures. This form should include space for the following:

   - Computer/server name and location
   - Type of backup to be performed each day of the week, along with the user responsible for backup
   - Description of the tape rotation procedure–include any off-site storage sites and disaster recovery plan

3. Use WordPad or your choice of word-processing software to create a Users and Groups form that contains the following information:

   - User full name, logon name, and level of access for each user
   - Group name, purpose, and membership information for each group

16

4. Use WordPad or your choice of word-processing software to create a Local Folder Security form that can be used to record permissions for each secured folder on the local computer. The form should include space for the following information (other information can be added at the discretion of your instructor):

■ Drive and path to the secured folder

■ Typical and maximum size of shared folder

■ A section to record user and group permissions and inherited permissions in the folder

■ A section to record user and group permissions assigned to the folder

5. Use WordPad or your choice of word-processing software to create a Shared Folder form that can be used to document information about each shared folder. The form should include space for the following information (other information can be added at the discretion of your instructor):

■ Share name of folder

■ Computer hosting the folder

■ Drive and path to the shared folder

■ Typical and maximum size of shared folder

■ User and group shared permissions assigned to folder

6. Use WordPad or your choice of word-processing software to create a Maintenance form that includes the following:

■ Computer identification information

■ Frequency of maintenance

■ Date of maintenance activity

■ Maintenance checklist that includes a minimum of the following items:

  - Display cleaning

  - Fan and mechanical checkout

  - Memory test

  - Disk scanning and defragmentation status

  - Warning messages

  - Network status

■ Space to document any new hardware installations including device manufacturer, model, and configuration

■ Space to include the date, identification, and location of any service pack or upgrade applied to the system

7. Use WordPad or your choice of word-processing software to create an Application Software form that includes the following:

- Application name and date of installation
- License information
- Location of software files

8. Use WordPad or your choice of word-processing software to create a Service Support Contact form that includes space for the names of support providers, phone numbers, email addresses, Web URLs, and comments.

9. Use WordPad or your choice of word-processing software to create a Problem and Solution form that includes space for the following:

- Date problem occurred
- Description of problem
- A space of each problem resolution attempt, along with results of that attempt

10. Use WordPad or your choice of word-processing software to create a Computer Information File heading page that provides space for the computer's name and location, along with a checklist for all forms and other items such as manuals, software copies, and licenses that are included in the computer's information file.

11. Print out and assemble the forms you've created in Steps 1 through 10. You will be using them to complete the labs in this chapter.

LAB 16.2   TROUBLESHOOTING NETWORK PROBLEMS

Objective

In this lab, you will work with a partner to practice using the Computer Information File along with troubleshooting techniques to solve some common network problems. To do this, the lab is broken down into three activities. In Activity 1, you will set up and document a simple network environment for the Wiggerts and Son Heating Company. In Activity 2, you will create a "typical" network problem on your system to simulate the client's problem, and then fill out a Problem and Solution form reporting the trouble. In Activity 3, you will act as the Computer Technology Services support specialist and attempt to solve the problem on your lab partner's computer. After completing this lab, you will be able to:

➤ Set up a simple network environment that includes a shared folder, printer, and several users.

➤ Identify common network problems and then "bug" your system by including one of these problems.

➤ Using troubleshooting techniques and tools to identify and solve a common network problem.

Requirements

➤ Blank disk to be used as an Emergency Repair Disk (ERD).

➤ To simulate printer problems, you should have access to the Windows 2000 Professional CD or other source of printer drivers.

➤ A lab partner to work with to troubleshoot network problems.

➤ An IP address that you can use to communicate with your partner's computer. If using a manually assigned IP address, record the IP address information here:

IP address: _____._____._____._____

Mask: _____._____._____._____

➤ A second IP address you can use to create an IP address conflict:

Conflicting IP address: _____._____._____._____

Mask: _____._____._____._____

Estimated completion time: **30 minutes**

Activity 1

The Wiggerts and Son Heating Company based in Duluth, Minnesota, has been a supplier of specialized furnace parts and accessories since 1892. They have been using a Unix-based central computer system to perform all business-processing needs, but now want to implement a small peer-to-peer Windows 2000 network in their office located in your city. There are three sales reps and an administrative assistant who will have Windows 2000 Professional systems. The three sales reps need access to shared customer files and price quotations located on the administrative assistant's computer. Although the sales reps will need to be able to create and modify their own files, they should be able to read only files created by other sales reps. The administrative assistant will need to rights to modify or delete any of the shared files. The printer attached to the administrative assistant's computer will be shared by all users, but controlled only by the administrative assistant. In this activity, you will establish the Wiggerts and Son network system, and then use the forms you developed in Lab 16.1 to document the system.

1. If necessary, start your computer with Windows 2000, and log on as an administrator.

2. Using the techniques you learned in Chapter 5, create the following user accounts by supplying your own user names and passwords:

   - Create restricted user accounts for the three sales representatives.

   - Create a standard user account for the administrative assistant.

   - Create a power user account named **PowerMan**.

3. Create the following folder structure on the drive containing your Windows 2000 operating system:

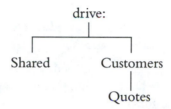

4. According to the scenario, the shared laser printer for the sales office is to be located on the administrative assistant's computer. In this step, use what you learned in Chapter 10 to simulate the shared laser printer by creating and sharing a printer, named SalesLaser, on your computer.

5. Create the necessary groups, and provide the following NTFS permissions to the groups:

   - Give the Users group Read, Execute, and List folder permissions to Customers and Shared. Be sure that the group Users inherits these permissions in the Quotes folder.

   - Give the Sales representatives group the Modify and Write permissions to both the Quotes and Shared folders.

   - Give the Administrative assistant user Full Control to the Customers and Shared folders.

   - Give the Sales representatives group basic printer permissions to the shared printer.

6. Using what you learned in Chapter 4, share the Shared and Customers folders with the Everyone group that has all shared permissions.

7. Remove the group Everyone from the SalesLaser printer permission, and include the sales rep group you created in Step 5.

8. Using what you learned in Chapter 7, remove all protocols except TCP/IP. Assign the IP address and Mask information recorded in the Requirements section.

16

9. Assemble all your forms and any other documents relevant to your computer, and fill in a Computer Information heading sheet for your computer. You will use some of these forms to complete the remaining steps in this lab.

10. Use the Computer Management tools, along with My Computer and My Network Places, to fill in the Computer and Network Information form you created in Lab 16.1.

11. Use the User and Groups form you created in Lab 16.1, and document the users and groups for the Wiggerts and Son network.

12. Use the Shared Folder form to document your shared folders and permissions.

13. Use the Backup Schedule form to document a backup procedure to be used by the administrative assistant.

14. Use the Backup program described in Chapter 15 to create an Emergency Repair Disk (ERD). Record the backup activity on your Backup Schedule form.

15. Fill out a Service Support Provider form, showing yourself and Computer Technology Services as service providers.

Lab
Activity

Activity 2

One of the most challenging tasks is to simulate computer problems. Often, during an attempt to simulate a problem, you can learn more about the operation of the system than you would by fixing the problem. In this activity, you will select one, or at most two, of the following "bugs" and then attempt to simulate them in your network system. Although steps are provided to help you implement the problem, you might want to carefully experiment with other ways you can make your computer "misbehave" in the prescribed manner. After you have successfully implemented the problem, you will then fill out a Problem and Solution form describing the symptom(s) of your problem for your partner, who then will act as the computer technician and attempt to fix the problem in Activity 3.

1. Sometimes adding new hardware to a computer or changing hardware configurations can cause an interrupt or memory resource conflict with the LAN card. When this occurs, the LAN connection is removed from My Network Connections window. Follow the steps below to simulate a problem where new hardware added to one of the sales rep's computers causes a conflict of resources with the LAN card.

   a. Right-click **My Network Places** and click **Properties**.

   b. Right-click **Local Area Connection** and click **Properties**.

c. Under the Connect using text box, click the **Configure** button to display the network card driver properties.

d. Click the **Resources** tab, and click to remove the check mark from the **Use automatic setting** check box.

 You may not be able to change your LAN card resources if the card is integrated into the motherboard or automatically configured by the Plug and Play BIOS.

e. Record the existing settings on your Computer and Network Information form.

f. If your network card allows, click either the Interrupt Request or Input/Output range resource, and click the **Change Setting** button.

g. If possible, select a value that shows a conflict with another device, as shown in Figure 16-1.

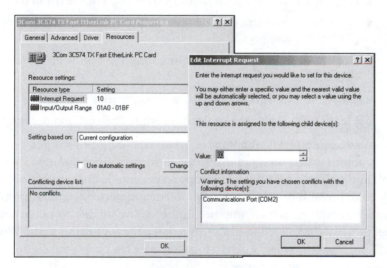

Figure 16-1 Interrupt Request window

h. Click **OK** and click **Yes** to continue using the conflicting resource.

i. Restart your computer, and document the error condition on your Problem and Solution form.

2. When IP addresses are assigned manually, adding a new device to the network with the same IP address as one of the existing computers can disable that computer's communication. The computer's communication can also be disabled if the TCP/IP protocol is accidentally disabled. Follow the steps below to simulate a network problem by either disabling the TCP/IP protocol, or changing the IP address to one that conflicts with another computer on the network.

a. To create a conflicting IP address, follow these steps:

- Right-click **My Network Places** and click **Properties**
- Right-click **Local Area Connection** and click **Properties**.
- Click the **Internet Protocol (TCP/IP)** component, and click the **Properties** button.
- Enter the conflicting IP address you identified in the Requirements section.
- Click **OK** twice, and click **OK** to respond to the IP conflict warning message.
- Close the Network and Dial-up Connections window.
- Identify and record the problem on your Problem and Solution form.

b. Follow these steps to disable the TCP/IP protocol:

- Right-click **My Network Places** and click **Properties**
- Right-click **Local Area Connection** and click **Properties**.
- Click to remove the check mark from the **Internet Protocol (TCP/IP)** component.
- Click **OK** and respond with **No** to the Do you want to respecify your selection warning.
- Close the Network and Dial-up Connections window.
- Identify and record the problem on your Problem and Solution form.

3. When setting up new computers, or when changing IP configurations, communication between computers can be disrupted either through physical cabling problems or incorrect network addressing. It can sometimes be difficult to distinguish between a cable problem and network address problem because in both cases the computer cannot communicate to other devices. Select one of the following problems to simulate a situation at the Wiggerts and Son network where a newly installed sales rep's computer is unable to communicate on the network

a. Follow the steps below to select a different network address or mask:

- Right-click **My Network Places** and click **Properties**
- Right-click **Local Area Connection** and click **Properties**.
- Click the **Internet Protocol (TCP/IP)** component, and click the **Properties** button.
- Record the existing IP address information on your Computer and Network Information form.
- Change either the first number in the IP address, or in the network mask.

- Click **OK** twice, and then close the Network and Dial-up Connections window.
- Identify and record the problem on your Problem and Solution form.

b. Disconnect the network cable and restart. Identify and record the problem on your Problem and Solution form.

4. Users will not be able to connect to a network printer and send output if they do not have access permissions, or if the print server is not operating. To simulate a problem where one of the sales representatives is unable to print documents, do one of the following:

a. Follow the steps below to stop the print server:

- Open **Control Panel** and double-click **Administrative Tools**.
- Double-click **Services**.
- Scroll down and right-click the **Print Server** service.
- Click **Stop**.
- Attempt to access the printer from your computer or your partner's, and identify and record the problem on your Problem and Solution form.

b. Follow the steps below to remove the sales rep user from the group you created in Activity 1:

- Open **Control Panel** and double-click **Users and Passwords**.
- Click the **Advanced** tab, and then click the **Advanced** button.
- Double-click the **Groups** folder to display all group names in the right-side results pane.
- In the right-side results pane, double-click the sales rep group.
- Click the member to be removed, and then click the **Remove** button.
- Click **OK** and close the Local Users and Groups window.
- Log on as the sales rep user, and attempt to access the SalesLaser shared printer from your computer or your partner's computer.
- Identify and record the problem on your Problem and Solution form.

5. Garbled output on a printer can be caused by a defective print device, incorrect printer language setting, bad cable, or an incorrect printer driver. In this step, you attempt to generate garbled output on the printer attached to your computer by either changing the printer driver or using the wrong language by sending an incorrect separator page. For example, send a Postscript separator page if you have a PCL print device, or send a PCL separator page to a Postscript print device. Follow the steps below to either change your printer driver or separator page.

16

    a. Click **Start**, **Settings**, **Printers** to open the Printers dialog box.

    b. Right-click your **SalesLaser** shared printer, and click **Properties**.

    c. Click the **Advanced** tab.

    d. Follow the steps below to change your printer driver:

- Click the **New Driver** button, and click **Next** to start the driver wizard.

- Highlight an incorrect driver by selecting a driver for a different printer of similar type. (You might need to experiment with a few different drivers to obtain the desired garbled output.)

- Click **Next** and then click **Finish**.

- If necessary, insert the CD or provide a path to the selected driver.

- After the new driver files are copied to your computer, click **OK** to return to the Printers window.

    e. If you have a printer that supports multiple languages, follow the steps below to send an incorrect separator page:

- Click the **Separator Page** button to display the Separator Page dialog box.

- Click the **Browse** button and, if necessary, navigate to the **WINNT\system32** folder on your Windows 2000 operating system drive.

- If the printer attached to your computer is set for PCL language, double-click the **pscript.sep** file. If the printer is set for Postscript language, double-click the **pcl.sep** file.

- Click **OK** to save your separator page, and return to the printer properties window.

- Click **OK** to return to the Printers window.

    f. Close the Printers window.

6. Booting errors often can be caused by an incorrect partition number in the boot.ini file, or by missing or corrupt loader or kernel software. Simulate a booting problem that prevents the system from starting by performing one of the following (Step 6a, 6b, or 6c):

    a. Follow the steps below to modify the partition number in the boot.ini file:

- Use My Computer or Windows Explorer to open the C: drive window.

- Double-click the **boot.ini** file, and edit it with Notepad.

- Follow the instructions from Chapter 14 to increase the partition number of the Windows 2000 operating system by one.

- Save the file and exit Notepad.
- Restart your computer.
- Identify and record the problem on your Problem and Solution form.

b. Follow the steps below to rename the NTLDR or NTDETECT.COM programs. (Be sure you have an operational Windows 2000 Professional boot disk such as the one you created in Chapter 14.)

- Use My Computer or Windows Explorer to open a window to the root of your C: drive.
- Right-click either the **ntldr** or **ntdetect.com** program, and rename it using the extension **.BUG**.
- Press **Enter** to save the new name.
- Restart your computer.
- Identify and record the problem on your Problem and Solution form.

c. To simulate a corrupted operating system kernel, follow the steps below to rename the kernel program ntoskrnl.exe.

- Use My Computer or Windows Explorer to open a window to the WINNT\system32 folder of your Windows 2000 operating system drive.
- Locate the ntoskrnl.exe file, and rename it to **ntoskrnl.bug**.
- Open the **dllcache** folder.
- Locate the ntoskrnl.exe file, and rename it to **ntoskrnl.bug**.
- Close all windows, and restart your computer.
- Identify and record the problem on your Problem and Solution form.

7. Incorrect permissions or conflicting permission assignments are often the cause of users being unable to perform certain network actions. In this step, you prevent one of the sales rep users from accessing files in the Quotes folder by setting up one of the following permission problems.

a. Provide the sales representative group with only the Read shared permissions to the Customers folder.

b. When a group is denied access to a resource, all members of that group also have no access, regardless of what other permissions that group or the members of that group might be assigned. This can sometimes cause a problem if you attempt to secure a resource by denying access to a group. For example, in this step you simulate an access problem caused when the administrative assistant attempts to increase security by adding the group Everyone to the permissions list of the Customers folder.

c. Another permissions problem can be caused accidentally by preventing a subfolder from inheriting rights from its parent. For example, in this

16

step you simulate an access problem caused by preventing the Quotes folder from inheriting rights from its parent Customers folder.

- Use My Computer or Windows Explorer to open the Customers folder.
- Right-click the **Quotes** folder, and click **Properties**.
- Click the **Security** tab, and record or verify the permission assignments in the inherited permissions section of your Local Folder Security form.
- Click to remove the check mark from the **Allow inheritable permissions from parent to propagate to this object** check box.
- Click the **Remove** button to remove the inherited permissions, and keep only the permissions explicitly specified.
- If necessary, modify the inherited permissions section of your Local Folder Security form to include only those users or groups that were removed from the Quotes Properties window.
- If necessary, modify the assigned permissions section of your Local Folder Security form to only include those users and groups appearing in the Quotes Properties window.
- Click **OK** to save your changes, and return to the Customers folder window.
- Attempt to access the Quotes folder.
- If you made the permission assignments specified in Step 5 of Activity 2, only users in the sales rep group will be able to access the Quotes folder. All other users, including the administrator, will be denied access.
- Identify and record the problem on your Problem and Solution form.

Activity 3

In this activity you are to move to your partner's computer and, using only their Problem and Solution form, identify and correct the problem(s) created in Activity 2. After you have solved the problem(s), use the Problem and Solution form to record the solutions.

Activity 4

Repeat Activities 2 and 3 as time permits.

LAB 16.3   APPLYING SERVICE PACKS

Objective

Obtaining and applying service packs is a necessary part of maintaining operating system software. After completing this lab, you will be able to:

➤ Download the latest Windows 2000 service pack.

➤ Install a service pack.

➤ Uninstall a service pack.

Requirements

➤ Access to the Internet to download a Windows 2000 service pack, or access to a downloaded service pack on your local network. If using an already downloaded service pack, record the network path to the service pack:

Estimated completion time: **40 minutes**

ACTIVITY

1. If necessary, start your computer with Windows 2000, and log on as an administrator.

2. Download the service pack.

   a. If necessary, open a connection to the Internet.

   b. Start **Internet Explorer**.

   c. Go to the *ftp:\\ftp.microsoft.com/bussys/winnt/winnt-public/fixes/usa/* site.

   d. Locate the folder containing the Windows 2000 service pack(s) and then, on your Maintenance form record the name of that folder, along with the name and date of any service packs.

3. Install the service pack.

   a. Copy the service pack file into an empty directory.

   b. Close all applications and windows.

   c. Locate and execute the **Update.exe** file using the **Start**, **Run** command.

   d. Follow any prompts that appear. Be sure to select the **Uninstall** option.

   e. Restart your computer when instructed.

4. Verify service pack installation.

5. Delete service pack files and temporary directory from your hard drive.

16